GI

THE US INFANTRYMAN IN WORLD WAR II

ROBERT S. RUSH

Illustrated by ELIZABETH SHARP & IAN PALMER

GI

THE US INFANTRYMAN
IN WORLD WAR II

ROBERT S. RUSH

Illustrated by ELIZABETH SHARP & IAN PALMER

First published in Great Britain in 2003 by Osprey Publishing,
Elms Court, Chapel Way, Botley, Oxford OX2 9LP, UK.
Email: info@ospreypublishing.com

Previously published without additional material as Warrior 45:
*US Infantryman in World War II (1) Pacific Area of Operations
1941–45*; Warrior 53: *US Infantryman in World War II (2)
Mediterranean Theater of Operations 1942–45*; Warrior 56: *US
Infantryman in World War II (3) European Theater of Operations
1944–45*

A CIP catalogue record for this book is available from the
British Library

ISBN 1 84176 739 5

Editor: Sally Rawlings
Digital Artwork by Ian Palmer
Design: Ken Vail Graphic Design, Cambridge, UK
Index by Susan Williams
Originated by Grasmere Digital Imaging, Leeds, UK
Printed in China through World Print Ltd.

03 04 05 06 07   10 9 8 7 6 5 4 3 2 1

All photographs are US Army images unless otherwise
credited.

Front cover photograh: American troops of the 28th
Infantry Division march down the Champs Elysees, Paris, in the
"Victory" Parade. (NARA)

FOR A CATALOGUE OF ALL BOOKS PUBLISHED BY OSPREY MILITARY
AND AVIATION PLEASE CONTACT:

Osprey Direct USA, c/o MBI Publishing, P.O. Box 1, 729
Prospect Ave, Osceola, WI 54020, USA
E-mail: info@ospreydirectusa.com

Osprey Direct UK, P.O. Box 140, Wellingborough, Northants,
NN8 2FA, UK
E-mail: info@ospreydirect.co.uk

www.ospreypublishing.com

CONTENTS

CHAPTER 1

INTRODUCTION 7

CHAPTER 2

THE INFANTRY REGIMENT 20

CHAPTER 3

CHRONOLOGY 37

CHAPTER 4

PACIFIC OCEAN AREA OF OPERATIONS, 1941–45 42

CHAPTER 5

MEDITERRANEAN THEATER OF OPERATIONS, 1942–45 96

CHAPTER 6

EUROPEAN THEATER OF OPERATIONS, 1944–45 156

CHAPTER 7

SOUTHWEST PACIFIC THEATER OF OPERATIONS, 1944–45 214

CHAPTER 8

CONCLUSION 248

CHAPTER 9

FORMATIONS AND POSITION SCHEMATICS 251

NOTES AND ABBREVIATIONS 257

BIBLIOGRAPHY 259

INDEX 263

Prewar equipment for National Guard infantry units consisted of
equipment used in World War I. This 1927 picture shows soldiers
posed clockwise from top left, with an 81mm mortar, a soldier in firing
position with a rifle grenadde, a soldier with a bipodless Browning
Automatic Rifle (BAR). In the foreground stands a soldier with the
M1903 Springfield rifle and bayonet. To his right kneels a grenadier
throwing a defensive "pineapple" hand grenade

CHAPTER 1

INTRODUCTION

To the everlasting glory of the Infantryman ...

This book provides an overview of how the US infantryman in World War II was organized, equipped, trained, and led. Rather than fill this book with just the dry details of soldiering, I use four vignettes of infantrymen fighting in the major war theaters (Pacific Ocean Area, Mediterranean Theater, European Theater, and Southwest Pacific Area) with combat markedly different in each area. The perspective the average infantryman had while fighting the different battles of World War II was my guiding principle. At the level of the common soldier, grand strategies beyond the next objective are of little matter because all he experiences is hardship, fear, death – and only afterwards does he reflect on loss and gain. These infantrymen were the reality behind the symbols that staff officers moved with such alacrity on the map board; where a ten-centimeter move might mean kilometers of hard marching through rain and mud over extremely rugged terrain.

The best plan is only as good as the soldiers who execute it. It was in the trenches that wars were won and lost – depending on how well the soldier was trained, equipped, led and how he was motivated to put his life on the line. What motivated this soldier to fight as he did, how did he enter service, what was his training, and what might have been his attitude when going into battle. From the common soldier's viewpoint, a unique perspective of the US infantryman during World War II emerges.

All military organizations operate under the rubric of regulations and doctrine. Every condition under which soldiers operate, the uniforms they wear and the weapons they carry are all prescribed by regulation. The different regulations, field manuals, unit reports, and histories written by individual participants all form the basis of our infantryman's narrative. While the focus of each vignette is on one hypothetical soldier – in a fully realistic timescale and experience – the generalities and experiences of the many are also examined and carefully woven into the individual narrative thread.

The Pacific Ocean Area vignette follows "Michael" through his enlistment into, and training with, the 165th Infantry Regiment (New York National Guard). It takes him through the 1941 maneuvers the 27th Infantry Division participated in, the transfer to Oahu, and into the reality of daily life and combat in the Pacific theater from 1942 to 1945, including Makin, Saipan, and Okinawa. His experience reflects the everyday experience of many soldiers in the POA Theater of operations. This composite soldier has been drawn by examining the social and demographic environment of a National Guard regiment, the US army regulations under which the soldiers operated, the uniforms they wore and the weapons they carried, company diaries and official reports of the actions.

In the Mediterranean Theater narrative, we follow "John" as he enlists in February 1942, trains at a Replacement Training Center (RTC), and is assigned to the 76th Division. It provides the reader with a general overview of how American infantrymen in the Mediterranean were organized, equipped, trained and cared for, and deals particularly with the problems these soldiers faced while fighting the Germans and Italians in North Africa and Italy. In December 1942 John ships overseas as a replacement, and joins the 133d Regiment in early March 1943 when he fights his first battle in the Fondouk Pass. More than two years later, he fights his last battle in the Po Valley of northern Italy.

This soldier's story includes activities similar to those experienced by most replacement infantrymen; his enlistment, testing and selection as an infantryman, training, shipment overseas, promotion and demotion, weapons, injury and illness, as well as the everyday occurrences of eating, resupplying, and fighting across North Africa and Italy. A key focus is on the Heavy Weapons Company, which consisted of two .30 caliber machine gun platoons, and an 81mm mortar platoon. The training and combat roles of the machine gunner's Military Occupational Specialty (MOS) are discussed in detail.

The European Theater vignette follows "Joe" through his induction, assignment and training in the 22d Infantry Regiment in 1941. It takes him from draftee, through the tactical operations at squad, platoon, and company level, and into the reality of daily life and combat in Northern Europe in 1944–45. Joe along with his unit prepares for D-day, assaults Utah Beach, and fights toward Cherbourg. He enters the Hürtgen forest in late 1944 as a squad leader, and is awarded a battlefield commission as a second lieutenant: here he is again wounded and evacuated, and his condition is exacerbated by battle fatigue. The title ends with Joe's death on April 4, 1945: the soldiers who had known him since 1941 briefly mourn his passing, and when the war ends those high in the "point" system return home.

Lastly, the fully endnoted Southwest Pacific vignette follows "Gordon" from his induction in mid-1942, through assignment and training in the 88th Infantry Division before being selected to attend the Infantry Officer Candidate School. Upon completion in July 1943, he is assigned to the 96th Division as a platoon leader in the 382d Infantry, with which he enters combat on Leyte. Later, he is severely wounded on Okinawa during the battle on Tombstone Ridge and evacuated to a Veterans Hospital in the US. The training and combat roles of the infantry platoon leader MOS 1542 are discussed in detail. Within each theater the administrative procedures for replacements, and medical and psychiatric care of the soldier will be examined.

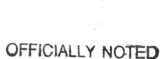

Between 1940 and 1945, the US Army expanded from eight to 73 active infantry divisions (including the cavalry and airborne divisions), with infantry regiments increasing from 42 to 299 (rifle, armored, mountain, glider, and parachute) on active duty, as well as an additional 99 separate infantry-type battalions. The vast majority, 204, were standard rifle regiments and included 57 Regular Army (RA) (including Philippine Scouts and the four dismounted cavalry regiments of the 1st Cavalry Division), 79 National Guard and 125 regiments of the Army of the United States (AUS).

On December 7, 1941, there were 80 National Guard infantry regiments, 44 regular army regiments (16 of which were overseas in Alaska, Panama, Iceland, Hawaii, and the Philippine Islands), and six regiments of the AUS on active duty. During the hectic days of early 1942, units went overseas with their last maneuvers being those of October 1941, and without any opportunity to correct their deficiencies. National Guard (NG) and RA divisions traveled overseas first, with most initially going to the Pacific, and the rest earmarked for the campaigns in Europe and North Africa.

The first Army seaborne invasion occurred in November 1942, when three RA infantry divisions (1st, 3d, and 9th, with two sailing from the US) and one regiment of the 34th Infantry Division (NG) assaulted North Africa. These organizations were at the optimum personnel strengths, but they lacked advanced training and much of their necessary modern equipment. Their shortcomings in training and equipment were readily apparent in the opening phases of the Tunisian campaign and casualties were higher than expected. The established RTCs could not keep pace with demand so untrained soldiers in some forming divisions went overseas as replacements.

THE REGULAR ARMY

In 1939, there were only five RA divisions (1st, 2d, 3d, Hawaiian, and Philippine) and 189,488 soldiers on active duty. By Pearl Harbor, RA infantry divisions numbered 11 (1st, 2d, 3d, 4th, 5th, 6th, 7th, 8th, 9th, 24th and Philippine) divisions. Although RA in name, on 7 December, 1941 most units comprised only 20 percent regulars, the remainder being draftees, and the majority of platoon leader positions and many company commanders were Reserve officers called to active duty.

Unlike World War I, when half of the RA regiments stayed home to train the National Army (NA), all saw overseas duty in World War II, with 24 serving in Europe, 17 in the Pacific, and others in the Caribbean and in Alaska. Of the 45 RA regiments active on December 7, 1941 (including the Philippine Scouts), 16 were outside the continental US. Nine others shipped overseas in 1942 along with numerous National Guard infantry regiments.

Others remained in the US until 1943 and 1944, providing trained cadres for newly forming units, and in turn receiving and training drafts of men destined to fight within the regiments when they were shipped overseas.

NATIONAL GUARD

Each recognized state possesses a National Guard, which serves as the governor's military force in time of civil disturbances, natural disasters or other emergencies. Many of these state organizations predate the establishment of the United States and the RA. During World War II, 39 states as well as the territories of Alaska, the Hawaiian Islands, and Puerto Rico provided at least one rifle regiment and some as many as five, such as New York.

When the NG federalized in 1940 and 1941, its divisions were organized under the WWI square division concept of two brigades of two infantry regiments each. Between February and September 1942, when the 27th Division (New York National Guard) reorganized, the 18 federalized Guard divisions converted to a triangular organization of three infantry regiments, which dramatically increased mobility as well as improving command and control.

During the 1930s, National Guard armory life consisted of 48 drill periods spread out as a weekly drill lasting between one and a half and four hours, for which privates were given one day's pay, payable every three months. On mobilization and during their two-week summer camp, guardsmen received the same pay as their RA counterparts.

Drill itself consisted of a few hours of training, mostly dismounted drill, and some weapons firing on the armory shooting range, after which soldiers congregated in the company canteen to drink beer and play cards, or in the drill hall to watch various sports. Soldiers were outfitted from supplies left over from World War I: they were armed with M1903 Springfield rifles, .30 cal. Browning Automatic Rifles (BAR), and .45 cal. pistols. Machine guns and mortars, though authorized, were rarely seen. In 1940, armory drills were boosted from 48 to 60 periods per year, and home station field training was increased. For a newly recruited guardsman there was no basic training per se. He trained with the company drill sergeant until he knew basic soldiering, and then drilled with his squad or section thereafter.

When the regiments mobilized in 1940 and 1941, their soldiers were taken through a 13-week period of mobilization training (eight hours per weekday, four hours on Saturday) which included two weeks of recruit, eight weeks of company, two weeks of battalion, and one week of regimental level training. Of the 572 hours, only 20 hours were devoted to close-order drill, and 111 hours to rifle marksmanship.

THE ORGANIZED RESERVE AND ARMY OF THE UNITED STATES

Soldiers going "over the top" during training in 1940. They wear World War I equipment, save for the canvas leggings replacing wrap leggings. Also note the massed formation, which is symbolic of platoon drill of the 1920s and 1930s.

Unlike the National Guard, the Organized Reserve (OR) was a Federal entity. During the interwar years, the OR divisions were skeletons consisting primarily of WWI era officers with the junior grades filled by Reserve Officers' Training Corps (ROTC) graduates, and very few enlisted men. There was little opportunity to train with troops and, like NG officers, the Reserve officers remained current in their speciality by taking correspondence courses that qualified them for promotion.

The 39 infantry divisions organized in the US after Pearl Harbor in 1942 and 1943 were either OR or AUS. They were built around the cadre concept; with older more established divisions supplying officers and soldiers who provided the core organization and training element of the new division around which the recruits from the reception stations formed. The new division's junior officers came from officer candidate and service. Germany used this same process in forming new divisions in late 1940 and early 1941.

The Army Ground Forces (AGF) estimated that divisions required ten to 12 months' training to be fully prepared for combat. Responsibility for training rested with commanders, who continually emphasized those tasks necessary for basic mission accomplishment,

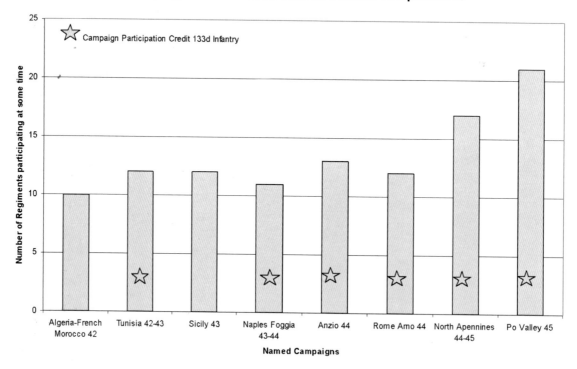

Campaigns in the Mediterranean Theater of Operations

stressing drills and techniques for the small units. They wanted soldiers to be able to walk before they ran. Training progressed through four phases: basic and individual training – 17 weeks devoted to individual up through battalion level training; 13 weeks of unit training primarily at regimental level; 14 weeks of combined arms training, which included at least one division-against-division maneuver. Another eight weeks were devoted to correcting deficiencies.

Every division organized after 1941 had at least one year of training and most more, although many divisions suffered severe personnel upheaval with soldiers leaving as replacements as soon as they were basically trained. With an authorized strength of just over 14,000, the 89th Infantry Division trained 40,000 soldiers before shipping overseas in 1945. All OR and AUS divisions except one saw combat in 1944 and 1945, with five in the Mediteranean Theater of Operations (MTO), six in the Pacific Theater of Operations (PTO), and 27 in the European Theater of Operations (ETO).

The 76th Infantry Division, one of the divisions of the OR, was activated in June 1942 from a small cadre of 185 Regular and Reserve officers and 1,190 enlisted men, most of whom were specialists in the different technical services. There were not enough noncommissioned Officers to fill all the positions and consequently many newly trained graduates of the RTCs found

themselves rapidly promoted to NCO positions with no military background outside their 13 weeks of training. Due to the massive upheaval both in forming new units and filling units preparing to go overseas, the 76th Division was designated a Replacement Pool Division in October 1942. Unit training stopped and concentration was placed instead on housing soldiers until it was their turn to ship overseas as replacements. Some recruits who arrived from reception centers in June and July 1942 to fill the forming division received very little infantry training before shipping overseas to North Africa, and this ultimately created a great uproar overseas. Unit training began again in March 1943 when the 76th Division refilled and restarted its basic training cycle. Twenty-two months later, in January 1945, the division shipped overseas to France and entered combat immediately.

Soldiers in dungarees fire M1903 Springfields on an unimproved range in 1940/41. A coach kneels on the firer's right, observing the strike of the round as well as the firer's body position. Note not only the sparseness of the range, but also its size, large enough for a battalion to fire in one order.

THE ONSET OF WORLD WAR II

In summer 1940, France and the Low Countries had fallen, the Battle of Britain was raging, and the US had placed its first embargo on war trade against Japan. By the fall of 1940, President Roosevelt had signed the Selective Service Act, which provided for the registration of male citizens and aliens between the ages of 21 and 36 and authorized the induction of up to 900,000 men for a period of 12 consecutive months of training and service; National Guard organizations were federalized. The draft and mobilization were to last for only one year, but in August 1941, Congress extended the term of service for draftees and mobilized guardsmen for up to 18 months. This prewar army formed in 1940 and 1941 from the standing army of 296,437 regulars, 241,612 guardsmen, and 106,000 Reserve officers, was the tool that fought the US' first battles of World War II.

The War Department developed standardized training plans for both units and individuals in 1939 and 1940, and as the war progressed these were modified and refined, taking on board the most recent information and lessons learned from the overseas combat areas. When training commenced in earnest, a rifleman training at the Infantry Replacement Center at Camp Wheeler, Georgia, received the same hours of instruction on the same subjects as did riflemen training at other Infantry Replacement Centers throughout the country, or for that matter within any of the organizing divisions.

Additionally, with the realization that the RA was too small to provide enough proficient trainers to build the expanding army, masses of new manuals appeared in 1940–41 that addressed every aspect of army organization and operations from the individual soldier through corps and army operations. If something was to be done, there was a manual demonstrating how to do it. From 1940, every soldier received FM 21–100, *The Soldier's Handbook*, and the higher rank a soldier achieved the more manuals he accumulated. A good sergeant might have FM 7–20, *Rifle Company*; FM 21–20, *Physical Training*; FM 21–25, *Map and Aerial Photograph Reading*; FM 22–5, *Infantry Drill Regulations*; FM 23–5, *US Rifle Caliber .30*, and FM 23–15, *Browning Automatic Rifle with Bipod Cal. 30*. Countless millions of manuals rolled off the presses, and as the war wore on, whenever new lessons were learned, the Army published updates and appendices.

THE ENLISTED SOLDIER

There were three types of enlisted soldier within the US Army. The regular who enlisted for adventure, patriotism or need; the guardsman, who had signed up for the same reasons as the regular, and was part-time until his unit federalized and he laid down the wrench to pick up the rifle; and the draftee or inductee, who after November 1940 was selected by his county draft board.

During 1940 and 1941, the average age of the soldier was 26; more soldiers were over 40 than under 21, and most had not finished high school, although this was typical of the rest of the white male population.

The first draft
The draft provided the lifeblood of the Army, and between November 1940 and June 1945, 7,420,082 men entered the Army through conscription.

On September 16, 1940, after one year of war in which Germany had run roughshod over Europe – driving Britain to the brink of defeat – and driven deep into the Soviet Union, President Franklin D Roosevelt signed the Selective Service Act, which called to service 900,000 single men aged 21–35 for a one-year period. The first draft registration in 1940 called for all men aged 21–35, resident or alien,

to register. In mid-October, over 16,000,000 men registered, were tentatively classified after filling out an eight-page questionnaire, received their draft numbers, and waited for the National Lottery. The draft began when Secretary of War Stimson drew number 158 on October 29, 1940.

For its soldiers, the Army wanted young, single men who met the prewar physical and mental standards; and for the most part it received what it wanted in the first draft call. Most of the men called were reasonably healthy, unattached, and often unemployed. On average, the selectees were an inch taller and eight pounds heavier than those drafted in 1917.

Just under 17,000 men entered service through Selective Service in November and December 1940 with another 289,000 between January and March 1941; the majority arriving untrained to increase RA units to wartime authorizations. Later, inductees filled the National Guard divisions and, after Pearl Harbor, they formed OR and AUS divisions. By mid-1941, basic training was consolidated in replacement centers with tactical units drawing their personnel from the centers.

On August 18, 1941, President Roosevelt extended the inductees' period of service to 18 months, releasing those aged 28 and older to the reserves, with most called back to duty after Pearl Harbor just months later. By the end of 1942, the draft was in full swing, with 3,364,000 inductees entering the Army that year, more than in any other year of the war. On February 16, 1942, 20-year-olds began registering and shortly thereafter became eligible for the draft and on June 30, 1942, 18- and 19-year-olds registered, becoming liable for service shortly thereafter, with 19-year-olds drafted first. That said, there were more soldiers aged over 40 than under 20 on active duty that year.

By late 1941, the Army began lowering the mental and physical standards for draft-eligible men. By February 1942, the Army accepted those who required glasses, as well as men who had just enough teeth to eat the standard Army rations. In 1943 and 1944 standards were further lowered and civilians were accepted with physical defects that would have disqualified them in 1941 and 1942. Prewar fathers, who up until late 1943 only made up about six percent of those drafted, supplied almost 50 percent of all men drafted after April 1944.

Beginning in 1941, polls showed that most Americans thought it was more important to stop the Axis powers than to remain at peace, although even more preferred that the US not go to war, hoping that material aid alone to Britain, and later the Soviet Union, might bring about victory. However, that was not to be. December 7, 1941, the day Japan attacked Pearl Harbor, ended any discussion as to whether the US should enter the war.

Soldiers enlisting

Most of the men enlisting in the US Army December 1941 through February 1942 did so out of patriotism. The Japanese attack on

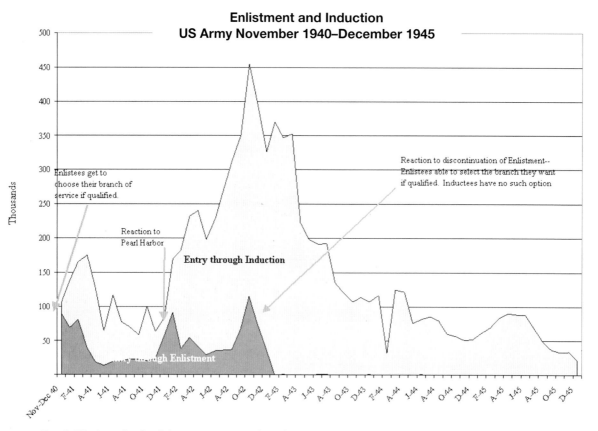

**Enlistment and Induction
US Army November 1940–December 1945**

Enlistees get to choose their branch of service if qualified.

Reaction to Pearl Harbor

Entry through Induction

Reaction to discontinuation of Enlistment-- Enlistees able to select the branch they want if qualified. Inductees have no such option

Entry through Enlistment

Pearl Harbor ignited in many a passion for revenge. Although Germany and Italy declared war against the US on December 11, the main object of American rage was Japan.

Between December 1941 and February 1942, 186,360 men enlisted in the US Army. Although the average age of a soldier in 1941 was 26, the newly enlisted soldier was typically younger than the draftee in the next bunk over, with 39.9 percent of those enlisting between the ages of 18 and 21, while only 14.7 percent of the draftees were as young.

THE OFFICER

In 1940, before the US Army's buildup, there were approximately 14,000 RA officers on active duty, and 22,000 National Guard and 180,000 Organized Reserve Corps (ORC) officers. In 1941, large numbers of reserve officers were called to active duty to assist in officering the expanding Army.

Prewar RA officers entered commissioned service either through graduation from the United States Military Academy (USMA); for a select few, through a direct commissioning process for enlisted men and warrant officers; or as a Distinguished Military Graduate of the Reserve Officers' Training Program. During the war years of 1942 to

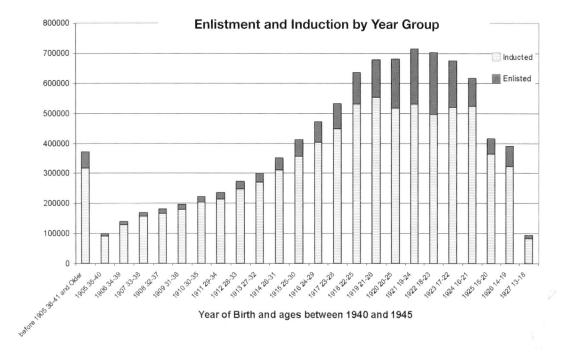

Enlistment and Induction by Year Group

Year of Birth and ages between 1940 and 1945

1945, only graduates of the USMA received RA commissions, which accelerated its classes so that both the classes of 1943 and 1944 graduated in 1943.

Most ORC officers were commissioned through the four-year ROTC program while in college. This instruction consisted of primarily classroom instruction, drill instruction, and a summer camp held between their junior and senior years. Others were National Guard officers appointed by their state governors. Although the majority of ORC officers received their commission during the 20s and 30s only a few entered active duty for resident branch training before 1940; the remainder staying current in their field and qualifying for promotion through military correspondence courses.

Officer candidates and officers "battlefield commissioned" received appointments as officers in the AUS. The officer's candidate schools (OCS) placed practical application over teaching theory in the view that continuous practice led to theoretical understanding. The Infantry OCS, which produced 62,968 infantry lieutenants during the war, trained aspiring officers in the technique and tactics of the rifle platoon and squad and to a lesser extent battalion and regimental level operations using tactical exercises. Leadership training comprised theoretical instruction and practical training with candidates serving in student leadership positions within the student company; and as patrol leader, platoon leader, and company commander during tactical problems. The most important question each tactical officer asked himself when evaluating the candidates was: "Would I be willing to follow this man in battle?"

The officers candidate course was short because the AGF believed that actually leading soldiers was more valuable than learning it from a lecture and through canned exercises, and so fought to keep officer training programs short, preferring to train through experience with troop duty. It was only in July 1943 that the infantry course lengthened from 13 to 17 weeks.

Soldiers needed a minimum score of 110 on the Army General Classification Test (AGCT) to qualify for officer training. There was no formal educational requirement; soldiers only needed enough education or military experience that would reasonably insure satisfactory completion of the course. Initially, only warrant officers and enlisted men with at least four to six months of service were eligible for entry. Beginning in the summer of 1942, men who had not completed the full college ROTC were, once inducted into the Army and after their basic training, given the regular OCS course. Later in 1944, the OCS policy changed to accept soldiers directly from the RTCs, which because of the younger draft ages, lowered the average age of candidates to something less than the mid-20s. The popular image of the beardless 90-day wonder leading other baby-faced soldiers, though partially true in 1945, was not in 1944. Before deploying overseas, officers shipping as replacements

Young men read the "Defend your country" poster outside their town's recruiting station, circa 1941.

spent, by AGF policy, at least three months with company-level tactical units in the US. It was this combination of school and unit training that produced the successful infantry junior officer. With skilled field-grade officers and time to train in the US, these lieutenants made competent combat leaders.

The last source of commissioning was through a battlefield commission. Here soldiers who, regardless of education or AGCT score, had proven themselves as outstanding leaders under battlefield conditions, received appointments as second lieutenants in the AUS.

CHAPTER 2

THE INFANTRY REGIMENT

Each infantry regiment was practically a miniature division and with attachments was more properly referred to as a combat team, with the same types of combat organizations as a division, only smaller. Weapons requiring prime movers were in regimental heavy weapons companies, all those in a battalion heavy weapons company could be hand-carried for short distances and all weapons in a rifle company were capable of being hand-carried. The regimental and three battalion headquarters provided the organization's command and control, while Service Company and the regimental medical detachment provided combat service support. Regimental heavy weapons companies consisted of a field artillery battery, known as Cannon Company, and an Antitank Company. A 105mm field artillery battalion was normally in direct support, and in combat when required, the regiment received engineer, field artillery, armor, and tank destroyers.

REGIMENTAL HEADQUARTERS AND HEADQUARTERS COMPANY

The Regimental Headquarters consisted of the regimental commander (colonel), executive officer (lieutenant-colonel), S-1 Adjutant (captain), S-2 Intelligence (major), S-3 Operations and Training (lieutenant-colonel), S-4 Supply (a major from Service Company), assistants and liaison officers.

Infantry Rifle Regiment table of organization, 1920–45					
	Oct 7, 1920	Nov 1, 1940	Aug 1, 1942	Jul 15, 1943	Jan 24, 1945
Total Strength	3041	3449	3333	3118	3068
HQ & HQ Co	119	210	132	108	104
Band			29		
Service Co	225	152	132	114	111
Antitank Co		185	169	165	159
Cannon Co	104		123	118	114
Rifle Battalion (3)	831	932	916	871	860
HQ & HQ Co	70	52	139	126	121
Rifle Co (3)	205	223	198	193	193
Machine Gun Co	146				
Heavy Weapons Co		211	183	166	160
Medical Detachment	*100*	*106*	*136*	*135*	*136*

The Headquarters Company consisted of a company headquarters, an intelligence and reconnaissance platoon, and a communications platoon grouped into one unit primarily for administrative purposes.

The company headquarters was similar to that of all other infantry companies with a company commander, executive officer (XO), first sergeant, transportation NCO, messengers, drivers, bugler in the command group, supply and mess section, and company clerk in the administration section. The company commander also served as the headquarters commandant, responsible for the administrative functioning of the tactical operations center. The executive officer served as the second-in-command, with additional duties as regimental gas officer. The first sergeant assisted the commander in administering the company and as headquarters commandant.

The intelligence and reconnaissance platoon operated under the supervision of the regimental intelligence officer and was organized into a platoon headquarters and two reconnaissance squads.

The communications platoon established, maintained, and operated the radio and wire communications systems of the headquarters' message center. The platoon leader also served as the regimental communications officer. The platoon was composed of a headquarters, message center, wire section and radio and visual sections.

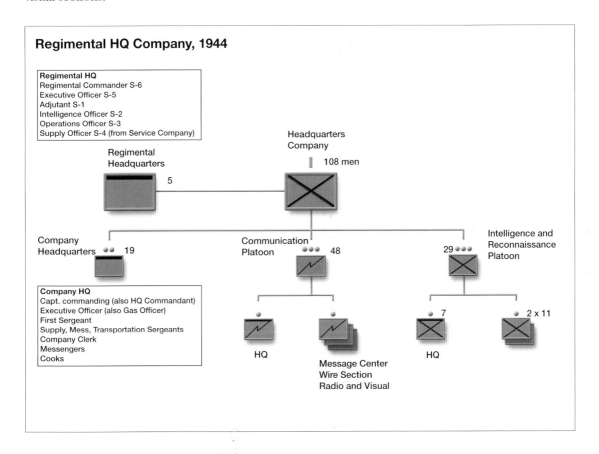

Regimental HQ Company, 1944

Regimental HQ
Regimental Commander S-6
Executive Officer S-5
Adjutant S-1
Intelligence Officer S-2
Operations Officer S-3
Supply Officer S-4 (from Service Company)

Regimental Headquarters

Headquarters Company

108 men

5

Company Headquarters   19

Communication Platoon   48

29   Intelligence and Reconnaissance Platoon

Company HQ
Capt. commanding (also HQ Commandant)
Executive Officer (also Gas Officer)
First Sergeant
Supply, Mess, Transportation Sergeants
Company Clerk
Messengers
Cooks

HQ

Message Center
Wire Section
Radio and Visual

7   HQ

2 x 11

SERVICE COMPANY

The Service Company's primary mission was to be the regimental supply unit. It comprised a company headquarters, a regimental headquarters platoon, and a transportation platoon.

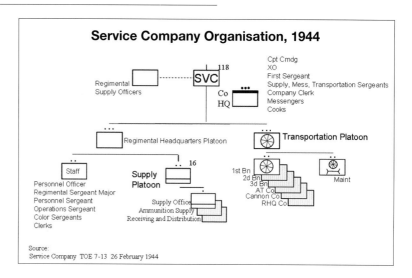

The Company Headquarters was divided into a command and an administrative group, similar to the regimental headquarters described earlier, except that the commander also served as assistant to the regimental Supply Officer and there was no executive officer.

The Regimental Headquarters platoon consisted of a headquarters section and a supply section. The headquarters section contained soldiers who served in the different command posts. It had the personnel officer, regimental sergeant-major, operations sergeant, intelligence sergeant, color sergeants, clerks, drivers, and messengers. The supply section consisted of the regimental and three battalion supply officers, a supply office group, receiving and distribution group, and ammunition supply group.

The transportation platoon constituted the regimental trains. It consisted of a headquarters section, three battalion sections, a headquarters company section, antitank company section, cannon company section, and maintenance section.

MEDICAL DETACHMENT

The Medical Detachment provided the doctors, dentists, medics, and litter bearers necessary to conserve the strength of the regiment. It was organized into a headquarters section and regimental aid station group of doctors, dentists, and medics, three battalion sections organized into an aid station group, litter bearer group, and company

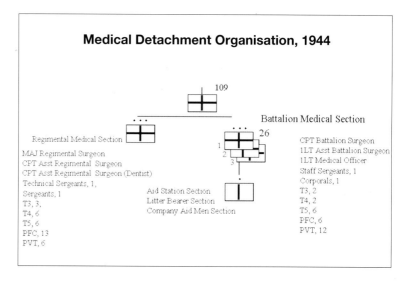

aid man group. Patients received only emergency treatment at the aid station: bleeding was stopped, bandages readjusted, and wounds dressed only as necessary.

CANNON COMPANY

The Cannon Company provided close and continuous indirect fire support to the regiment by destroying or neutralizing enemy troops that posed the greatest threat, and that could not be readily engaged by supporting artillery. The company consisted of a company headquarters, and three 105mm (4.1in.) firing platoons. Most infantry divisions contained towed howitzers; however, those divisions landing on D-Day contained 105mm (4.1in.) howitzers on self-propelled carriages.

The company headquarters was divided into a command and an administrative group similar to all infantry company headquarters.

The cannon platoons each contained a headquarters and two howitzer sections of one 105mm (4.1in.) howitzer each. Each cannon platoon was capable of independently supporting a designated infantry unit be it a battalion or company.

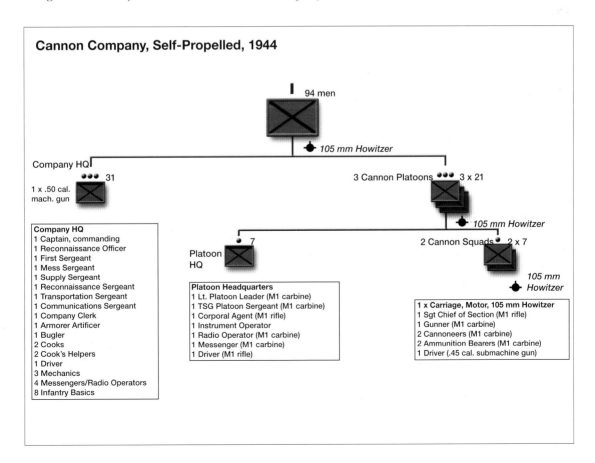

Cannon Company, Self-Propelled, 1944

94 men

105 mm Howitzer

Company HQ

1 x .50 cal. mach. gun — 31

3 Cannon Platoons — 3 x 21

105 mm Howitzer

Platoon HQ — 7

2 Cannon Squads — 2 x 7

105 mm Howitzer

Company HQ
1 Captain, commanding
1 Reconnaissance Officer
1 First Sergeant
1 Mess Sergeant
1 Supply Sergeant
1 Reconnaissance Sergeant
1 Transportation Sergeant
1 Communications Sergeant
1 Company Clerk
1 Armorer Artificer
1 Bugler
2 Cooks
2 Cook's Helpers
1 Driver
3 Mechanics
4 Messengers/Radio Operators
8 Infantry Basics

Platoon Headquarters
1 Lt. Platoon Leader (M1 carbine)
1 TSG Platoon Sergeant (M1 carbine)
1 Corporal Agent (M1 rifle)
1 Instrument Operator
1 Radio Operator (M1 carbine)
1 Messenger (M1 carbine)
1 Driver (M1 rifle)

1 x Carriage, Motor, 105 mm Howitzer
1 Sgt Chief of Section (M1 rifle)
1 Gunner (M1 carbine)
2 Cannoneers (M1 carbine)
2 Ammunition Bearers (M1 carbine)
1 Driver (.45 cal. submachine gun)

ANTITANK COMPANY

The Antitank Company provided, in conjunction with the battalion antitank platoons, protection against mechanized forces threatening the regimental elements. The company consisted of a company headquarters, three 57mm (2.22in.) antitank platoons, and an antitank mine platoon.

Most infantry divisions contained antitank guns towed behind one and one half ton cargo trucks. However, those divisions landing on D-Day in Normandy had halftracks as prime movers for added mobility.

The company headquarters was divided into a command and an admin group similar to all infantry company headquarters.

The antitank platoons each contained a headquarters and three antitank squads, each containing one 57mm (2.22in.) antitank gun and one 2.36in. (60mm) bazooka. Each antitank platoon was capable of independently supporting a designated infantry unit.

The antitank mine platoon contained a headquarters and three antitank mine squads capable of emplacing and removing minefields as well as basic engineering tasks.

The infantry regiment's main combat power resided in its three infantry battalions, with each containing a headquarters and headquarters company, three rifle companies (A, B, and C in 1st Battalion; E, F, G in 2d Battalion and I, K and L in 3d Battalion; and a heavy weapons company (D in 1st Battalion, H in 2d Battalion and M in 3d Battalion).

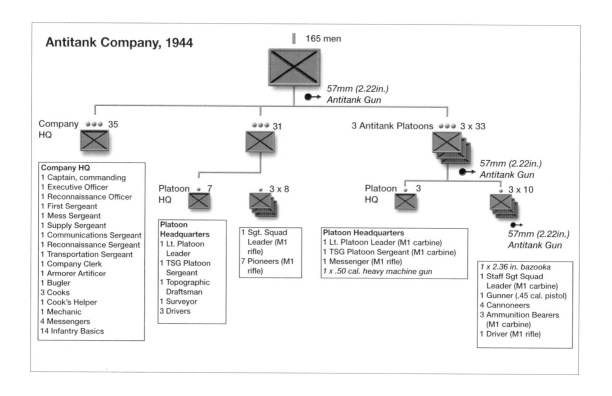

BATTALION HEADQUARTERS AND HEADQUARTERS COMPANY

The Battalion Headquarters consisted of the battalion commander (lieutenant-colonel), executive officer (major), S-1 Adjutant (captain) – also headquarters company commander, S-2 Intelligence (lieutenant), S-3 Operations and Training (captain), S-4 Supply (captain) – from Service Company.

The Headquarters Company consisted of a company headquarters, a battalion headquarters section, a communication platoon, an ammunition and pioneer platoon, and an antitank platoon.

The company headquarters was divided into a command and an administrative group similar to the regimental headquarters described earlier, except that the commander also served as battalion adjutant and the executive officer served as the battalion motor officer.

The Battalion Headquarters section was composed of soldiers provided for the operation of the command post and observation posts. It consisted of the battalion sergeant-major, operations sergeant, intelligence sergeant, clerk, drivers, messengers, and scouts.

The communications platoon established, maintained, and operated the radio and wire communications systems of the headquarters' message center. The platoon leader also served as the battalion communications officer. The platoon was organized similarly to the regimental headquarters company.

The ammunition and pioneer (A & P) platoon maintained the battalion ammunition supply service, executed simple engineering tasks not requiring technical training, and installed and breached mine fields. The platoon consisted of a headquarters and three A & P squads.

Infantry Rifle Battalion table of organization and equipment, 1942–45			
	Aug 1, 1942	**Jul 15, 1943**	**Jan 24, 1945**
Rifle Battalion (3)	916	871	860
Headquarters (TO 7–16)	4/0	4/0	4/0
Headquarters Co (TO 7–16)	5 off/130 enl-men	5/117	5/117
Company Headquarters	2/29	2/25	2/23
Battalion Headquarters Section	15	13	13
Communications Platoon	1/22	1/22	1/22
Ammunition and Pioneer Platoon	1/23	1/22	1/22
Antitank Platoon	1/41	1/31	1/28
Rifle Co (3) (TO 7–17)	6/192	6/187	6/187
Company Headquarters	2/37	2/33	2/33
Rifle Platoons (3)	1/40	1/40	1/40
Heavy Weapons Platoon	1/35	1/34	1/34
Heavy Weapons Co (TO 7–18)	8/176	8/158	8/152
Company Headquarters	2(3)/35	2(3)/31	2(3)/28
81mm Mortar Platoon	1/59	1/50	1/47
.30 cal. Machine Gun Platoon (2)	1/41	1/35	1/35
Medical Section (from Regimental Medical Detachment)	2/23	3/23	3/23

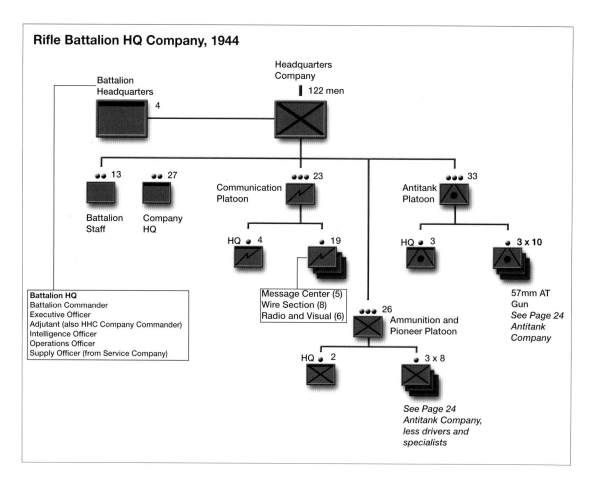

Rifle Battalion HQ Company, 1944

Battalion Headquarters

Headquarters Company — 122 men

4

Battalion Staff — 13

Company HQ — 27

Communication Platoon — 23

Antitank Platoon — 33

HQ 4

19

HQ 3

3 x 10

57mm AT Gun
See Page 24 Antitank Company

Message Center (5)
Wire Section (8)
Radio and Visual (6)

Ammunition and Pioneer Platoon — 26

HQ 2

3 x 8

See Page 24 Antitank Company, less drivers and specialists

Battalion HQ
Battalion Commander
Executive Officer
Adjutant (also HHC Company Commander)
Intelligence Officer
Operations Officer
Supply Officer (from Service Company)

The antitank platoon provided anti-mechanized protection to the battalion. The platoon was organized into a headquarters section and three 57mm (2.22in.) antitank gun squads.

RIFLE COMPANY

Infantry rifle company organization changed throughout the war, not so much in personnel but in new weapons systems and numbers of automatic weapons carried. Numbers and equipment within the rifle platoon remained stable throughout the war, and the M1 rifle was the primary weapon. These changes were always based upon the mobility and firepower of the units at the lowest level. A platoon's mobility centered on the soldiers carrying the BAR, with no weapon in a squad seen as a focus for enemy fire.

The rifle company in the 1940 square division was composed of three platoons. Lacking the mortars and machine guns of the later weapons platoon, the company commander had only to lead his rifle platoons. Each platoon contained two rifle sections of three squads.

Each squad contained eight men and a BAR, giving the company 18 BARs. With 58 men in a platoon, the units were well suited for

Rifle company organization, 1944

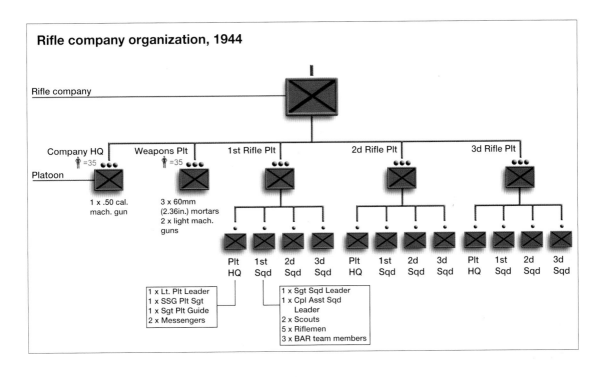

Rifle company, 1944

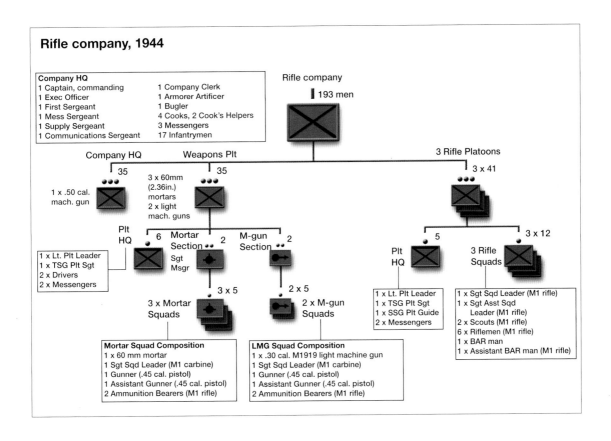

attrition-style combat, and platoons attacked with one section behind the other. When the divisions triangularized, platoons shrunk to three squads, although squad strength increased to 12 men. Rifle companies after 1941 contained a company head-quarters, a weapons platoon, and three rifle platoons, each with three rifle squads.

By September 1942, all infantry organizations within the rifle regiment were identical by Tables of Organization and Equipment (TOE), although most had to make do with antiquated equipment until production caught up and units received their full authorization of new equipment. Overseas divisions might have modified clothing issues for soldiers fighting in the different climates, but weapons and manpower were identical to those in the US.

For the Normandy invasion, some rifle companies in the assault divisions were reorganized for the initial landing, with one officer and 29 enlisted, or the number of soldiers able to fit into an LCVP. Each assault section was self-contained and had the capacity with its flamethrowers, bazookas and explosives to eliminate enemy strong points.

Company headquarters

Although equipment and personnel strength changed, the duties and responsibilities of the infantry leaders in a rifle company did not. The rifle company headquarters section comprised a command and an administrative group, with the commanding officer (CO), executive officer (XO), first sergeant (1SG), and communications sergeant making up the command group.

Infantry Rifle Company table of organization, 1942–45

Personnel	Jul 15, 1943		Jul 15, 1944		Jun 1, 1945	
	Officers	Enlisted men	Officers	Enlisted men	Officers	Enlisted men
Rifle Company (3) (TO 7–17)	6	187	6	187	6	236
Command Group					2	7
Administrative Group						33
Rifle Platoon (3)	1	40	1	40	1	40
Platoon Headquarters	1	4	1	4	1	4
Rifle Squad (3)		12		12		12
Weapons Platoon					2	75
Platoon Headquarters	1	5	1	5	2	7
60mm (2.36 in.) Mortar Section		2		2		2
60mm (2.36 in.) Mortar Squad (3)		5		5		5
.30 cal. Machine gun Section		2		2		2
.30 cal. Machine gun Squad (2)		5		5		5
Assault Section						1
Assault Squad (3)						7
Special Weapons Section						2
Special Weapons Squad (3)						5

Rifle Company armaments, 1943–45

Equipment	Jul 15, 1943	26 Feb, 1944 w/c	Jun 1, 1945
Rifle Company (3) (TO 7–17)			
Headquarters	9 carbines 26 M1 Rifles	9 carbines 26 M1 Rifles 6 BAR 6 submachine guns[1] 5 60mm (2.36in.) Bazookas	10 carbines 31 M1 Rifles 6 BAR* 6 submachine guns*
Rifle Platoon (3)			
Platoon Headquarters	1 carbine 4 M1 Rifles 1 1903A4 Sniper*	1 carbine 4 M1 Rifles 1 1903A4 Sniper*	1 carbine 4 M1 Rifles 1 M1C Sniper*
Rifle Squad (3)	11 M1 Rifles 1 BAR	11 M1 Rifles 1 BAR	11 M1 Rifles 1 BAR
Weapons Platoon			
Platoon Headquarters	4 carbines 2 M1 Rifles 1 .50 cal. HMG 3 60mm (2.36in.) Bazookas	4 carbines 2 M1 Rifles 1 .50 cal. HMG	5 carbines 4 M1 Rifles 1 .50 cal. HMG
60mm (2.36in.) Mortar Section	1 carbine 1 M1 Rifle	1 carbine 1 M1 Rifle	1 carbine 1 M1 Rifle
60-mm (2.36in.) Mortar Squad (3)	1 Mortar, 60-mm (2.36in.) 2 carbines 2 .45 cal. Pistols 1 M1 Rifle	1 Mortar 60-mm (2.36in.) 2 carbines 2 .45 cal. Pistols 1 M1 Rifle	1 Mortar, 60mm (2.36in.) 2 carbines 2 .45 cal. Pistols 1 M1 Rifle
.30 cal. Machine Gun Section	1 carbine 1 M1 Rifle	1 carbine 1 M1 Rifle	1 carbine 1 M1 Rifle
.30 cal. Machine Gun Squad (2)	1 .30 cal. LMG 2 carbines 2 .45 cal. Pistols 1 M1 Rifle	1 30 cal. LMG 2 carbines 2 .45 cal. Pistols 1 M1 Rifle	1 .30 cal. LMG 2 carbines 2 .45 cal. Pistols 1 M1 Rifle
Assault Section			1 M1
Assault Squad (3)			2 60mm (2.36in.) Bazookas 2 .45 cal. Pistols 5 M1 Rifles
Special Weapons Section 57mm (2.22 in.)			1 carbine 1 M1 Rifle
Special Weapons Squad (3)			1 Rifle, 57mm (2.22in.) 2 carbines 2 .45 cal. Pistols 1 M1 Rifle

Table notes
[1] Six BARs and six submachine guns added to TOE 6/44 to be distributed as mission necessitated.
* Sniper rifles were authorized one per platoon to be assigned by the platoon leader in lieu of M1 rifle.

The company commander (captain) was responsible for the discipline, administration, supply, training, tactical employment, and control of his company. Although he decided how best to employ his company, he did so in conformity with orders from higher headquarters. He could accept advice and suggestion, but he alone was responsible for his organization's success or failure. On the battlefield, the commander was located where he could most decisively influence the situation. The XO (lieutenant) was second-in-command. In combat he remained at the company command post maintaining contact between battalion and company, keeping abreast of the tactical situation and was prepared to assume command if the company commander was injured. He was in charge of the command post until called forward to assume either company command or command of one of the platoons. The XO frequently coordinated resupply of ammunition and rations to the platoons. The 1SG (pay grade 2, until 1944 when it became pay grade 1) assisted the company commander and XO in controlling the company. During combat, his duties varied from handling administrative and supply matters to commanding a platoon. Ordinarily, he took over the communication and administrative duties when the XO was absent.

The administrative group consisted of those headquarters elements not directly involved in the fighting, such as the supply sergeant, company clerk, and mess team, all of whom (except the supply sergeant) were normally back in the battalion trains area.

Rifle platoon

The rifle platoon was composed of three rifle squads and a command group. The platoon leader (lieutenant) was responsible for the training, discipline, control, and tactical employment of his platoon. In combat, he was located where he could most decisively influence the situation. The platoon sergeant (PSG, technical sergeant) was second-in-command. He assisted the platoon leader in controlling the platoon and acted as platoon leader when there was no officer present. In combat, the PSG was normally located at the second most decisive point. The platoon guide (staff sergeant) enforced the orders concerning cover, concealment, and discipline. He was normally located behind the platoon, where he could observe the flanks and rear. He managed the platoon's ammunition resupply.

Rifle squad

The rifle squad was made up of a squad leader, an assistant squad leader, an automatic rifleman, an assistant automatic rifleman, and eight riflemen, two of whom acted as scouts. The squad leader (a corporal prewar, a sergeant 1941–43, and a staff sergeant 1944–45) was always with his squad and was responsible for their employment, training, and sustenance. In combat, he ensured they fought. The assistant squad leader (private first class prewar, corporal 1941–43, sergeant 1944–45) assisted the squad leader in carrying out the squad's mission. In combat, he normally led a portion of the squad and acted as squad leader if the squad leader became a casualty. He might also ensure squad members remained resupplied with ammunition.

Weapons platoon

The weapons platoon was composed of a command group, a 60mm mortar section and a light machine gun section. The platoon leader (lieutenant) was responsible for the training,

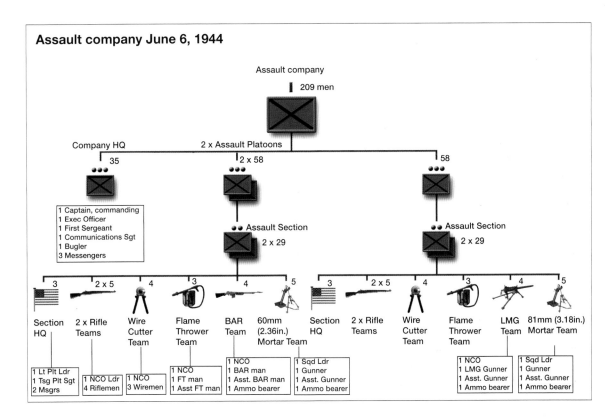

Assault company June 6, 1944

discipline, control, and tactical employment of his platoon. In combat, he was responsible for selecting primary, alternate, and supplementary positions; ensuring fire did not endanger troops as well as the delivery of ammunition to the guns. The platoon sergeant (PSG; staff, and later technical sergeant) was second-in-command. He assisted the platoon leader in controlling the platoon and acted as platoon leader when there was no officer present.

Mortar section

The mortar section leader (sergeant and later staff sergeant) was responsible for his three squads' employment, training, and sustenance. In combat he selected and assigned locations for the squads, assigned sectors of fire, and ensured the mortars were resupplied. The mortar squad leader (corporal, and later sergeant) selected the exact firing position, observed and adjusted fire. The difference was that usually only one NCO remained with the mortar section to supervise ammunition resupply and the execution of fire commands by the mortar crews. The two other NCOs served as observers for their respective mortars.

.30 Caliber Light Machine Gun section

The section normally consisted of a section sergeant, and two machine gun squads. Each squad had a corporal leader, a machine gunner, an assistant machine gunner, and four ammunition bearers.

The section leader (sergeant, and later staff sergeant) was responsible for their employment, training, and sustenance. In combat he selected and assigned locations for the squads, assigned sectors of fire, and ensured the machine guns remained resupplied. The squad leader (corporal, and later sergeant) selected the exact firing position, observed and adjusted fire, enforced fire discipline, and ensured his ammunition bearers kept his crew resupplied with ammunition.

HEAVY WEAPONS COMPANY

Between 1941 and 1945, the heavy weapons company consisted of two .30 cal. heavy machine gun platoons, an 81mm (3.18in.) mortar platoon, and a headquarters section split between a command and an administrative group. It was similar to the rifle company, and although equipment and personnel strength changed during the war years, duties and responsibilities of the leaders did not.

The command group consisted of the CO, XO, 1SG, and reconnaissance/signal sergeant.

The company commander (captain) was responsible for the discipline, administration, supply, training, tactical employment, and control of his company. He decided how best to employ his company in conformity with the battalion commander's scheme of fire support. Although he could listen to advice, he alone was responsible for his organization's success or failure. The reconnaissance officer (lieutenant) was second-in-command. During combat, he reconnoitered for initial and subsequent firing positions, targets, and routes for ammunition resupply. He kept abreast of the company situation and was prepared to assume company command. The 1SG (initially pay grade 2, changed to pay grade 1 in 1944) assisted the company commander in controlling the company. His duties varied from handling administrative and supply matters to maintaining the company command post or commanding a platoon in combat.

The administrative group consisted of those headquarters elements not directly involved in the fighting, such as the supply sergeant, transportation sergeant, company clerk, and mess team, of which all except the supply sergeant and transportation sergeant were normally back in the battalion trains area.

.30 Caliber Heavy Machine Gun platoon

The platoon normally consisted of two sections and a command group. The platoon leader (lieutenant) was responsible for the training, discipline, control, and tactical employment of his platoon. In combat, he was responsible for selecting primary, alternate, and supplementary positions; ensuring fire did not endanger troops as well as the delivery of ammunition to the guns. The platoon sergeant (PSG; staff, and later technical sergeant) was second-in-command. He assisted the platoon leader in controlling the platoon and acted as platoon leader when there was no officer present. In combat, the PSG was normally located in the rear of the platoon command post where he could supervise the ammunition bearers. The two corporals assisted in reconnaissance, served as liaison between the platoon and supported company, controlled the fire control equipment, and prepared firing data.

.30 Caliber Heavy Machine Gun section
The section normally consisted of a section sergeant and two machine gun squads. Each squad had a corporal leader, a machine gunner, an assistant machine gunner, and four ammunition bearers.

The section leader (sergeant, and later staff sergeant) was responsible for their employment, training, and sustenance. In combat he selected and assigned locations for the squads, assigned sectors of fire, and ensured the machine guns remained resupplied. The squad leader (corporal, and later sergeant) selected the exact firing position, observed and adjusted fire, enforced fire discipline, and ensured his ammunition bearers kept his crew resupplied with ammunition.

81mm Mortar platoon
The duties of the mortar platoon command group were identical to those of the heavy machine gun platoons.

Much like the duties of the section leader in the machine gun platoon the mortar section leader (sergeant and later staff sergeant) was responsible for his squad's employment, training, and sustenance. In combat he selected and assigned locations for the squads, assigned sectors of fire, and ensured the mortars were resupplied. The mortar squad leader (corporal, and later sergeant) selected the exact firing position, observed and adjusted fire. The difference was that usually only one NCO remained with the mortar section to supervise ammunition resupply and the execution of fire commands by the mortar crews. The two other NCOs served as observers for their respective mortars.

WEAPONS

Soldiers in rifle companies carried the same type of weapons whether they fought in the Pacific or European theaters, the primary weapon being the M1 Garand rifle, carried by all riflemen except snipers. The one sniper in each squad wielded an M1903 Springfield and later an M1C Sniper Rifle.

The BAR was the principal automatic weapon with one in each squad. Officers were issued .45 cal. pistols until 1943, when they began carrying M1 carbines instead of the pistol; leaving the pistols to be carried only by gunners and assistant gunners. Company heavy weapons consisted of two M1919A3 .30 cal. light machine guns, one .50 cal. heavy machine gun and three 60mm (2.36in.) mortars. Additional weapons available to the company on a

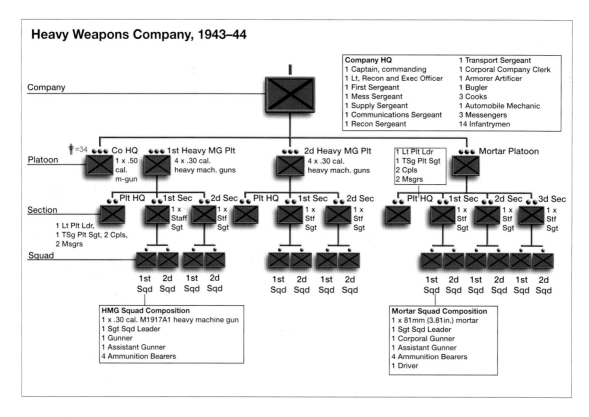

Heavy Weapons Company, 1943–44

Company HQ
1 Captain, commanding
1 Lt, Recon and Exec Officer
1 First Sergeant
1 Mess Sergeant
1 Supply Sergeant
1 Communications Sergeant
1 Recon Sergeant
1 Transport Sergeant
1 Corporal Company Clerk
1 Armorer Artificer
1 Bugler
3 Cooks
1 Automobile Mechanic
3 Messengers
14 Infantrymen

Company

Platoon — Co HQ (1 x .50 cal. m-gun) · 1st Heavy MG Plt (4 x .30 cal. heavy mach. guns) · 2d Heavy MG Plt (4 x .30 cal. heavy mach. guns) · Mortar Platoon
1 Lt Plt Ldr
1 TSg Plt Sgt
2 Cpls
2 Msgrs

Section — Plt HQ · 1st Sec (1 x Staff Sgt) · 2d Sec (1 x Stf Sgt) · Plt HQ · 1st Sec (1 x Stf Sgt) · 2d Sec (1 x Stf Sgt) · Plt HQ · 1st Sec (1 x Stf Sgt) · 2d Sec (1 x Stf Sgt) · 3d Sec (1 x Stf Sgt)
1 Lt Plt Ldr, 1 TSg Plt Sgt, 2 Cpls, 2 Msgrs

Squad — 1st Sqd · 2d Sqd · 1st Sqd · 2d Sqd · 1st Sqd · 2d Sqd · 1st Sqd · 2d Sqd · 1st Sqd · 2d Sqd · 1st Sqd · 2d Sqd · 1st Sqd · 2d Sqd

HMG Squad Composition
1 x .30 cal. M1917A1 heavy machine gun
1 Sgt Sqd Leader
1 Gunner
1 Assistant Gunner
4 Ammunition Bearers

Mortar Squad Composition
1 x 81mm (3.81in.) mortar
1 Sgt Sqd Leader
1 Corporal Gunner
1 Assistant Gunner
4 Ammunition Bearers
1 Driver

mission-by-mission basis from the battalion weapon's pool were Thompson submachine guns and flamethrowers. Many squad leaders in the Pacific carried the Thompson instead of an M1, giving squads two automatic weapons. By 1943, the 60mm (2.36in.) bazooka was added to the armory, and in many organizations the M3 submachine "grease" gun replaced the Thompson.

The M1919A4 air-cooled machine gun was a tripod-mounted, air cooled, belt-fed, fully automatic .30 cal. machine gun that fired at a nominal rate of 400 to 550 rounds per minute. It weighed 32lbs (14.5kg). The M1919A6 was a wartime modification that substituted a bipod in place of the tripod and added a shoulder stock and carrying handle. The M1919A6 had a lighter barrel than the M1919A4 and fired at a nominal rate of 400–500 rounds per minute.

The M19 60mm (2.36in.) mortar fired high explosive, white phosphorous and illuminating shells. The maximum range with a 3lbs.(1.36kg) HE shell was 1,985 yards (1,815m). The sustained rate of fire was 18 rounds per minute, with 30–35 rounds per minute the maximum rate of fire.

Soldiers in heavy weapons companies (D, H, and M companies of an infantry regiment) carried the same type weapons whether they fought in the Mediterranean (MTO), European (ETO) or Pacific (PTO) theaters of operations. In 1942, the company's primary heavy weapons systems were eight M1917A1 .30 cal. Browning water-cooled heavy machine guns, six M1 81mm mortars, and one M2 .50 cal. Browning air-cooled heavy machine gun. Individual weapons consisted of the .45 cal. automatic pistol, the M1 rifle, and the M1 (and later M2) carbine.

The gunners and assistant gunners carried pistols; the officers, senior NCOs, drivers, and some ammunition bearers the M1 carbine; all others carried the M1 rifle. Beginning in 1943, each of the three heavy weapons platoons received two 60mm (2.36in.) bazookas as part of their platoon equipment and these were carried within the platoon headquarters. The heavy weapons company, because of its numerous heavy weapons systems, also contained 19 quarter-ton trucks (jeeps), 14 quarter-ton trailers, and one three-quarter-ton weapons carrier.

The M1917A1 .30 cal. heavy machine gun was fully automatic, recoil-operated, and water-cooled, firing a 175-grain bullet to an effective range of 1,100 yards (1,005m) from 250-round belts. The machine gun weighed about 93lbs (42kg) with tripod and water, and could fire longer, more sustained bursts before overheating than its air-cooled cousins.

The basic design of the M1 81mm mortar was the same as that of the French Brandt-designed mortar. The mortar weighed 136lbs (61.7kg) and fired rounds weighing between nine and 19lbs (8.6kg) each, depending whether the round was high explosive (heavy or light), smoke (white phosphorous), or illuminating. The 81mm (3.18in.) mortar's range varied depending on the type of shell used, from a minimum of fewer than 200 yards to a maximum of 3,290 yards (3,008m). Three men could

Rifle Company weapons

US submachine gun, .45 cal., M1 "Thompson"

Browning machine gun, .30 cal., M19114A4

Mortar and mount, 60mm, M2

US pistol, .45 cal., M1911A1

US carbine, .30 cal., M1

US rifle, .30 cal., M1903 "Springfield"

US rifle, .30 cal., M1 "Garand"

US M1918A2 Browning Automatic Rifle

Heavy Weapons Company weapons
*In both Heavy Weapons and Rifle Companies

M1 81mm mortar

M1917A1 Browning .30 cal.
water-cooled heavy machine gun

M2 HB Browning .50 cal.
machine gun*

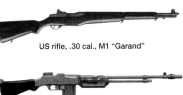

easily carry the mortar for short distances: one carrying the tube, the second the bipod and sight, and the third the base plate.

The M2 .50 cal. heavy machine gun (heavy barrel) was belt-fed, crew-served and air-cooled, and capable of single-shot as well as automatic fire; its functioning was similar to the .30 cal. Browning. The .50 cal. machine gun's primary use was defense against aircraft, with a secondary mission of protecting organic vehicles from ground attack.

The 57mm (2.22in.) M1 antitank gun was designed after the British six-pound antitank gun. It fired fixed armor-piercing rounds that could penetrate 86mm (3.4in.) of armor at 20° slope at 500 yards (457m). The gun's approximate rate of fire was 30 rounds per minute, depending upon its crew's skill. The antitank gun was towed either by a one-ton cargo carrier or by one of the series of halftracked carriers with off-road capability.

The 105mm (4.1in.) M2A1 howitzer was mounted on either the M2A2 towed carriage or the M7 howitzer motor carriage and was commonly referred to as the "Priest." The howitzer's rate of fire was four rounds per minute with a maximum range of 12,500 yards (11,430m). Ammunition included high explosive, smoke, armor-piercing, and chemical rounds. The towed version was pulled by a two and one half ton truck at speeds up to 35 miles per hour (56km/h) on improved roads. The M7B1 version was a lightly armored open-topped vehicle based on the M4A3 tank chassis. It carried a basic load of 69 105mm (4.1in.) rounds and traveled at a maximum speed of 26 miles per hour (42km/h).

CHAPTER 3

CHRONOLOGY

<u>1931</u>
Sep 18   Japanese Kwantung Army seizes Mukden, Manchuria

<u>1933</u>
Jan 30   Adolf Hitler appointed German Chancellor

Oct 1   Hitler announces withdrawal of Germany from the League of Nations

<u>1934</u>
Jun 30   "Night of the Long Knives" in Germany

<u>1935</u>
Mar 16   Hitler decrees universal military service for Germany

Oct 3   Italians invade Ethiopia

<u>1936</u>
Mar 7   Germans reoccupy Rhineland
Jul 17   Outbreak of Spanish Civil War

<u>1937</u>
Jul 7   Sino–Japanese War begins
Dec 12   Japanese attack US and British gunboats in Yangtze River, sinking *Panay*
Dec 13   Japanese take Nanking

<u>1938</u>
Mar 12   Germans march into Austria
Jul 28   Soviet and Japanese forces fight in Far East
Sep 29   Hitler and Chamberlain, meeting in Munich, partition Czechoslovakia
Sep 29   Munich Conference opens (to September 30)
Nov 3   Japanese announce a "New Order in East Asia"

<u>1939</u>
Mar 1   Germans enter Prague, Czechoslovakia
Mar 29   Madrid falls to Franco forces – end of Spanish Civil War
Mar 31   British Government abandons appeasement policy, announces aid to Poland

May 29   Germany and Italy sign "Pact of Steel"
May 28   New Soviet–Japanese fighting erupts at Khalkhin Gol
Aug 23   Soviet–German Nonaggression Pact signed
Sep 1   Germany invades Poland – War again comes to Europe
Sep 1   George C. Marshall becomes US Army Chief of Staff
Sep 8   Roosevelt signs emergency proclamation expanding the Regular Army to 237,000, and increases the National Guard to 235,000
Sep 17   Soviets move into Poland
Sep 29   Soviet–German Boundary and Friendship Treaty signed
Nov 3   US Congress passes "cash and carry" amendment to Neutrality Laws
Nov 30   USSR invades Finland – beginning of Soviet–Finnish (Winter) War

<u>1940</u>
Mar 12   Finland capitulates, ending Soviet–Finnish War
Mar 30   Japanese establish puppet Chinese government (Wang Ching-wei) at Nanking
Apr 9   Germany seizes Denmark, invades Norway
May 10   Germany invades Low Countries and France
May 14   The Netherlands surrender
May 26   Allied evacuation at Dunkirk (to June 4)
May 28   Belgium capitulates to Germans
Jun 9   Norway surrenders
Jun 22   France Falls, armistice signed with Germany
Jun 26   First US embargo on war trade with Japan
Aug 15   Eagle Day – Battle of Britain
Aug 27   Authorization for Federalization of National Guard for 12 months
Sep 3   US–British destroyers bases deal
Sep 7   German bomber "Blitz" on London begins
Sep 13   Italian Army advances into Egypt
Sep 16   Roosevelt signs Selective Service Act
Sep 22   Japanese forces move into Indochina

Sep 23	Discharge granted enlisted men who are sole support for dependents (51,501 enlisted men leave Guard – about 1 in 5)
Sep 27	Japan signs Tripartite Pact
Nov 5	Roosevelt elected to third term as US President
Dec 9	British attack Italians in Western Desert
Jan 22	British capture Tobruk

1941

Feb 5	British victorious at Beda Fomm
Feb 12	Rommel arrives in Tripoli
Mar 11	US Lend–Lease Act signed
Mar 24	Axis (Rommel) takes El Agheila
Apr 6	Germans invade Balkans
Apr 9	Axis captures Bardia
Apr 10	Axis siege of Tobruk begins
Apr 22	British begin withdrawal from Greece
Apr 23	Greek Army surrenders to Germans
Apr 27	Axis occupies Halfaya Pass
May 2	British complete evacuation from Greece
May 20	Germans invade Crete
May 22	British withdraw from Crete airfields
May 27	*Bismarck* sunk
Jun 1	British complete evacuation of Crete
Jun 15	British launch Operation Battleaxe offensive in Western Desert
Jun 22	Germany invades USSR
Jul 5	US forces begin occupying Iceland
Aug 5	Germans eliminate Russian resistance in Smolensk pocket
Aug 9	Roosevelt and Churchill meet in Atlantic Conference (to August 12); Atlantic Charter proclaimed
Aug 17	Germans take Kiev
Sep 1	Germans complete investment of Leningrad
Oct 31	US Destroyer *Reuben James* sunk by U-boat
Nov 18	British open Crusader desert offensive
Nov 30	British Eighth Army links up with Tobruk garrison
Dec 7	War comes to the US. Japanese attack on US Naval Base at Pearl Harbor
Dec 8	US bases in the Philippines and British bases in Malaya attacked by Japanese; US declares war on Japan
Dec 10	Japanese sink HMS *Prince of Wales* and *Repulse* off the Malay Peninsula
Dec 10	Japanese take Guam; make first landings on Luzon, Philippine Islands
Dec 10	Siege of Tobruk is lifted Dec 11, 1941 Germany and Italy declare war on US, which takes reciprocal action
Dec 16	Japanese invade Borneo
Dec 19	Hitler assumes personal command of German Army
Dec 23	Wake Island falls
Dec 24	Arcadia Conference begins in Washington (to January 14)

Dec 24	British reenter Benghazi

1942

Jan 1	Declaration of the United Nations signed
Jan 7	Siege of Bataan begins
Jan 17	Halfaya garrison surrenders to British
Jan 22	In new Axis offensive, Rommel retakes Agedabia
Jan 24	US destroyers sink Japanese shipping in Makassar Strait
Jan 31	1st Battalion 133d Infantry, elements of the first division (34th) sent to the European Theater, arrive in Northern Ireland
Feb 22	MacArthur ordered to leave Philippines
Feb 27	Battle of Java Sea ends Allied naval resistance in Netherlands East Indies
Mar 7	Japanese land in New Guinea
Mar 9	Japanese secure Java completing conquest of East Indies
Mar 20	27th Division arrives in Hawaii. First division to arrive overseas in the Pacific since war's outbreak
Mar 30	General MacArthur appointed Supreme Commander Southwest Pacific Area, Admiral Nimitz as Commander in Chief Pacific Ocean Area
Apr 3	Bataan surrenders
Apr 18	US (Doolittle) B-25 raid on Japan
May 4	Naval Battle of the Coral Sea (to May 8)
May 6	Corregidor surrenders
May 27	Rommel attacks Gazala Line in large-scale Axis offensive
Jun 3	Naval Battle of Midway (to June 6)
Jun 7	Japanese invade western Aleutian Islands
Jun 9	Japanese conquest of Philippines completed
Jun 17	British withdrawal in Libya leaves Tobruk isolated
Jun 18	Churchill arrives in Washington for meetings
Jun 21	Tobruk falls to Rommel's forces
Jun 28	Axis takes Mersa Matrüh in Egypt
Jul 1	First battle of El Alamein begins (to July 17)
Aug 7	US 1st Marine Division lands on Guadalcanal
Aug 8	Naval Battle of Savo Island
Aug 19	Canadian and British force raids Dieppe
Aug 22	Brazil declares war on Germany and Italy
Aug 24	Naval battle of the Eastern Solomons
Aug 31	Battle of Alam Halfa (to September 7)
Sep 7	Japanese defeated in Milne Bay area, New Guinea
Sep 12	Eisenhower assumes post as C-in-C Allied Expeditionary Force (for Northwest Africa)

Sep 12	Fighting on Bloody Ridge, Guadalcanal
Sep 25	Allied counteroffensive opens on Papua
Oct 11	Naval battle of Cape Esperance
Oct 23	Second battle of El Alamein begins (to November 4)
Oct 26	Naval battle of Santa Cruz Islands
Nov 3	Axis begins retreat at El Alamein
Nov 8	Allies land in Northwest Africa (Operation Torch)
Nov 11	British Eighth Army takes Bardia
Nov 11	French cease resistance in Northwest Africa
Nov 11	Germans occupy southern France
Nov 11	Naval battle of Guadalcanal
Nov 11	British take Tobruk
Nov 19	Russians open counteroffensive at Stalingrad
Nov 30	Naval battle of Tassafaronga
Dec 13	Axis begins retreat from Al Agheila

1943

Jan 14	Allied Casablanca Conference begins (to January 23)
Jan 15	British Eighth Army opens drive on Tripoli
Jan 22	Allies complete victorious Papuan campaign in Sanananda area
Feb 9	US forces complete Guadalcanal campaign
Feb 19	German attack and breakthrough US units at Kasserine Pass
Mar 1	Naval battle of the Bismarck Sea
Mar 1	Von Arnim replaces Rommel as Axis C-in-C in Africa
Mar 26	British Eighth Army breaks through Mareth Line in Tunisia
Mar 27	34th Infantry Division begins attack on Fondouk Pass (to 31 Mar) but fails in effort
Apr 8	133d Infantry Regiment seizes Fondouk Pass
Apr 29	Elements of 34th Infantry Division seize Hill 609
May 7	Allied 18th Army Group captures Tunis and Bizerte
May 7	Axis forces in northeast Tunisia surrender unconditionally
May 11	US 7th Division lands on Attu
May 12	Trident Conference (Anglo–American) begins in Washington (to May 25). All Axis resistance in North Africa ends
May 30	Japanese resistance on Attu ends
Jun 30	Operation Cartwheel (Rabaul) launched in Southwest Pacific
Jul 5	Battle of Kula Gulf (Kolombangara)
Jul 10	Allies invade Sicily
Jul 12	Battle of Kolombangara
Jul 22	Palermo falls to US Seventh Army
Jul 25	Mussolini resigns; Badoglio becomes Italian Prime Minister

Aug 6	Battle of Vella Gulf
Aug 14	First Quebec Conference opens (to August 24)
Aug 15	US force invades Kiska
Aug 17	Axis resistance ends in Sicily
Sep 3	Allies land on Italian mainland
Sep 3	British 8th Army lands on Calabrian coast of Italy
Sep 3	Italians surrender
Sep 8	Allies land at Salerno
Sep 8	Eisenhower announces Italian surrender
Sep 9	US Fifth Army lands at Salerno
Sep 10	German forces occupy Rome
Sep 22	133d Infantry lands at Salerno
Oct 6	Battle of Vella Lavella
Oct 12	US Fifth Army attacks across Volturno River; 133d Infantry's first crossing of Volturno River
Oct 13	Italy declares war on Germany
Oct 18	133d Infantry's second crossing of Volturno River
Oct 31	US 3d Marine Division lands on Bougainville
Nov 4	133d Infantry's third crossing of Volturno River
Nov 5	Allies begin assaults on Winter Line in Italy
Nov 20	US 165th Infantry lands on Makin Island and Marine 2d Division assaults Tarawa
Nov 22	Allied Cairo Conference (to November 26)
Nov 25	Battle of Cape St. George
Nov 28	Allied Big Three begin Teheran Conference (to November 30)
Dec 1	Allies begin assaults on Winter Line in Italy
Dec 3	Allied meetings resume at Cairo (to December 7)
Dec 26	US 1st Marine Division lands at Cape Gloucester, New Britain

1944

Jan 15	Winter Line Campaign ends
Jan 16	Eisenhower assumes duties as Supreme Commander, Allied Expeditionary Force
Jan 22	US Fifth Army lands at Anzio
Jan 24	34th Infantry Divison begins its battle for Cassino (to Feb 21, 1944)
Jan 31	US 4th Marine and 7th Infantry Divisions land on Kwajalein
Feb 13	Combined Chiefs of Staff order intensive bomber offensive against Germany
Feb 15	Allies bomb abbey of Monte Cassino
Feb 17	22 Marine Regiment and 106th Infantry Regiment land on Eniwetok
Feb 29	Elements of US 1st Cavalry Division lands in Admiralty Islands
Mar 25	133d Infantry lands at Anzio

Apr 22	US 24th and 41st Infantry Divisions land in Hollandia area, New Guinea	**Aug 23**	US Seventh Army battles Germans at Montélimar (to August 28)
May 11	Allies open drive on Rome with attack on Gustav Line	**Aug 25**	Aitape operation (New Guinea) ends in Allied victory
May 18	163d Infantry Regiment lands on Wake off New Guinea	**Aug 25**	Paris liberated. 4th Division enters Paris from south. 22d Infantry establishes bridgehead across the Seine south of Paris
May 23	US Fifth Army breaks out at Anzio beachhead		
May 27	41st Infantry Division lands on Biak	**Sep 4**	British Second Army takes Antwerp
Jun 3	Lanuvio falls to 133d Infantry	**Sep 8**	First V-2 rocket falls on England
Jun 4	US Fifth Army enters Rome	**Sep 8**	Fifth Army begins attack on Gothic Line
Jun 6	Allies invade Normandy (Operation Overlord); 4th Infantry Division lands on Utah Beach	**Sep 11**	Allied Normandy and southern France invasion forces meet near Dijon
Jun 6	D-Day – Allies land in Normandy, France, 4th Division assaults Utah Beach	**Sep 12**	Second Allied Quebec Conference opens
		Sep 14	4th Infantry Division penetrates West Wall in the Schnee Eifel
Jun 13	First V-1 bomb falls on England	**Sep 15**	1st Marine Division and later 81st Infantry land on Peleliu
Jun 14	4th Division captures Quinéville		
Jun 15	2d and 4th Marine Divisions, followed by 27th Infantry Division invade Saipan	**Sep 15**	31st Infantry Division land on Morotai
		Sep 17	First Allied Airborne Army units dropped in Holland (Operation Market Garden)
Jun 19	Naval Battle of the Philippine Sea (Great Marianas Turkey Shoot) (to June 20)	**Sep 21**	British Eighth Army takes Rimini
Jun 25	Elements of the 4th Division enter Cherbourg	**Oct 2**	US First Army assaults West Wall
		Oct 16	133d Attacks Mount Belmonte (to 23 Oct 43)
Jul 3	US First Army opens "Battle of the Hedgerows" in Normandy	**Oct 20**	US Sixth Army invades Leyte with 1st Cavalry and 24th, 7th and 96th Infantry Divisions
Jul 6	4th Division begins its attack toward Périers		
Jul 9	Fighting ends on Saipan	**Oct 21**	US First Army occupies Aachen
Jul 17	Rommel severely wounded in strafing attack	**Oct 23**	Naval battle for Leyte Gulf (to October 26)
Jul 18	British Second Army opens offensive in Caen area (Operation Goodwood)	**Nov 7**	Roosevelt elected to fourth term as US President
Jul 20	German Army officers attempt to assassinate Hitler	**Nov 16**	4th Infantry Division attacks on broad front and attacks into the Hürtgen Forest
Jul 21	3d Marine Division, 77th Infantry Division and 1st Provisional Marine Brigade invade Guam	**Nov 16**	US First and Ninth Armies open offensive to clear Roer plain
		Nov 23	French armored force enters Strasbourg
Jul 24	4th and 2d Marine Divisions invade Tinian	**Nov 24**	US begins B-29 raids on Japan
Jul 25	US First Army breaks out at Saint-Lô (Operation Cobra); 4th Infantry Division as part of VII Corps attacks across Périers–St Lô road on narrow front. 22d Infantry attached to 2d Armored Division acts as armored infantry	**Nov 27**	Fighting ends on Peleliu
		Nov 29	22d Infantry in frontal and flanking attacks supported by armor, takes Grosshau and cuts the road to Gey
		Dec 3	4th Infantry Division is relieved by 83d Division in the Hürtgen Forest and moves to quiet sector in Luxembourg
Aug 1	Organized resistance ends on Tinian		
Aug 1	US 12th Army Group becomes operational in France	**Dec 13**	US Third Army completes capture of Metz
Aug 3	British Eighth Army takes Florence	**Dec 15**	19th Infantry and 503d Parachute Infantry Regiments invade Mindoro
Aug 7	Germans in Normandy begin counterattack toward Avranches	**Dec 16**	Germans attack in Ardennes (Battle of the Bulge);106th Divisions, 28th Divisions, 9th Armored Divisions, and elements of 4th Divisions all fall back under enemy onslaught
Aug 9	Eisenhower establishes HQ in France		
Aug 10	Organized resistance ends on Guam		
Aug 12	German counterattack at Avranches ends in failure		
Aug 15	Allies land in southern France (Operation Dragoon)	**Dec 26**	US Third Army armored relief column reaches Bastogne
Aug 19	US Third Army reaches Seine River	**1945**	
Aug 20	Canadian, First Army forces seal Germans in Falaise–Argentan pocket	**Jan 1**	Germans launch offensive (Operation Nordwind) against US Seventh Army

Jan 9	US Sixth Army invades Luzon with 46th, 37th, 6th and 43d Infantry Divisions
Jan 12	Major Soviet winter offensive opens
Jan 16	Allied counteroffensive reduces German bulge in Ardennes
Jan 17	Soviet Army takes Warsaw
Jan 18	4th Infantry Division attacks north across the Sauer River and reaches the Our River between Longsdorf and Hosdorf
Jan 20	Hungary signs armistice with Allies
Feb 3	US Army reaches Manila
Feb 4	4th Infantry Division breaches outer defenses of West Wall along the Schnee Eifel ridge northeast of Brandscheid
Feb 4	Yalta Conference begins (to February 12)
Feb 12	4th Infantry Division completes capture of Prüm
Feb 13	Budapest falls to Red Army
Feb 19	4th and 5th Marine Divisions followed by 3d Marines invade Iwo Jima
Feb 25	B-29 raid on Tokyo demonstrates effectiveness of incendiary bombs
Mar 3	Japanese resistance in Manila ends
Mar 5	US First Army units enter Cologne (secured March 7)
Mar 7	Troops of US 9th Armored Division cross Rhine on bridge at Remagen
Mar 9	US B-29s begin incendiary campaign against Japanese cities
Mar 11	41st Infantry Division lands on Mindanao
Mar 18	40th Infantry Division lands on Panay
Mar 22	In surprise action, troops of US Third Army cross Rhine at Oppenheim
Mar 23	British Second Army begins crossing Rhine near Rees
Mar 25	AMERICAL Infantry Division assaults Cebu
Mar 26	Fighting ends on Iwo Jima
Mar 27	Last V-2 rocket lands in England
Apr 1	US Tenth Army, with 6th and 1st Marine Divisions and 7th and 96th Infantry Divisions invade Okinawa. 77th and 27th Infantry Divisions as well as 8th Marine Regiment follow landing forces
Apr 7	US Navy planes sink Japanese battleship *Yamato* in East China Sea
Apr 9	Allies begin major attack on Gothic Line (Italy)
Apr 11	Japanese begin two-day kamikaze onslaught against US ships at Okinawa
Apr 12	Roosevelt dies; Truman succeeds as US President
Apr 13	Soviets complete capture of Vienna
Apr 14	Allies begin major attack on Gothic Line (Italy)
Apr 16	Soviets begin final offensive toward Berlin
Apr 18	US forces complete Ruhr operations, taking more than 300,000 prisoners

Apr 18	US Third Army troops enter Czechoslovakia
Apr 20	US Seventh Army takes Nuremberg
Apr 21	133d Infantry takes Bologna
Apr 21	Elements of 4th Infantry Division seize Crailsheim
Apr 23	Himmler makes surrender offer to Western Allies; Russians break into Berlin
Apr 25	First US Army and Soviet forces meet near Torgau, splitting Germany in two
Apr 25	United Nations conference opens in San Francisco
Apr 28	Mussolini is executed by partisans
Apr 30	Hitler dies in bunker; Dönitz is chosen as head of state
Apr 30	US Seventh Army takes Munich and elements of the 4th Divisions cross the Isar River in vicinity of Wolfratshausen
May 2	German forces in Italy, the Netherlands, Bavaria and northwestern Germany and Denmark surrender
May 2	Units of British Second Army reach Baltic and Berlin falls to the Soviet Army
May 7	All German forces surrender unconditionally (0241hrs at Reims)
May 8	President Truman declares V-E (Victory in Europe) Day
Jun 22	US Tenth Army completes capture of Okinawa
Jun 30	Luzon campaign concludes
Jul 25	Organized resistance ends on Mindanao
Aug 6	Atomic bomb dropped on Hiroshima
Aug 9	Atomic bomb dropped on Nagasaki
Aug 8	Soviets invade Manchuria; USSR declares war on Japan
Aug 14	Japan surrenders, ending World War II
Sep 2	VJ DAY Japan signs surrender documents on the deck of the USS *Missouri* and the Second World War passes into history
Jul 12	22d Infantry Regiment returns to the US
Nov 3	133d Infantry Regiment returns to the US and subsequently inactivated
Dec 31	165th Infantry Regiment returns to the US and subsequently inactivated

1946

Feb 2	382d Infantry Regiment returns to the US and subsequently inactivated
Mar 5	22d Infantry Regiment inactivated

CHAPTER 4

PACIFIC OCEAN AREA OF OPERATIONS, 1941–45

"It is impossible for the Nation to compensate for the services of a fighting man. There is no pay scale that is high enough to buy the services of a single soldier during even a few minutes of the agony of combat, the physical miseries of the campaign, or of the extreme personal inconvenience of leaving his home to go out to the most unpleasant and dangerous spots on earth to serve his Nation."
George C. Marshall, Chief of Staff of the United States Army

In 1942, the Pacific Theater split into two major combat areas for Americans: the Southwest Pacific Area commanded by General Douglas MacArthur, and the Pacific Ocean Area commanded by Admiral Chester Nimitz. The Pacific Ocean Area's (POA) war zone was a huge expanse that was subdivided for administrative purposes into the North, Central, and South Pacific, which encompassed the Japanese Mandates (islands put under Japanese protection during the 1920s and 1930s) as well as the Japanese main islands. In the POA, Army infantrymen fought alongside Marines in sharply contested, high-casualty battles, taking one heavily defended island after another as they edged ever closer to Japan proper. This high-intensity fighting combined with large numbers of non-battle casualties, primitive infrastructure, as well as the slow arrival of replacements and constrained shipping of resources lent a cyclical nature to combat.

Because of the vast distances covered in the Pacific, every move from one island to another required shipping, and resources were tightly stretched, due in large part to the emphasis on European operations and the shipping shortages. It was only in late 1944 that there was enough shipping to allow the major campaigns in the Philippines and on Okinawa, and US Army strength in the Pacific Ocean Area reached the half-million mark only in May 1945

The US Army entered combat in the Pacific Area of Operations on December 7, 1941 with its six prewar regiments stationed in Hawaii. Between that date and September 1945, US Army infantry units fought alongside those of the Marine Corps in five named campaigns, from Pearl Harbor in the Central Pacific to the Ryukyu Islands in 1945. There were 67 Army infantry regimental months of combat in the POA Theater, including combat on Kwajalein Atoll, Saipan, Peleliu, and Okinawa. The 27 Army infantry regiments in

US Army strength in the Pacific Theaters of Operation

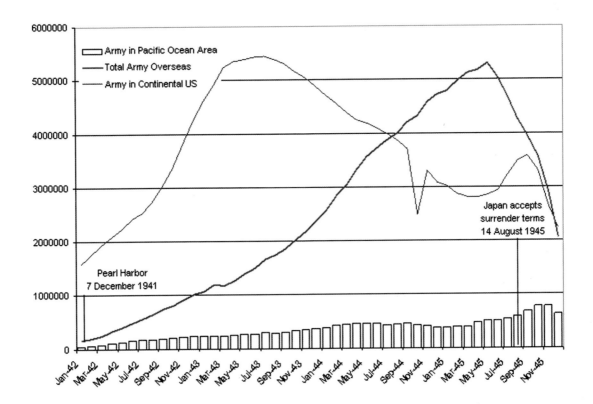

the Pacific Ocean Area of Operation accumulated 1,961 months in theater and 67 combat months. There were no more than 15 in combat at any one time and it was not until April 1945 that more than half of the regiments in the area were in combat. This much higher overhead was due primarily to the need to garrison outposts and the Hawaiian Islands as well as the cyclical nature of combat in this theater.

From 1942 on, most divisions arriving in the Pacific stopped in the Hawaiian Islands prior to entering combat – and after from one to six months of training and providing security they shipped to combat zone in either the PAO or Southwest Pacific Area – with their place being taken by units newly arrived from the US. The requirement to guard the Hawaiian Islands and the islands along the convoy route to Australia meant that more units were in training and guarding than were in combat, at least until April 1945.

Since all but two RA divisions had been heavily levied for soldiers to form new units, and 14 RA regiments were already overseas in December, it was the untouched federalized National Guard divisions and their regiments that first shipped overseas. Those traveling overseas in early 1942 were at the correct

Daily average non-effective rate (per 1,000 strength), Ocean Area			
	Disease	Non-battle injury	Battle injury or wound	Total daily admissions per 1,000
Pacific Ocean Area	33.89	5.85	6.31	46.05
Continental US	27.06	4.24	.01	31.31

personnel strengths but lacked advanced training and some vital modern equipment; some units had not yet reorganized under the correct tables of organization and equipment. Although some regiments entered combat as early as 1942, they were untrained in jungle warfare and had to learn how to combat the Japanese with the most brutal on-the-job training – simply fighting them. In much of the combat during 1942 and 1943, platoon and company operations were vital to the grand scheme, unlike later periods when whole armies fought across islands.

The incidence of disease on the tropical islands in the PAO was not high and malaria was rare – with dengue fever and dysentery the most noteworthy diseases. In the POA, for every soldier wounded or killed, 6.3 were lost to disease or other injuries. The average daily casualty rate for the worldwide US Army was one battle casualty for every four and one half rendered ineffective through disease or non-battle injury.

THE 165TH INFANTRY REGIMENT

The 165th (the "Fighting 69th") Infantry Regiment, New York National Guard, is the regiment in which our composite soldier enlisted during the summer of 1938. Michael O'Brien was born in

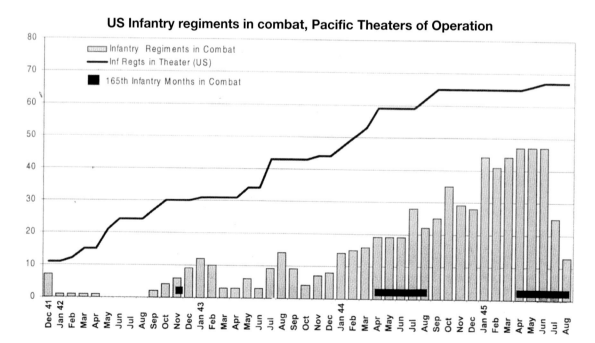

May 1921 in the Bronx, one of the boroughs of New York City. He was the youngest son of an Irish immigrant and, like the average family, had three brothers and two sisters, four of whom lived past age five. His father and three brothers worked in a nearby printing shop, as did Michael part-time after school. Once a weekend two weeks a year, his brothers drilled as members of the 165th Infantry Regiment, formerly the 69th Infantry of the American Civil War and World War I, which was headquartered at the 69th Regiment Armory located off Park Avenue on Lexington Avenue.

In 1938, when Michael was a senior in high school, the 165th Regiment consisted of a headquarters, three infantry battalions, three rifle companies, one machine gun company, a supply company, a howitzer company, and a medical and chaplains detachment; recruits were primarily citizens of Irish descent from the boroughs of the Bronx and Manhattan. Traditionally, the regiment received Mass at St Patrick's Cathedral before marching in the St Patrick's Day parade every year. Some of the 165th's companies traced their lineage to the American Revolutionary War and 20 campaign streamers from the different wars adorned the regimental colors.

In October 1940 the 165th Infantry Regiment was federalized along with the other organizations within the 27th Infantry Division, New York National Guard. Regiments called their guardsmen, accustomed to their weekly drills and two-week summer camps, to the colors. What had been a welcome distraction and additional income now became all-important. Uncertain about the future, the soldiers left their families and jobs behind.

The first day of federalization for the 165th Infantry. Note the widely varied uniforms of the soldiers pitching camp. In the right center rear are the vehicles that have brought them here.

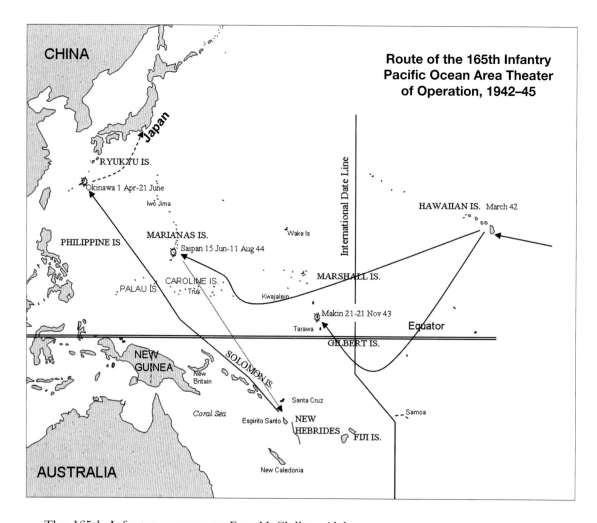

The 165th Infantry was sent to Fort McClellan, Alabama, on October 25 to begin a period of intense training interspersed with furloughs and maneuvers. After the attack on Pearl Harbor, the regiment went on high alert, and transferred by train to Englewood, California just eight days later. On March 8, the 165th Infantry sailed aboard the United States Army Transport (USAT) *President Grant* for Hawaii, where the regiment, along with the remainder of the 27th Division, spent the next year and a half guarding the Hawaiian Islands and training for combat. In October 1943, the regiment began amphibious training, making several practice assaults against the island of Maui. On November 4, the men boarded the USS *Calvert* for their first combat action on Makin Atoll, Butaritari Island. Later, in June 1944, the 165th earned a richly deserved campaign streamer for its work on Saipan, and another in April 1945 for Okinawa. At war's end, the regiment was preparing for occupation duties on the Japanese main island of Honshu, but in December 1945 returned to the US where it inactivated on December 31, 62 months after federalization and 46 months after shipping overseas.

Campaigns in the Pacific

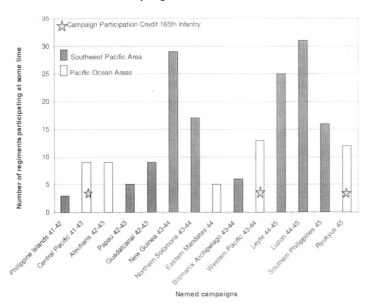

MICHAEL'S STORY

Michael was only 17, and the minimum age for a guardsman was 18, but, with the Great Depression, limited enlistments, parents' tacit permission, and sometimes older brothers in the same company, recruiting sergeants and officers sometimes turned a blind eye and enlisted young men before their time. The wink of his brother was all it took and Michael was soon filling out the necessary paperwork and being told of his enlistment bonus and subsequent pay for each drill, which as a private was a dollar a drill plus $14 for summer camp. Michael, along with one other enlistee, raised his right hand and repeated the following oath: "I do hereby acknowledge to have voluntarily enlisted this 21st day of June, 1938 as a soldier in the National Guard of the US and of the State of New York for the period of three years under the conditions prescribed by law, unless sooner discharged by proper authority. And I do solemnly swear that I will bear true faith and allegiance to the United States of America and to the State of New York, and that I will serve them honestly and faithfully against all their enemies whomsoever, and that I will obey the orders of the President of the US and of the Governor of the State of New York, and of the officers appointed over me according to law and the rules and Articles of War."

His brother shook his hand, as did the others witnessing the ceremony, and the recruiting officer handed Michael his enlistment bonus of two dollars. The first sergeant escorted them to the supply room to draw uniforms and equipment. Here Michael received the standard allocation of: "Breeches, cotton;

Coats, woolen; Drawers, cotton, Drawers, woolen; Hat, service with infantry cord; leggings, field; Overcoat, Raincoat, Shirts flannel, Shoes field, Stockings, Trousers, woolen; Trousers, elastic; undershirts cotton and undershirts elastic." His field equipment consisted of a shelter half, pins and poles, a cartridge belt, a haversack and pack carrier, a canteen, canteen cup and cover, a steel bonnet and mess gear.

The only things that fitted properly were his campaign hat and leggings. Everything else was too large for a boy's body and smelled of disuse and camphor, although it was obvious by the various mendings that the equipment had had previous owners. Every item, except his nearly new trousers and coat, was of World War I vintage and older than he was. The arms room contained Springfield rifles, BARs, and .45 cal. pistols, all left over from World War I. Machine guns and mortars, though authorized, were nonexistent.

Many of the company leaders were veterans of World War I and long National Guard service. It was a spit and polish organization: officers and men well turned out in the uniforms of the day, with gleaming leather and spotless uniforms, but lacking in tactical acumen. Officers and NCOs took military correspondence courses to stay abreast, but had very little opportunity to polish their skills.

Discipline was also different from that of a full-time military unit. Subordinates during drill might very well be peers or supervisors during normal workdays, and discipline could not be too harsh or men would leave the unit. Although this was not a full-time unit, Michael learned early on to stay within the confines of his squad and not to become too well known. Like all privates, he saw his company commander and first sergeant at company formations and during inspections. For that matter, most just stayed out of any officer's way, interacting with their superiors only when absolutely necessary.

Michael's next two years consisted of weekly evening drills and a summer camp of two weeks at Camp Smith, just across from the Military Academy at West Point, New York. Much of the time during training was spent drilling and parading. Retreat parades were especially memorable, with the entire regiment formed in line, companies in column. Michael, deep in the ranks of his company, could not observe much, but he could hear the music and officers' commands. With the formations at present arms, he heard the colonel command "Sound Retreat." At the last note of the bugle call the evening gun fired and the regimental band began playing the National Anthem as the color bearers struck the post flag.

In the summer of 1940, while debate in Congress and across the nation centered on the necessity of a peacetime draft and federalization of the Guard, the 165th maneuvered at DeKalb, New York. Newsreels in theaters showed German tanks and Stukas sweeping across France, and smiling Japanese soldiers marching through Chinese towns with flags in their rifle barrels. By the end of the encampment and the final parade reviewed by President Roosevelt, everyone knew they would soon be on active duty. They just did not know when.

In September and early October, many guardsmen with dependents requested discharge, and only intensive recruiting drives extolling the virtues of army life in the Guard kept the companies at some modicum of strength. When soldiers gathered on October 15 for induction, most of the men in the companies were new untrained recruits.

Entry onto active duty was more rigorous than enlisting in the National Guard. Before induction, the guardsmen took a comprehensive medical examination, as well as a battery of intelligence tests. Standing in line became a way of life: there was a queue for physicals, for aptitude tests, for uniforms, for meals, and for pay. Although many Guardsmen left service in September and early October, more were discharged who were not physically capable, who did not meet mental standards, or had dependants. Of the 90 or so soldiers in each company, only about 50 actually entered active service. After two years, Michael found himself promoted by his company commander to private first class, meaning an increase in pay of six dollars per month, and designation as next in command of his eight-man squad.

Next, Michael and his comrades received their eight-digit Army Serial Number. Soldiers, standing in alphabetical order received sequential serial numbers. Brothers were separated so their numbers were not sequential. Being National Guardsmen, their numbers began with 2025, the first 2 representing Guard, then a 0 and the next 2 representing the 2d Corps Area of New York, New Jersey and Delaware, and the 5 showing they were among the first 50,000 Federalized Guardsmen in the area. Those arriving later would have different codes representing the RA and draftees.

On October 26, Michael's battalion boarded trains for the long circuitous trip to Fort McClellan, Alabama, arriving five days later. Fort McClellan was quite different from Camp Smith and the summer camps of the last few years. Tent life was the same, but tactical training and marksmanship replaced drill. Soldiers adjusted to the bugle calls which regulated their day. They filled out rapidly from exercise and a calorie- and carbohydrate-intensive diet. There was plenty to eat, with every soldier able to return for additional helpings in their mess kits. Michael learned early on to balance and eat out of his two-piece mess kit without spilling his food. The lid of the pan was designed so that it hooked by way of a ring on the handle to the pan itself, allowing a soldier one hand free to carry his carton of milk.

Training intensified as all the men began the process of becoming trained soldiers. The first two weeks were dedicated to uniform issue, basic soldiering, rifle marksmanship, and schooling of the soldier. The next eight weeks began with squad operations and progressed through company training, followed by two weeks of battalion training and one week dedicated to regimental training.

Throughout the 13-week period, only 26 hours were devoted to drill, with 246 hours spent on tactical training and 111 hours on marksmanship. Training lasted eight hours Monday through Friday, and four hours on Saturdays, which were normally set aside for inspections. On Sundays, Catholic chaplains conducted field Mass.

Michael soon learned how to adjust the loop on his Springfield rifle's sling, so that the lower band passed around the right of the left wrist, and then round his left upper arm, with the loop so tight that the position was uncomfortable. However, with practice the discomfort soon passed. This convolution bound the sling to the left forearm to the rifle and to the ground so that it formed a dead rest for the rifle, with the wrist as its universal joint. It not only increased accuracy but also dramatically reduced the recoil of the Springfield. Although the soldiers used the sling during their firing practices, many could not see themselves using it in combat.

Rifles had to be cleaned immediately after firing and for three consecutive days thereafter because the corrosive propellant would rust the bore. Everyone knew that "A dirty or rusty rifle means that the soldier does not realize the value of his weapon and that his training is incomplete," and that it was the quickest way to lose pass privileges. Michael and the others were forbidden to take their Springfields farther apart than the bolt and magazine mechanism, and concentrated primarily on keeping rust and carbon out of the bore and chamber.

Training stopped in December, and the soldiers boarded trains back for holiday furlough in New York, with only a smattering of unmarried soldiers remaining to pull the necessary camp details. On return, they found that the first draftees from Selective Service were arriving in February. Everyone looked forward to their units being filled to wartime strength, not only for training, but to reduce the number of details that each man currently had to perform. Some Reserve officers from the ROTC also arrived to replace those officers who were either too old or could not sustain the training pace.

As soon as the first group of inductees arrived they were issued clothing and equipment and formed into uneven but manageable rows. Every inductee was senior to Michael in age, with some in their thirties. Since Michael had been with the company for two years, and was a high school graduate, his company commander selected him to assist in training the new draftees; almost all Irish Catholics from New York like him. The word was that the division commander had selected from the draftees all those with Irish surnames and assigned them to the 165th Infantry to carry on its Irish heritage. Just basically trained himself, Michael studied the manuals during the night so that he could instruct the next day. Everyone learned together.

One Monday morning, Michael and his squad mates formed up with full pack and gear. The company commander took the lead and set a swift pace for the company's first 15-mile march. Michael and some of the older hands realized the march was coming and had lightened their haversacks. Unfortunately for the "old timers", the

Service (bugle) calls, December 1941

The following list of service call is announced:

Calls	Duty Days	Saturdays	Sundays and Holidays
Reveille, 1st Call	0600hrs		0715hrs
Marches	0625hrs		0725hrs
Assembly	0630hrs		0730hrs
Mess (Breakfast)	0645hrs		0745hrs
Drill, 1st Call	0745hrs		
Assembly	0800hrs		
Church Call			1130hrs
Sick Call	1300hrs	1100hrs	0900hrs
Recall, drill and fatigue	1130hrs		
1st Sergeants Call	1130hrs		
Mess (Dinner)	1200hrs		1200hrs
Drill, 1st Call	1250hrs		
Assembly	1300hrs		
Fatigue	1300hrs		
Recall, drill and fatigue	1600hrs		
Guard Mounting, 1st Call	1600hrs	1250hrs	1250hrs
Assembly	1610hrs	1300hrs	1300hrs
Retreat	1700hrs		1700hrs
Mess (Supper)	1715hrs		1715hrs
Tattoo	2200hrs		2200hrs
Call to Quarters	2245hrs		2245hrs
Taps	2300hrs		2300hrs

end of the march culminated in a full field layout of equipment and tentage. Those who had "forgotten" to bring all their equipment had to dig the company latrines and kitchen garbage pit, while those more inexperienced at soldiering watched.

After participating in a mock St Patrick's Day parade, athletics and hearty celebratory toasts to the patron Saint of Ireland, Michael, his company and all units of the 27th Division began preparing for the season of maneuvers. Uniforms were still in short supply and there was a mixture of khaki and older olive drab uniforms in the formations. There was little heavy weapons training outside mechanical drill because there was a severe shortage of mortars and machine guns, so stovepipes and wooden facsimiles had to suffice.

Michael's division left Fort McClellan in the last week of May, beginning its period of field training in preparation for the fast-approaching Second Army maneuvers. Foot marches became the norm, as did establishment of field camps. The VII Corps staff handled battalion-level training for advance guards and conducting defenses, but Michael and his comrades at squad level

got little out of the training outside observing the Tennessee countryside as they marched from one locale to another. There was a short break back to Fort McClellan to clean up, followed by a trip to the Alabama maneuver area for more training at company, battalion, and regimental level. Here, Michael and his mates practiced overnight marches, where the only thing visible in the dark was the back of the man's head marching in front. Minds slept while feet marched. By the end of August, all was ready and the soldiers were loaded on to trucks for the long drive to Arkansas, the staging area for General Ben Lear's Red Army, of which the 27th Division was a part.

Soldiers of the 165th attend Mass during Second Army maneuvers. They wear a mixture of khaki and olive drab uniforms.

Pay of Enlisted men of the Army as of September 16, 1940					
	Less than 4 years	**Over 4 years**	**Over 8 years**	**Over 12 years**	**Over 16 years**
1 Master Sergeant	$126.00	$138.60	$144.90	$151.90	$157.50
2 Technical Sergeant or First Sergeant	$84	$92.40	$96.60	$100.80	$105
3 Staff Sergeant	$72	$79.20	$82.80	$86.40	$90
4 Sergeant	$60	$66	$69	$72	$75
5 Corporal	$54	$59.40	$62.10	$64.80	$67.50
6 Private First Class	$36	$39.60	$41.40	$43.20	$45
7 Private	$30	$33	$34.50	$36	$37.50
Privates with less than 4 months service	$21				

An infantry rifle company advances during Second Army maneuvers. The soldiers carry World War I-era equipment.

While Congress debated on extending the call-up of the National Guard, Reserve officers, and draftees, Michael and many others in every unit listened to discussions from their fellow soldiers on going AWOL if the measure passed. Many enjoyed listening to the song, "I'll be back in a year, little darling" and "OHIO" was a watchword which meant "Over the Hill in October." Soldiers scrawled the acronym on vehicles, latrine walls and any other available canvas. Many wanted to go back home to their businesses and their families. Some signed a petition to ask their congressmen to oppose the legislation proposed by the War Department to extend the service of the National Guard, Reserve officers, and selectees.

The draft extension was passed in August by one vote in the House of Representatives and signed in September by President Roosevelt, giving the Guardsmen and selectees another 18 months of active duty. In October, soldiers over 28 could ask for discharge, and Michael's brother took the opportunity to go home. Little did he know he would be recalled in December after Pearl Harbor, and although he tried to rejoin the 165th, he was assigned to a unit bound for Europe.

The Second Army maneuvers began in earnest on September 16, and the 165th Infantry fought battles throughout the pine forests northwest of Alexandria, Louisiana. Officers learned to deploy and maneuver their soldiers, while soldiers in squads mostly learned about field living at the basest level, experienced seemingly endless marches on dirt roads, and dealt with the attentions of ever-present mosquitoes and snakes.

Umpires adjudicated combat between the Red and Blue armies by considering manpower, armament, and disposition of forces to decide which side had won or lost, and then waved different colored flags to tell one force to retreat. Michael and his comrades often found themselves marching to and fro with no idea whether they were winning or losing. The only way to tell who was winning was by reading the civilian newspapers from the nearby towns.

With maneuvers over, Michael's division returned to Fort McClellan, and the routine guard and details began again. With more than a year to go on active duty, there seemed little hurry to correct the deficiencies found during the exercises. Large sumptuous Thanksgiving Dinners were held in company messes, and men prepared for their Christmas furloughs.

Michael first learned of the attack on Pearl Harbor while standing guard on a bridge along a deserted stretch of road: the sergeant of the guard brought another soldier to double the guard. Back at the barracks, soldiers gathered around any available radio to listen to President Roosevelt's speech to Congress asking for a declaration of war. "Yesterday, December 7, 1941 – a date which will live in infamy – the United States of America was suddenly and deliberately attacked by naval and air forces of the Empire of Japan …

During the 1941 maneuvers every aspect of warfare was practiced. Here a POW is interrogated. The Geneva Convention stipulated that while in the combat area, prisoners were allowed to keep their helmets and gas masks.

Hostilities exist. There is no blinking at the fact that our people, our territory, and our interests are in grave danger. With confidence in our armed forces – with the unbounded determination of our people – we will gain the inevitable triumph – so help us God … I ask that the Congress declare that since the unprovoked and dastardly attack by Japan on Sunday, December 7, a state of war has existed between the US and the Japanese Empire."

Soldiers broke out arms and equipment, and officers and NCOs armed with clipboards went through detailed inspections and inventories of equipment. Those available attended Mass with a service for those who died at Pearl Harbor. On December 16, 1941, Michael and his regiment left Fort McClellan after 14 months, taking the Southern Railroad through Texas and New Mexico to Englewood, California. The rails were filled with military units moving, and it took a week to cross the country. Once there, Michael's company guarded an aircraft plant against sabotage.

January passed with soldiers living in tents, not eating with the relish they once did, and reacting to the constant myriad of rumors. This was not how Michael and his mates imagined war would be.

Training began again in February, with soldiers using the M1 rifle for the first time. More inspections were held and preparation for overseas movement began. Soldiers who failed the overseas physical and for other reasons were dropped from the unit, and a large group of untrained inductees from California joined the company, the first members not from New York. On March 7, 1942, Michael and his unit moved to Pier 22, San Francisco, where Red Cross workers served coffee and donuts as they mustered before climbing the gangway and boarding the USAT *President Grant*. Michael's company filled one of the holds that had berths five high, with about 18in. of headspace for each. The next day the ship set sail on a southwest course and joined a convoy bound for Hawaii.

Defense of Hawaii and preparation for combat, 1942–43

On March 16, 1942, Michael's company arrived on the island of Kauai, Hawaiian Islands, and immediately began providing security and preparing beach defenses. For the next 20 months, the various islands were home to the 165th Infantry, who built beach defenses and guarded the islands against an invasion that never came. War here was different from on the mainland. There was less food to eat, as most of it had to be shipped from the continental United States, and with the build-up of military traffic, there were not as many luxuries. Milk, especially was in short supply, and most of the food arrived in cans. There was an 1800hrs curfew: if soldiers were not on guard they had to be in their garrisons. At least initially, there were many instances of soldiers firing in the darkness at imagined targets, both offshore and on the beaches. Vehicle convoys driving under blackout conditions were especially dangerous and some soldiers were killed or injured in crashes.

Michael and his mates spent much of their time digging foxholes, building machine gun bunkers, and erecting concertina and double-apron barbed wire fences along all the beaches. About the only leisure activity was swimming in the surf, as in the beginning everyone worked seven days a week, stopping only to sleep. However, the high-intensity schedule died down and in May, they finally received day passes, although these were limited toward the end of the month when there were numerous anti-invasion drills. Soldiers scrambled from their bunks to

Men in five-tiered bunks on a troopship. Although these men are Army Air Corps, as noted on the insignia of the sergeant on the topmost bunk, the conditions shown were typical of such transfers.

A soldier stands guard, in the midst of barbed wire. He is wearing the M1 helmet and carries an M1 rifle.

man the positions they had built along the coastline, hauling ammunition and weapons back and forth seemingly without purpose. Michael and the others were unaware of the great naval battles being fought in the Coral Sea, and found out about Midway only after the victory was secured.

Michael received his first daytime pass and immediately headed for one of the open bars in Kekaha. There was not much else to do. The whiskey was expensive, but it was better than the 3.2 "near" beer they had at their canteen, and in the end cheaper to get drunk on.

By June, everything had settled into a routine: a period of beach defense when soldiers lived near their positions without luxuries, followed by airfield defense with showers, a canteen, and other amenities. In August 1942, the company finally changed from the old Table of Organization and Equipment to one with three squads in three platoons and a weapons platoon. Squad leaders, once corporals, were now sergeants, and their assistants became corporals. Company weapons remained essentially the same, except now they carried the M1 rifle instead of the Springfield, and the weapons platoon had the authorized M1919A3 light machine guns and M2 60mm (2.36in.) mortars. The new M1 helmet and liner replaced the old-style M1917A1 steel bonnets. Everyone quickly found additional applications for the outer-shell: as a shaving basin, something to boil water in, and as an expedient entrenching tool.

FITNESS AND TRAINING, HAWAII, MAY 1943
(1) "I do push-ups every morning and my body's a rock". Soldiers are shown here performing exercises in formation. The normal uniform was the white undershirt, HBT trousers, and shoes. (2) A soldier negotiates a barbed wire obstacle known as a double-apron fence. Chicken wire has been thrown over the fence to aid in crossing. The soldier is equipped with an M1 rifle and cartridge belt, and wears heavy leather gloves. (3) Soldiers leap obstacles on a bayonet assault course. In line with standard practice they wear the olive drab plastic helmet liners for training (without the protective steel exterior used in combat); they also wear infantry cartridge belts and carry the M1 rifle and M1942 20in. bayonet.

ABOVE The conditioning march: this rear view shows the M1928 haversacks carried.

LEFT A conditioning march in the Hawaiian mountains.

On the negative side, they also found that it affected the needles in their magnetic compasses. Different uniforms also appeared for testing, and just as rapidly disappeared.

After six months of beach defense, the 165th began training for offensive combat operations, on both Kauai and Oahu. Some soldiers shipped to the officers' school at Fort Benning, while others attended the Hawaiian Department Ranger School. The first long marches through the mountains on Oahu left everyone gasping for breath, as the dramatic changes in altitude accompanied by the heat and humidity wasted even the heartiest soldier. Some soldiers could not take the grinding existence of an infantryman and were replaced, as were some officers.

In May 1943, Michael's regiment began intensive instruction in amphibious operations, and spent weeks aboard amphibious transports practicing loading LCVs (Landing Craft, Vehicles), forming into waves and assaulting the Hawaiian islands of Kauai and Maui. In between, they went through jungle obstacle courses, weapons ranges, and company problems. In June, there was a parade where the company received two silver rings for its guidon, the first for participation in the Revolutionary War and the second for participation in the War of 1812. Live fire maneuver exercises began in August, where soldiers assaulted objectives using live ammunition and overhead mortar, artillery and machine gun fire. During this high-risk training, some of the regiment's soldiers were killed by "friendly" fire. Soldiers quickly learned from their own as well as others' mistakes.

Some squad leaders received the Thompson submachine gun that fired the standard .45 cal. round. Although it was hard to clean, difficult to maintain, and inaccurate at longer distances, the heavy bullet and high rate of fire made it a choice weapon in close combat. Michael also practiced with the Mark 2 grenade; 2oz (57g) of TNT, surrounded by a serrated cast-iron casing which gave it the appearance of a "pineapple". It had an effective bursting radius of about 30 yards (27m) but small, casualty-producing shards could travel as far as 100 yards (91m). Michael could throw one about 35 yards (32m), about the norm for soldiers in his company. The drill was to assume a good throwing position with the non-throwing side of the body toward the enemy, grasp the grenade with your thumb over the safety lever, pull the pin with the non-throwing hand, throw the grenade with an arcing motion, and immediately get behind cover. This worked well in practice on a range, but when faced with dense foliage and fellow soldiers on the right and left, often as not the exploding grenade wounded friend as well as foe.

An early-type, one-piece camouflage uniform. This soldier carries a gas mask, a machete (on his left hip), and a K-bar (on his right).

By late October and early November 1943, after extensive amphibious training aboard the USS *Calvert* and multiple practice landings on the beaches of Kauai and Maui, every soldier realized their stay in Hawaii was drawing to a close, and that they would soon be in action. On November 9, Michael's regiment set sail for Makin Atoll in the Gilbert Islands. When the *Calvert* crossed the Equator, Michael and the other 164 "pollywogs" of his company underwent the traditional naval rite and became "shellbacks" (person who has crossed the Equator by boat), after having paid the appropriate respect to Neptune.

The bayonet course. This soldier wears M1938 leggings, what appears to be the first pattern herringbone twill (HBT), and a white t-shirt. Here he practices attacking the "enemy" with his M1 rifle, fitted with either an M1905 or M1942 bayonet.

Makin: First blood

By November 1943, Michael was a sergeant squad leader and had been on active service more than three years, entitling him to a 5 percent pay raise and a hash mark on the left sleeve of his service coat. The vast majority of his company had been on active duty for more than two and a half years. The combat which began November 20 was to be their first.

Michael's heart was in his throat every time he climbed down a cargo net. Although he kept his hands on the vertical ropes, he was always afraid the soldier above him would step on his hands and send him falling either to the deck of the landing craft bobbing

The LCV was a small, wood-hulled vehicle carrier capable of carrying 36 soldiers, one 1-ton truck, or 10,000lbs of cargo.

below or, worse, between the hulls of the two vessels. There was a real skill to getting into the landing craft. About three rungs from the bottom of the net, Michael waited until the surge of a wave lifted the landing craft before he could step into the bottom. One had to time one's step, though: letting go when the LCV was falling meant a 6ft or more drop onto the hard deck, and with a heavy haversack, ammunition and weapon, this could result in injuries such as sprained ankles, dislocated backs or broken legs.

The second part was when the landing craft began their run-in to the shore, the waves lifting up and smacking down the bow with such violence that the soldiers inside felt as if their muscles were separating from their skeletons. An open mouth might very well result in broken teeth and a bleeding tongue. Saltwater spray drenched everything, while everyone aboard prayed they would ground on the beach, rather than on a bar and have to wade in from offshore – while avoiding the bullets they knew were coming.

Michael's first combat landing was an anticlimax; the run-in was rough, but thankfully there was no Japanese fire against the beaching LCVs. His company landed split between the second and third waves on Red Beach, but the LCVs grounded on coral reefs

Landing on Red Beach 1. Jagged rocks prevented LVTs from landing on the beach, and forced soldiers to go over the sides into deep water.

extending 20 yards (18m) from the beach, and were unable to push forward or even lower their ramps. Soldiers went over the sides into the surf chest and neck high. The coral was slippery and any misstep caused shredded HBT uniforms and gashed limbs. This was not as they had practiced, and instead of rushing off the beach, everyone clustered together as they worked their way through the rocks, and waited for the remainder of the company before moving into the tree line. Michael discovered that the cardboard surrounding the ammunition in the two bandoleers that he and every rifleman carried was wet and stuck to the ammunition clips, rendering the bullets useless until the cardboard was scraped off. Many of the soldiers dropped the bandoleers on the beach rather than spend time cleaning ammunition.

After reorganizing, they fixed bayonets and Michael's company moved forward in column of platoons along the trail heading to the center of the island. His platoon, last in order of movement, was greeted by about 50 Gilbertese wishing them a "Good Morning" in English. Surprised to see friendly faces, Michael and some of the others gave cigarettes to the adults and candy to the children and pointed them in the direction of the beach. After marching about 600 yards (548m), Michael's company commander directed his platoons to drop their haversacks. Much lightened and encumbered now with only their weapons, ammunition, one-third of a K ration and two canteens of water, the men continued toward the central part of the island. Whenever the occasional bullet whizzed over their heads, everyone ducked and looked to see where it came from – although most of the rounds were "overs" from the 2d Battalion, which had landed in the center of the island and was advancing toward them.

Everyone began digging in when they arrived at the designated reserve position; but it was in a marsh, and as the water table was too high, the slit trenches filled with water as soon as they dug them, so soldiers crouched and sat along the sides rather than occupy them.

Soldiers of the 165th prepare to enter the jungle from Red Beach, Makin Atoll.

Around 1400hrs, Michael's squad was sent out on patrol to find bypassed Japanese. They began on the road but soon took to the bush on either side when they heard the distinctive hissing whistle of Japanese Model 98 .25 cal. rounds passing by. Michael and his men felt intimidated by their first taste of enemy fire, which although not heavy, was enough to keep them alert.

The thick brush created gaps between individuals and units, and provided openings that enabled the Japanese to infiltrate the rear areas, causing great consternation and breakdowns in weapons discipline. Units in the rear firing at infiltrators often pinned down the advancing Americans in the front lines with fire.

The worst part about never having been in combat was the uncertainty of what to expect, as Michael's senses were not yet

Makin, an infantryman crouches down, his first taste of sniper fire.

accustomed to notice that which would keep him alive. No amount of training in Hawaii could teach what it was really like to be under fire. The only time they had experienced overhead rifle and machine gun fire before was when pulling targets on the rifle ranges and when crawling under barbed wire on the infiltration course. This day, none seemed remotely similar.

Soldiers quickly learned to tell the difference in sound between the .30 cal. weapons of the Americans and those of the Japanese. The only disconcerting note was that the M1 carbine sounded too much like the Japanese rifle. Soldiers firing their carbines into the bush many times found themselves hugging the earth, trying to avoid returning M1 and BAR fire.

Although most of the snipers were on the ground, Michael and his squad spent much of their time searching the treetops of palms. After careful study, they found they could spot sniper roosts by looking for signs on the tree trunks and ground. The Japanese notched the trunks for easier climbing, and cached rifles, water, and sake in the fronds. They marked the trees they had equipped with palm fronds located just off the ground. All a Japanese soldier had to do was run to the tree, knock down the identifying fronds, and climb the tree using the notches to find everything waiting for him. And all a GI had to do was to look for the fronds and notches.

The dense terrain on Makin Atoll made it very difficult to maintain contact to the left and right. Note the soldiers are carrying M1928 haversacks and canteens.

MICHAEL'S SQUAD ENGAGES A JAPANESE PATROL, MAKIN, NOVEMBER 1943
It is the morning of the second day of Michael's combat experience. The Japanese officer leading the patrol attacks with his samurai sword, but he and all but one of the privates with him will die in this encounter. Michael makes his thrust at a Japanese private with the M1 and M1905 E1 Bayonet. Training taught the infantryman to thrust the rifle from the hip and drive it into the enemy. The bayonet was then twisted and withdrawn along the same line. Although seen by many as old-fashioned, most infantrymen in the Pacific Area of Operations kept the bayonet fixed to the muzzle of their rifle.

Soldiers digging foxholes under palm fronds on Makin Atoll. One soldier pulls security while the others work with shovels.

The company moved forward again when all the patrols returned and set up a nighttime perimeter on the battalion's right flank in the corner of the tank trap and the beach, with one company on their left and another behind them to their west. Michael and the others were tired and stressed, and expected the next day to be worse. They had woken well before dawn, had made their first combat landing, had marched through marsh and jungle and had eaten little all day. Many did not properly dig their positions, and although it was hot and muggy, no one took off their HBT shirts because their white T-shirts were very conspicuous in the dark green jungle. Perhaps the prevailing thought was "God, if you only let me live until tomorrow, I'll guarantee that this damned foxhole will be deeper by morning." Everyone bedded down for

Palm fronds litter the floor of this forest partially destroyed by naval gunfire. The soldiers are by now without their M1928 haversacks.

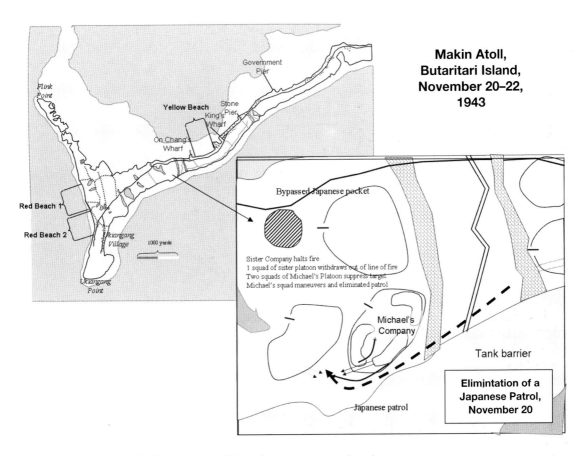

Makin Atoll,
Butaritari Island,
November 20–22,
1943

Government
Pier

Flink
Point

Yellow Beach   Stone
King's Pier
Wharf

On Chang's
Wharf

Red Beach 1

Red Beach 2

Ukiangang
Village

1000 yards

Ukiangang
Point

Bypassed Japanese pocket

Sister Company halts fire
1 squad of sister platoon withdraws out of line of fire
Two squads of Michael's Platoon suppress target
Michael's squad maneuvers and eliminated patrol

Michael's
Company

Tank barrier

Japanese patrol

**Elimintation of a
Japanese Patrol,
November 20**

the night without their knapsacks, although no one was sleeping. Company leaders warned the men not to talk or cough so they did not give their positions away.

During the night, the Japanese used various subterfuges to find the American foxholes. One came close to the perimeter whispering "Hey, Sarge." Someone shot him, but the firing gave away the American positions, which were soon peppered by rifle fire and hand grenades. Michael's platoon also reacted with rifle fire to exploding firecrackers, which provoked Japanese grenades and rifle fire. Calls of "Medic!" and "Hey, Charlie, where's my buddy?" broke through the stillness throughout the night.

One Japanese patrol slipped along the ocean to a position between Michael's company and the company positioned just behind it. This group kept up a patter of small arms fire throughout the night. The companies responded by engaging each other while trying to eliminate the Japanese. There was no fire discipline.

When dawn broke, Michael saw the Japanese in a small depression just 20ft away and began firing at them, as did positions up and down the line and across the way in the other company. There was an immediate danger of Americans killing Americans – and some soldiers in both perimeters fell killed or wounded by someone's fire, Japanese or American. Bullets thudded into the earth, tree trunks shredded and a rain of leaves and palm fronds fell onto the soldiers huddled in their foxholes. The indiscriminate shooting died only after Michael's platoon leader contacted the other company, and had one of the squads from another platoon pull back. Then, while two squads from Michael's platoon kept the Japanese heads down, Michael took his squad, bayonets fixed and adrenaline pumping, around the enemy flank using fire and maneuver until they were close enough to finish the action with bayonets.

Bayonet training took over, and Michael lunged at the nearest soldier with his rifle stock in close to his right hip, with a partially extended left arm, and guided the point of the bayonet into the enemy soldier's body, quickly completing his arm extension as his leading foot struck the ground, hearing the moan, and withdrawing his bayonet by twisting it to the right and pulling out along the same line of penetration. It was just like the bayonet range, except that this time the bayonet was stained with bright red blood. The shock of what he did came later. There were no prisoners and only one Japanese soldier escaped.

Later that morning the companies along the western tank ditch received heavy machine gun fire from the north shore of the island across the tank trap into the 1st Battalion positions. What they did not realize was that it was "overs" from American LVTs (Landing Vehicle, Tracked) firing their machine guns at what they thought were Japanese positions in the shipwrecks offshore.

When the company moved later that day to the front lines near the Stone Pier, the previous feelings of intimidation were replaced more by a nervous anticipation. Michael's company followed behind the M3 Lee tanks of the 193d Tank Battalion, with their short 75mm (2.95in.) gun in the hull and 37mm (1.45in.)gun in the turret, but they soon passed them when they became bogged in a traffic jam. The roads were filled with vehicles.

There seemed to be too many vehicles for the small island. Michael saw regimental and battalion vehicles ranging from $2^1/_2$ton trucks to the ever-present GP (Jeep), artillery prime movers from the 105th Field Artillery Battalion, tanks from the 193d Tank Battalion, as well as vehicles from the many different companies supporting the operation.

Michael's company halted behind the lead elements and formed a screen across the island in anticipation of forward companies pulling back into nighttime defensive positions. Later in the afternoon, Michael heard soldiers in the forward companies breaking through brush on his right and left and digging in for the night.

This second night, using lessons learned from the night before, word went out to use grenades instead of rifle fire against Japanese probing the perimeter. During the night, there was a lot of activity outside the company perimeter, but the only casualty in Michael's company was sleep. Snipers, hand grenades, and shells from the Japanese Model 10 50mm (1.9in.) grenade launcher, commonly referred to as a "knee mortar", kept everyone awake again. Although warned to use grenades instead of rifle fire, soldiers in the platoons returned fire, with no definite result apart from alerting the Japanese to their position.

The first night soldiers had tried to stifle their coughs by biting on handkerchiefs and sleeves. The second night the medics provided a concoction of codeine, glycerin, alcohol and coconut. Even if their throats were not sore, everyone sipped on what must have been a mind-numbing cocktail just in case.

Soldiers quickly learned from their experiences. Many found the admonitions about keeping their weapons clean were correct. Sand and rust quickly accumulated in magazine wells and weapons chambers, jamming rifles and machine guns. Only constant attention kept them clean. Flamethrowers did not work because the batteries got wet and would not spark, and there was not a mechanical method to ignite them. K ration cooking with the GI cooker carried in the canteen covers, or burning the cardboard ration box proved adequate to heat soldiers' rations. By the end of the second day soldiers realized their tall M1938 canvas leggings were too long and chafed their legs, especially since they never seemed to dry. Many cut them down so that they came just over the calf muscle. Later, the Army shortened the legging to this size (with eight eyelets instead of 12). Many also dyed their white T-shirts brown with coffee, not waiting for the Army solution after they were home.

Michael's company was relieved by another company early on the third day, and moved to King's Wharf where everyone, except the mortar section and two squads of infantry, one Michael's squad, boarded LVTs to conduct an amphibious flanking movement down the coast and behind the Japanese lines. The men left behind went to work collecting company equipment discarded the first day.

In the afternoon, Michael watched as the company marched down the road toward him. They had gone 3,000 yards (2,743m) by LVT, landed and formed a blocking position and killed or captured 45 Japanese forced onto them by the frontal attack of the 3d Battalion.

Equipment secured, Michael's company, the remainder of the 1st Battalion and the 2d Battalion loaded onto LSTs (Landing Ship, Tank) and transferred to their respective ships in the harbor. Michael's first combat was over. The three days' combat had taught him many of the finer aspects of staying alive; and although the three years of previous training was good, it was not the same. Casualties had been light, his company suffering only a few killed and his platoon only a few wounded. Only 113 men of the 3,000 or so landing with the 165th Infantry Regiment were battle casualties, of which only 32 were killed, one of whom Michael learned was Colonel Gardiner J. Conroy, the regiment's senior officer who had been its commander since 1940.

Saipan

Returning to Hawaii on December 2, the 165th moved to Hut City, Schofield Barracks and later to Bellows Field to rest, relax, and perform base security. Here Michael celebrated his fourth

Christmas on active duty with Christmas dinner in the mess hall and Mass at the regimental chapel.

Training resumed in January, with an emphasis on jungle training, where many of the lessons learned on Makin were incorporated into the school's instructional plans. In February, Michael's unit began amphibious training again, from rubber boats to the newer LCVPs (Landing Craft, Vehicle, Personnel) and during exercises on shore they practiced methods of eliminating Japanese fortified positions.

In March, the 165th celebrated its second year overseas; some new replacements arrived for the unit, but not many. They celebrated St. Patrick's Day in fine company fashion, with games, beer, and drinking of the regimental cocktail, which consisted of one part Irish whiskey to two parts champagne, although the ingredients were in such short supply every man received only a sip. Michael and the others stood a regimental review where medals for the Makin operation were awarded.

The unit then had more amphibious training around the island of Maui – scene of many previous practice landings. Michael felt as though he knew every rock and tree near the training site, and maps were not needed. All he had to do was tell his men, "We'll be setting up our squad position at the fork in the road with three taro plants," and they knew where to go.

There was a regimental formation for church service on Mother's Day. Michael was surprised that it was not a Mass, but he knew that both the regiment's and his company's composition had changed. By May 1944, he would bet that almost 40 percent of the regiment was from somewhere other than New York, with a good portion non-Catholic. The New York Guardsman flavor remained, however, as most of the officer and NCO leadership had been with the unit since the 69th Street Armory, although there were many Reserve officers serving alongside the remaining National Guard officers. Four of the seven company officers were veterans of Makin and Guard and Reserve. As for the enlisted leadership, a good percentage of the noncommissioned officers were draftees, although most were still from the New York area. There were a few long service RA soldiers, but they were all privates, with most having been busted in grade and coming to the company from other units in Hawaii.

On May 30, the men of the 165th conducted memorial services for their fallen comrades and on May 31 boarded the USS *Harris* at 1300hrs. Before dawn the next morning the *Harris* set sail and soldiers waited below decks for permission to go topside to catch a last glimpse of what they called the Paradise Isles. After the initial "abandon ship" drill, the ship's intercom system blared forth with the message, "Good morning, this is the Captain of the ship speaking. This task force is out to capture Saipan, Tinian, and Guam." More briefings followed as the days passed. There was a brief delay at Kwajalein Atoll for supplies and mail, something that cheered everyone up immensely.

Conditions aboard the transport were poor. There was little room and no space large enough to accommodate company-sized briefings, so platoons took turns poring over the terrain models, listening to the intelligence briefings and preparing for combat. There was no room to conduct physical training, and the days at sea without exercise weakened everyone. Michael and the others were stacked five deep in the hot and humid holds, or if lucky on deck under blankets and shelter halves. To pass the time, soldiers painted camouflage patterns on their helmets and lined up with the company barber for buzz-cut haircuts. There was no need for long hair in combat.

Operation Forager, Saipan, Marianas Islands

The *Harris* arrived in the target area on the morning of June 16, and the soldiers sat and stood on its decks watching from afar the battles along the beaches and the shelling of inland targets by the supporting battleships, cruisers, and destroyers. Michael and the others knew full well that they would soon be too immersed in their own troubles to watch others.

At approximately 1800hrs that day, about two-thirds of Michael's company, including his squad, loaded three LCVPs, believing they were heading straight to the beaches. Instead, they spent six miserable hours aboard the bouncing little craft waiting for word as to which beach they were to land on. It was nearly midnight before the ramps lowered and the wobbly-legged men stepped onto the shores of Saipan. They marched along the beach in a long open column of twos, threading around the destruction and supplies littering the beach. Exhaustion already setting in after almost

Saipan, June 17, 1944. Engineers flame the last of three bunkers. The two soldiers (bottom right) are medics with the engineers. One wears two medical pouches with suspenders, the other carries a collapsible litter.

Soldiers waiting to advance.

24 hours awake, they found the assembly area about 1600hrs and proceeded to dig their foxholes and await the rest of the company. The remainder of the company arrived early in the morning and at 0730hrs jumped off in its first assault, its right flanks against the coast.

Michael's platoon was in support of the lead platoons, clearing Japanese positions bypassed during the attack. Initially, their task focused on three bunkers just offset from the beach, which were well protected by thick overhead cover and interlocking fields of fire. Michael and the others could suppress with rifle and BAR fire, but could not get close enough to destroy them. Soon engineers and an amphibian tank mounting a 37mm gun arrived. While each squad suppressed their designated bunker, the tank and engineers moved from bunker to bunker. Michael's squad along with the tank first suppressed the Japanese in the bunker with rifle, cannon, and machine gun fire. The engineer carrying the flamethrower maneuvered close enough and squirted liquid fire onto and into the bunker, forcing the Japanese away from the apertures. Then one of Michael's soldiers tossed a satchel charge built of blocks of TNT after it. After the explosion, the engineer ran close and squirted flame directly into the bunker, filling it with an oily fire. When the bunker cooled, soldiers entered to check for any information they might find.

The attack continued up to the ridge overlooking Aslito airfield, where Michael's company, hit by automatic weapon and cannon fire as well as Japanese infiltrating between them and the adjacent company, withdrew from the hill by leapfrogging platoons. After laying down suppressive fire, Michael's squad was the last to pull back, with the company commander last off the ridge and close

A company advances in a column with security on right and left. The first soldier, probably an NCO, carries an M1 with fixed bayonet, and wears the M1928 haversack, infantry cartridge belt, K-bar, and jungle aid kit.

behind. Once off the ridge the soldiers fell back almost to the morning's starting point. Company casualties for the day were four dead and 18 wounded, or almost two full-strength rifle squads.

The next 17 days went much like the first day: an attack for several hundred yards, met by mortar, artillery and machine gun fire driving soldiers to ground; the elimination of the Japanese bunkers holding them up, or recoiling without success. Some days Michael's company took its objectives, some days not. Some days there were heavy casualties, some days not. Some days, at least initially, they took prisoners.

All the men knew that they, their company, and their friends were being worn down by the prolonged combat. It appeared to be a never-ending cycle: an all-round alert at first light; clean weapons while others guard, then exchange roles; the platoon leader gets the day's order from the company commander and assigns missions to each squad; the jump-off; attack; more casualties and offensive combat, once the enemy or someone up the chain decides the company goes no farther, then halt and prepare the perimeter defense. Digging foxholes, soldiers half-awake, half-asleep except when the Japanese try to infiltrate, all through the night until first light when it begins all over again.

Every afternoon before it grew dark, Michael's company would halt and prepare for what they knew was coming later: Japanese probes of their position, night attacks, and infiltration. Before the deep darkness fell, the company pulled into an all-round defensive

A bazookaman and his loader fire at a target on Purple Heart Ridge during mopping-up operations.

perimeter, with the company commander assigning defensive sectors to each platoon, as well as positioning the light machine guns. The platoon leaders designated squad positions and fields of fire for the automatic weapons so that the machine guns and BARs were locked into protective crossfires around the perimeter.

The soldiers grouped themselves into two- and three-man foxholes, with the assistant squad leader or squad leader with the BAR.

After several days of attack, Michael's company might get a day in battalion reserve to rest, maintain weapons and equipment, and to fill in the blank leadership positions caused by casualties; in some cases privates first class became platoon sergeants. Unfortunately, many times this day off lasted only a few hours, because the company had to quickly saddle up and march to assist another company in trouble or to fill a gap in the line.

There were no replacements beyond those just lightly wounded enough to require a night's stay at the battalion or regimental aid station, and the company's front-line strength dropped from about 165 to probably fewer than 100. Some squads and platoons were much harder hit than others were. Michael's squad had been fortunate so far, with few casualties, although the soldiers were spent. Michael remembered little of the past few days. They all seemed to merge together – attacking up hills and ridgelines called Love Hill, Purple Heart Ridge, Kagman Point, Papako Ridge, Karabara Pass, and Hill 760, the last overlooking Tanapag harbor; and clearing bunkers and caves of Japanese; capturing Aslito airfield. He could not put a date on any of these, he only knew that he had been there.

Michael only remembered the extraordinary. About nine days into the fight they had received a much longed-for gratuitous issue of cigarettes, and another day they watched P-47s land for the first time on Aslito airfield. He also remembered his first sergeant being wounded, but that was in the recent past. After almost 20 days on Saipan, infantrymen, soldier and Marine, wild eyed and bearded, all had the look and smell of death. The body moved, but the mind was numbed. Little things were significant – a night's sleep without being sniped at, the next meal, the next sunrise, or just surviving. Long-time friends had fallen and been forgotten, at least for now.

Finally, on July 5, Michael's company went into regimental reserve several thousand yards behind the front lines. The platoons immediately prepared a perimeter defense, but there was no sniper fire, and the soldiers could take off their blouses, sit in the sun, clean their equipment, and read their mail. One of the Catholic chaplains arrived and conducted Mass and non-denominational services for others. Both were well attended. Everyone knew they were going back up on the line the next day for what they hoped was the final push.

On July 6, nine men remained of the original 12 in Michael's squad. The squad had all been very lucky in the days since June 17, with only two battle casualties and one injury, none serious. For this operation, Michael's was the extreme right squad in the company, tied in with C Company on the left for the assault on the gulch ahead. If all went well, his platoon would cross the high ground north of the gulch, disappear over the crest and be above and behind the Japanese-occupied caves on the opposite face.

The slopes leading to the gulch looked like a tilted washboard, with what seemed to be drainage ditches cut into the sides. The near slope was a bit more gentle than the far one, with broad-trunked trees and huts that appeared to be made of straw about 30–40 yards (27–37m) apart.

Michael listened to the crump of the 60mm (2.36in.) and battalion 81mm mortars against the opposite slope about 200 yards

Saipan. The combat infantryman.

(183m) ahead. On signal, everyone began moving down the hillside, moving in rushes from cover to cover. Without gunfire, it was eerily quiet. Then, Michael heard off to his left a series of explosions and saw smoke in the straw huts. The entire company line went to ground while the explosions continued for about 15 minutes and then stopped. Michael and the soldiers on the right flank watched soldiers in the center crawl up and peer into the huts. Soon the word passed that about 60 Japanese soldiers had put grenades to their abdomens and committed suicide.

Just as they began moving again, Japanese sniper fire began pattering against the hard-baked ground. Everyone jumped into the ditches for protection. Yelling, Michael got his men moving again, but everyone stopped when they saw the men in Charlie Company pinned down. They waited for a tank to free Charlie, but the tank only made it halfway down the slope without getting a bearing on the enemy position. Michael's platoon again began moving over the ridge. Walking up and down over the washboard, they missed the camouflaged Japanese trench dug into the gulch about 25 yards (23m) away. All hell broke loose when a Japanese machine gun on the opposite ridge opened up and a hail of rifle fire from the trench caught Michael's squad in a crossfire.

Within moments, two of Michael's men were casualties, one hit in the leg and another more seriously injured. The attack halted; but Michael was so preoccupied with directing his squad that he was oblivious to the danger, unaware that everyone else was facedown in the dirt. He had to do something about his squad's position, but there was not much he could do except see that the two wounded were pulled out of the line of fire. One required immediate evacuation, but the heavy fire made that suicidal. Michael knew that his commander had stressed pushing the attack forward and for soldiers to return later for the wounded, but Michael had seen wounded soldiers mutilated by bypassed Japanese and wouldn't have that happen to his own men.

When he saw friendly machine gun and mortar fire landing on the slope ahead and in the gully, he realized this was the time to get his wounded out of harm's way. He called for help and with one of the nearby riflemen, grabbed an arm of the more seriously wounded man and ran for the crest. Michael and the soldier were almost at the ridge's crest when a bullet passed through Michael's hand, the wounded man's shoulder and the rifleman's chest, killing him instantly and spraying a gout of blood. Michael felt no immediate pain, just a sudden shock, and then numbness as they all fell to the ground. He wondered if this was a bad one.

Michael dusted his wound with Sulfa powder and pulled his compress out of his first aid kit, holding the package between his wrist and thigh and ripping it open with his unwounded hand. He opened the compress and pushed it against his wound to stanch the spurting flow of blood, which he knew was arterial bleeding. He then opened and wrapped his second compress on the exit wound, tying the bandage as best he could around his hand. He looked around for the platoon medic, who should have been there treating the wounded. Michael had no way of knowing he had been killed.

Through his haze, Michael watched as his assistant squad leader pushed the remaining five men of the squad forward onto a part of the ridgeline hidden from the Japanese fire, although the squads to the right and left were pinned down. Two men crawled to the lip of the crest and began rolling grenades down on the Japanese position. Reacting quickly, the Japanese soon pinned them down with return fire. The rifleman carrying the squad's M1903 Springfield with grenade launcher joined them, crawling into a firing position where he could engage the enemy below. He was killed before he got one round off.

Michael watched as his assistant squad leader gestured toward the BAR man to lay down a suppressive fire so that the two men could withdraw. What remained of the squad fell back to the location of the wounded man, who had not been evacuated and could go no farther because of the heavy fire. Suddenly one of the men jumped up and bounded over and down the ridge in the direction of C Company, with rifle fire following him. He was still on his feet when he disappeared from view.

A few moments later the platoon guide appeared with two soldiers to help drag Michael and the other wounded to safety, and then went back and provided covering fire for the remainder of the squad to withdraw.

While Michael was being treated at the company aid station before being evacuated, he realized that the soldier who had jumped across the ridge was not there, and begged that someone go back for him. The company commander refused at the time, but later when it was dark two lieutenants and six men went back down into "Harakiri Gulch" and found the soldier with a man from another company hiding in the bushes. Both had given up hope. Michael's squad member died of wounds at the aid station, the other lived.

Before Harakiri Gulch, Michael's squad numbered nine, only three short of full strength. By late afternoon, only three remained with the company. Of the others, three were dead, two of whom had been guardsmen with the company while it was at the 69th Regiment Armory, and three wounded. A squad that had trained and lived together for three years was gone.

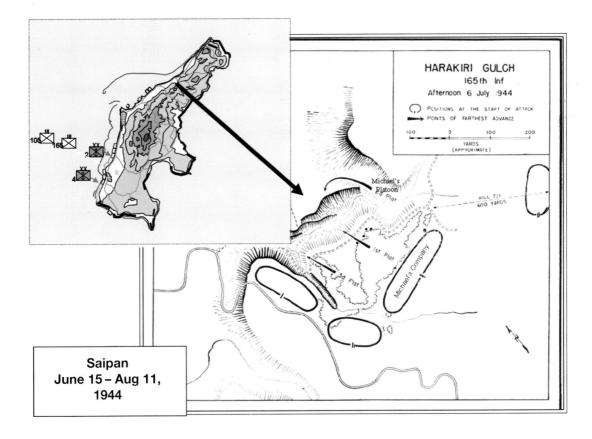

By nightfall, Michael and the other wounded had processed through the battalion aid station where his wound was dressed, then to a beach hospital, on to an amphibian and finally on to a "Green Dragon" LST outfitted as a hospital. Although his wound was relatively minor, there was no place on shore during the battle where he could have surgery and recuperate, so when the LST left for Kwajalein Atoll, he went with it, hoping that he would not have to return.

The aftermath on Saipan

Although the battle was over, some sniping still occurred and patrols walked the terrain looking for hidden Japanese troops. Not much else occurred outside routine duties, care and cleaning of equipment, and a half-day training schedule. Otherwise the company was very subdued, and still far below strength. The depleted squads of between four and six men, with no new faces, impressed upon the remaining soldiers just how bad the fighting had been and emphasized the loss of their buddies.

Japanese equipment, arms, and ammunition littered the landscape and was piled high in dumps. Leisure activity besides bathing in the surf and playing poker, included walking over the battlefields, where soldiers talked through their actions. For Michael some trips were just bad memories. The company also set up weapons ranges where all the soldiers practiced using Japanese weapons and worked with the enemy mines and booby traps. Soldiers listened to the news over the short wave radios and followed the war's progress in Europe and the Pacific.

Saipan turned sickly with the coming of the rainy season, as shell holes, tree stumps and depressions filled with water, allowing mosquitoes carrying dengue fever to breed prolifically. Many soldiers, physically and emotionally weakened by the campaign, wound up in hospital, and although many returned within two weeks, they remained sick and weak for some time afterwards.

Michael boarded a resupply ship and returned to his unit on Saipan in August. He arrived just in time to attend his company's memorial service for their fallen comrades at the cemetery in the Saipan Bowl. To ease the grief caused by the loss of so many wounded and fallen, the regimental chaplains conducted daily services.

In late September, Michael paid a last visit to his friends at the 27th Infantry Division Cemetery before boarding the USAT *Robin Doncaster en route* to Espiritu Santo in the New Hebrides.

Casualties and medics

Michael was one of the lucky ones: his injury was not considered life-threatening and he was given medical attention relatively quickly. When he was pulled back to the lee side of the crest, Michael saw the litter bearers preparing to carry a more seriously wounded soldier back to the battalion aid station and the company medic coming closer. All were armed. In the PTO, the medics carried side arms or carbines to protect themselves and their patients. They wore the same equipment as medics in other theaters but they did not wear the protective Red Cross, because of the Japanese habit of targeting medics.

The medic's presence was a great comfort, because everyone knew that "Doc" left no one to die on the battlefield. The medic smiled, pulled out a morphine syrette, which contained 25 grains of morphine and looked like a miniature toothpaste tube with a sealed end, and used the needle attached to the syrette to puncture the seal before inserting it into Michael's thigh and then pinning the empty syrette to Michael's shirt collar. Michael immediately felt pain relief, euphoria, and a mellowness of spirit he thought long lost. After re-bandaging Michael's hand, Doc filled out an Emergency Medical Tag (EMT), with Michael's name and serial number, the nature of the wound, the approximate time he was wounded, and the treatment so far given. He attached the tag through a buttonhole in Michael's blouse, helped him to his feet and began walking him and the others down the hill toward the battalion aid station.

At the aid station casualties from companies throughout the battalion sat or lay quietly waiting to be seen among the bloody bandages and clothing littering the floor. A lieutenant walked among the wounded with the senior aidman, sorting who could be bandaged and sent back to the front, and who needed treatment further back. More morphine syrettes were utilized as necessary. Many times the combination of exhaustion and morphine put injured soldiers to sleep until they woke in the field hospital.

The battalion surgeon examined Michael; he did not change the dressings the medic had earlier applied, but he started a

Medics in the POA lift a casualty up a steep ridge. Note the 1944-style plywood pack board, personal weapons and lack of Red Cross armbands. Unlike the MTO and ETO, in the PTO there were no noncombatant privileges afforded medical personnel.

plasma drip. One of the medics taped Michael's fingers around a splint and immobilized the injury by taping Michael's arm to his chest. He recorded his actions on the EMT and sent Michael to join the other wounded waiting for transportation back to the clearing station. Soon medics with a jeep and stretchers loaded him and the others for the trip to the clearing station, where they were again triaged to decide who remained in the field hospital and who boarded the hospital ships in the harbor.

Had Michael suffered a less damaging wound, he might have spent a few days at the adjacent field hospital and then been sent back up on the line, not because he was completely healed, but because his bed was required by someone else. Instead, he boarded an LCVP from the field hospital, but the craft grounded on the reef and he and the others transshipped to another craft, to a hospital LST, and finally to one of the transports now being used to transport the lightly wounded. On board ship, Michael's wounds were dressed again, but it was only when he arrived at a general hospital on Kwajalein Atoll that he received specialized surgery on his hand. The hospital had over 1,000 beds with staff and equipment equal to any hospital in the US.

For a soldier expected to take more than 90 days to recover, Kwajalein Atoll would have been a stopover point *en route* to a hospital in Hawaii and probably later a hospital in the continental United States. Again, it was a matter of bed space; it was important to free the bed space near the battlefield, so casualties were evacuated to clearing stations and hospitals as quickly as possible. Every wounded soldier left in theater meant one less bed for a future wounded soldier. Dependent upon his recovery, the soldier might be re-deployed as a limited-duty soldier with an organization in the States, or discharged and assigned to a Veterans' Administration hospital until recovered enough to go home.

Wounded soldiers, closely spaced in landing craft, wait to be ferried to a floating hospital.

Other soldiers became psychoneurotic casualties, suffering from what was commonly called "combat fatigue", a condition which manifested symptoms mimicking such serious disorders as manic depression, schizophrenia, and Parkinson's disease. Had Michael been stricken with combat fatigue and sent back from the front line (tactical situation permitting), he would have received hot food, a cool shower, and the chance to shave. He would then have seen a psychiatrist who would have sedated him with sodium amytal, which prevented nightmares from interfering with rest. Those not responding to treatment within 36–72 hours were transferred to hospital ships. During the battle on Saipan, 74 percent of the 272 patients with battle fatigue from the 27th Infantry Division returned to duty by the end of the battle.

Rest and recuperation

Michael's company debarked from the USAT *Robin Doncaster* on October 7, 1944, and were hit immediately by the heat and humidity of Espiritu Santo. They climbed onto trucks and moved to one of the coconut plantations about 10miles (16km) away from the naval base. There was little there besides the palms, so Michael and the others set to building their living quarters. The beaches were made up of coral with the consistency of broken glass. It was nothing like Hawaii, with its women and reasonably free-flowing alcohol. Here was 3.2 "near" beer if you could get it, as well as an active trade in real or manufactured Japanese battle souvenirs which could be bartered for hard alcohol and other creature comforts. Orders came down from regiment to sew the divisional patch on their cotton khakis. The only real benefit to being veterans of Saipan was that Michael and his comrades received fresh meat, which was in extremely short supply.

By September 1944, Michael, along with about 75 percent of his division, had been overseas for two and a half years. Like the others, he felt he would live the rest of his life on some God-forsaken island, never again experiencing the familiarity of home: shoveling snow, taking a taxi, the smells of the city, and home cooking. Some soldiers who won the regiment's monthly draw for one of the few limited furloughs went home for 90 days, although most of that was spent traveling. One of Michael's friends computed that at the going rate; the last man would get his furlough in 1949! Everyone was both happy and envious when their friends left, even though they knew most would try hard not to return, hunting assignments in the US or working towards a compassionate discharge. Anything to keep from coming back.

Michael and the other members of his company learned through letters from home, enclosing the September 18, 1944 issue of *Time* Magazine and newspaper articles that their division had supposedly performed poorly on Saipan. Bitterly, they felt that their performance was well reflected by the butcher's bill of a casualty list. Their companies, platoons, and squads had been just as hard hit, as had the Marines they had fought alongside. Three

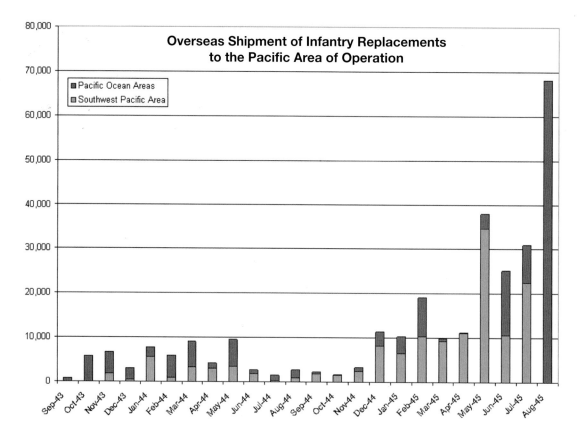

months after the battle, many rifle companies remained below 50 percent strength.

There was a change in company leadership: the captain who had led Michael's company through Makin and Saipan, and his executive officer both left to become staff officers in the battalion headquarters. A new commander and other officers joined. Some of the company NCOs, including the first sergeant, received commissions as second lieutenants, and others received promotions. Michael was happy to remain a squad leader. Sometimes, when he thought of Saipan, he wished that he only had responsibility for himself.

In November and December, 57 replacements arrived to fill many of the vacancies, but the company was still short about 40 soldiers from its authorized strength. The soldiers still in hospital remained on the company roster until they had been away 60 days, so there were fewer soldiers actually present than what the paper strength showed. The recovered wounded slowly trickled in, but for every two casualties, only one returned, the other too seriously wounded for further service. With four new men, Michael's squad increased to eight, with one man still in hospital. Even with everyone available, Michael lacked three men for a full squad.

Training in October was rigorous, intense, and professional. Michael and the others were battle-hardened and their training on

Espiritu Santo was more a honing of skills, in marked contrast to the period before their first fight on Makin, when they were only basically trained and thought they knew everything. Everyone requalified with their weapons and familiarized themselves with the company machine guns and mortars. They went through another jungle training school. Michael switched weapons from his faithful M1 to the Thompson submachine gun. Although not as accurate at long ranges and a real pain to clean and maintain, he wanted the firepower for close-in engagements.

Combat Infantryman badge.

Battle-wise officers set time aside for Michael and other NCOs to train their soldiers. They now knew what to emphasize to the new soldiers, although the real test was combat itself. They practiced squad battle drills, day and night patrolling, map reading, demolitions, mines and booby traps, and the employment of the flamethrower. Once squad training finished, they progressed to platoon, company, and battalion exercises that included fire and maneuver, attack, tank-infantry-artillery exercises, stream-crossing exercises, and more jungle and amphibious training. Michael and the others also practiced moving and attacking at night, which seemed doubly dark in the interior jungles of Espiritu Santo. It wasn't hard keeping soldiers awake because they had all heard of the headhunters and pythons inhabiting the jungle and didn't want to be supper for either.

The oppressive heat of January through March 1945 felled many soldiers, and tropical skin diseases were rampant. Soldiers who had survived Makin and Saipan without injury either found themselves in hospital recuperating or on their way home.

Michael remembered one exercise especially well, or at least its aftermath. The soldiers had been dragging back to camp in rout step, finding it difficult to put one foot in front of the other in the heat. The regimental band greeted them with "Garryowen", giving a lift to everyone's step and automatically putting every soldier in step with the other, even though many believed themselves too tired to be motivated by music.

When they were not training, it seemed they were parading. Reviews, parades, and awards ceremonies occurred monthly. It was not so bad if one was watching or receiving a medal, but standing in formation in the heat was grueling. Everyone was happy, though, when their unit and friends received the recognition they deserved. Michael received a Bronze Star and could have worn five medals: the Bronze Star, Purple Heart, Good Conduct Medal, National Defense Service Medal, and Asiatic Pacific Service Medal with arrowhead and two service stars. However, most of the infantrymen wore only their Combat Infantryman Badge, and left the medals and ribbons in their boxes. The prevailing thought was that anyone could get a medal but only a combat infantryman could wear the badge. The posthumous awards to soldiers brought back bitter memories. Of the 42 Silver Star and Bronze Star medals awarded members of Michael's company for Saipan, 15 were posthumous.

In early March, there was a final ceremony where the 165th's three battalions received the Combat Battalion Infantry Streamer, signifying that 65 percent of the battalions were recipients of the Combat Infantryman Badge. On March 19, in the midst of driving rain, Michael and the others boarded the USS *Missoula* for landing exercises at Turtle Bay and travel to Okinawa.

Soldiers peer into the undergrowth, while searching for Japanese in thick terrain. They are armed with M1 rifles and carbines. Typically, each soldier carries two canteens.

The last battle: Okinawa

This was not an assault landing like Makin or a six-hour LCVP ride at night like Saipan. Michael and the members of the battalion combat team climbed down cargo nets into the bouncing LCVPs, formed waves and then headed for the enemy-free Hagushi Beaches, landing on Brown Beach just after lunch. Soldiers munched on assault lunches that contained hard candy, chocolate bars, gum, cigarettes and matches. However, they were shocked by the cold drizzling rain, unprepared as they were after three years in the tropics. Many wished they had the woolen shirts they wore in 1941.

Also, unlike the two earlier battles, the unit was not at full strength, with the company numbering 152 rather than the authorized 193. Michael's squad stood at 75 percent strength or nine out of 12 before a shot was fired. This did not seem to matter: if the rumors were true they would act as the Ryukyu Islands garrison, detailed with mopping up.

Michael's company spent the next nine days patrolling the rear areas for bypassed Japanese, capturing some and killing others. There was a lot of talk about a new weapon some of the members of the Intelligence and Reconnaissance Platoon were carrying. It looked to many like one of Buck Rogers' ray guns, with a large dish mounted beneath an M2 carbine and a large flashlight on top with a power cable leading to a metal box carried in a backpack. They called it a "sniperscope" for good reason, and the Army had developed it for the sole purpose of thwarting Japanese infiltration. Using this weapon, a soldier could see in the dark to a range of about 70 yards (64m), with objects appearing in the scope in various shades of green. About 30 percent of the total Japanese casualties inflicted through rifle fire during the first weeks of the Okinawa operation were from the sniperscope and M2 carbine.

Michael's squad pulled security occasionally for the sniperscope teams. Although they were heavy and bulky, it was nice to sit in a concealed position and watch the green images of Japanese soldiers creep forward. A quick blast of automatic fire and another enemy soldier lay dead. After a few nights they discovered that rain and night illumination tended to cut down the scope's efficiency.

Word arrived that they were moving forward to launch an attack against Japanese positions guarding Machinato airfield. Michael's company's objective was the Gusukuma village, just down a ridge and across a gulch. Total distance was about 800 yards (731m). Orders were to move forward and bypass any Japanese resistance. With open terrain quite unlike the dense vegetation of Saipan, it appeared they might be on the airfield by that night.

Just before the attack began the next morning, mortar fire wounded Michael's company commander. The executive officer assumed command and started the company forward at 0730hrs, driving straight down the crest of the ridge into a pocket formed by high ground on three sides and the village on the other. They attacked through a maze of pillboxes and tunnels, knocking out each in turn with techniques perfected on Saipan using flamethrowers and explosives. By early afternoon, Michael and the others were at the nose of the ridge, but heavy machine gun fire forced them left across the road and into the railroad cut for cover, which they followed down to a deep gulch. Both the road and railroad bridges were blown and the Japanese had perfect fields of fire down the length of the narrow ravine from the ridge and the pocket.

Several soldiers threw smoke into the ravine, and while the Japanese fired blindly, the men crossed the ravine in pairs. But once they crossed the gulch they were on their own. The walls were too steep for any vehicles to cross. Forming on the hill on the other

Riflemen relax for a moment while advancing in thick undergrowth on Okinawa.

side, the infantrymen continued forward until the company was on a grass-covered, treeless hill just east of Gusukuma. Without tank support, heavy fire pinned them down, and as it was growing late in the day, they began digging in for the night. For ten days, until they were relieved, they fought for Gusukuma.

There was a little resupply during the night. Soldiers in carrying parties brought forward water cans, ammunition and rations over 1,000 yards (914m) of rough terrain. The extra BARs and Thompsons the squads now carried were good for night defense, but resupplying them over extended distances posed a real problem. A BAR could fire the equivalent of more than a 96-round .30 cal. bandoleer (weighing 9lbs (4kg)) in a minute and a Thompson could go through several .45 cal. 30-round magazines, each weighing more than $1^{1}/_{2}$lbs (0.68kg), in the same amount of time. An M1, for that matter, firing three to four eight-round clips, each weighing 1lb, added to the resupply problem. With 30 or so soldiers in Michael's platoon armed with M1s, BARs, and Thompsons, this amounted to a daily requirement or basic load of about 474lbs (215kg) of .30 cal. and 33lbs (15kg) of .45 cal. ammunition.

The wounded were carried out the same way, by bearer. There were no tanks or self-propelled mounts to help them push forward. As the men clustered under cover, a few rounds of mortar and artillery fire slammed into the village in front of them. It was not much, but with other fighting elsewhere, it was all they could get. Michael's platoon moved forward in an inverted wedge formation with two squads forward and one behind in support. There was little fire from the town and opposing ridgeline until they had crossed the road onto a bare rise just east of the village. Then all hell broke loose: Japanese machine guns from their front, left and right flanks opened up, pinning them in crossfire. Caught in the open between the village and the road in the killing ground between the interlocking fires of at least four machine guns, the two options were to go forward, or pull back. Michael's inclination was to pull back and try again later, but his platoon leader had other ideas, and motioned his squads to continue forward. The attack became a crawl: they positioned, then rushed to the next cover, with movement measured in feet rather than yards.

After about four hours of slowly moving forward, Michael had part of his squad clustered in the wrecked house on the village perimeter and the remainder under cover behind them. Miraculously, only one man was wounded, although there were casualties from other squads on the open ground. The word came to tie in with adjacent squads and wait for the company on the right to come up. Everyone began digging in and preparing for the night, fully expecting Japanese infiltration and mortar barrages.

About 2100hrs, Japanese mortar and artillery fire began landing throughout the area. Michael and the others had never experienced such a heavy barrage on Saipan. This was like a never-ending series of lightning flashes and thunder as rounds

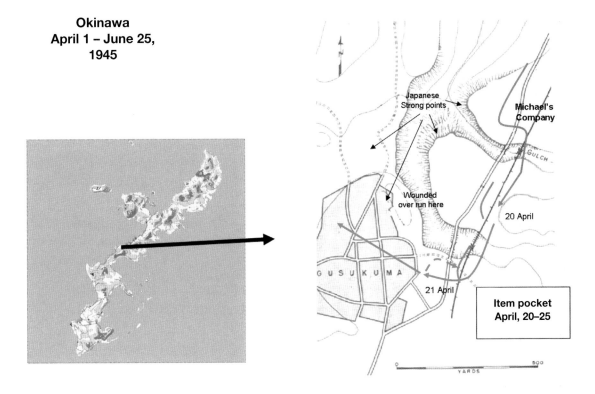

**Okinawa
April 1 – June 25,
1945**

Japanese
Strong points

Michael's
Company

GULCH

Wounded
over run here

20 April

G U S U K U M A

21 April

**Item pocket
April, 20–25**

YARDS

exploded around them. The barrage went on for hours and then
for an instant the air was deathly still. The shrill yells of a large
Japanese force attacking someone over on their right rent the
silence and then, in the muzzle flash of machine guns and rifles, it
appeared that hundreds of enemy soldiers were boiling out of the
pocket and northern half of the village. All Michael's squad could
do was sit hunkered down in their holes and wait for the attack to
hit them, firing at Japanese close by who were visible in the flashes.
It did not seem to be going well for the Americans on their flank,
and they watched as the men retreated up the hill. Although not
in heavy contact, word passed for Michael and the others to fall
back to the support platoon's line. No one slept that night.

The next morning they saw smoke and heard grenades going
off in the gulch followed by screams. Some of the wounded
Americans who could not be evacuated the night before had
hidden in caves. The Japanese attacked them with grenades and lit
fires at the entrances of the caves. They shot those who crawled
from the caves, while those who stayed within suffocated. Coursing
through the minds of those listening to the slaughter was the
thought, "No prisoners".

The next few days blurred into the haze of carrying
ammunition and water forward at night, supporting other
companies' attacks on the pocket, adjusting mortar and artillery
fire on Gusukuma, and finally assaulting and clearing the village in
a vicious day-long battle of hand-to-hand fighting. Opposing

enemy fire from the ridge cut off any means of retreat, so Michael and the others went forward. Casualties were high. There were still no tanks, and the ridge on the other side of Gusukuma was riddled with caves and tunnels. The only way to destroy the enemy within was to dig them out, or seal them in, both methods calling for the infantrymen to close with the Japanese.

Infantrymen shelter behind a tank from incoming artillery in the combat pocket.

To Michael and the others conducting the clearing, it seemed as if time flew; to those watching it stood still. The men scanned the ridge sides looking for what might be caves and taking turns at being the lead man. When Michael's turn came, he crawled forward until he could see inside the cave, watched for a few minutes, and then motioned the others to cover him while he crawled adjacent to the cave's mouth. With the others prepared to cover him, Michael took a deep breath, ensured his Tommy gun was on "fire", pivoted into the cave entrance and fired a long burst into the depths, and then pivoted back to the side. He then took a pineapple grenade, pulled the pin, released the safety lever, counted to three and tossed the grenade inside. He knew the grenade fuze was supposed to be five seconds. He also knew from experience that some of the fuzes were cut as short as three seconds by indifferent factory workers. Nevertheless, that was the chance he had to take, else the Japanese might throw the grenade back out. After the smoke and debris cleared, he watched and listened at the opening for any signs of movement. Satisfied, he then motioned the engineer to come up with his explosives, usually 30 or 40lbs (13–18kg) of TNT, watched him set them and then they both backed off. When the dust cleared, Michael climbed over the rubble to see that the cave mouth was sealed tight. Then the squad moved on to the next cave.

Ten replacements joined the company in the middle of the fight for Gusukuma, one new man going to each squad. Michael had never received replacements in combat before, and really did not know what to do with the new soldier, except to pair him with a veteran and tell him to watch what everyone else was doing, and not to do anything stupid. There wasn't much else he could do.

The fighting for the pocket continued for several more days. At the end tanks came up and assisted in clearing the remaining caves. On just about the last day, Michael watched Private First Class Alejandro Ruiz, one of the soldiers who had joined them on Espiritu Santo, clear what remained of the pocket by himself after

An infantryman with a child. Most soldiers showed an affinity towards children, especially after witnessing so much death.

watching seven of his squad mates wounded by a hidden pillbox. He charged the pillbox with a BAR; climbed on top of it only to find his weapon didn't work. He killed one Japanese soldier using the BAR as a club, then climbed down the bunker and ran back to obtain another weapon. He charged the pillbox again, killing everyone within, and then proceeded to move from cave to cave, destroying each one as he came to it. Ruiz was later awarded the Medal of Honor for this heroic action, the highest award for valor the US can bestow. He was the only member of the 165th Infantry to receive such a distinction in World War II.

At the end of April, Michael's unit was relieved by members of the 1st Marine Division. The smell of burnt, rotting, and decomposing flesh had filled their nostrils for so long that they had grown used to it. After a bath in the ocean to wash off the grime and the sweat, the putrid smell of decomposing bodies and the sweet smell of death had returned. After a few days' rest, they returned to patrolling the rear areas looking for Japanese. In mid-May, everyone learned the war was over in Europe. However, the fighting continued to rage on Okinawa, and with soldiers still dying, the good news did not have the same impact as it did elsewhere. The Okinawan monsoon, known as the "plum rain season", arrived and took much of the smell from the air. The roads turned to mud, and green began to sprout where brown had once been.

Going home

Things changed with the announcement that soldiers with more than 85 points or service credits were being sent home. Soldiers everywhere began adding up their points, figuring on the backs of C ration boxes just how many they had. Every soldier who had traveled overseas in February 1942 had more than 100 points of service and overseas credit alone. Moreover, adding in campaigns, medals, wounds and children, some had as many as 150 points. This contrasted with the soldiers who had arrived in November–December 1943 who had on average 21 service, overseas, and combat credits.

One of the problems, however, was that almost 75 percent of Michael's division had been overseas since 1942, meaning that

ABOVE Messing in the open on Okinawa.

BELOW Adjusted Service Rating, based on a number of factors including time in service, time overseas, combat service, and parenthood. (War Department Press Release May 10, 1945).

Adjusted Service Rating		
Group	**Remarks**	**Michael's points**
1. Service Credit	1 point per month in the service since September 16, 1940	65 x 1=65
2. Overseas Credit	1 point per month in the service since September 16, 1940	50 x 1=50
3 a. Combat Credits	5 points for ever Bronze Service Star (battle participation stars)	3 x 5=15
b. Decorations	5 points for the first and each additional award of the following for service performed since September 16, 1940 (Distinguished Service Cross, Distinguished Service Medal, Legion of Merit, Silver Star, Distinguished Flying Cross, Soldiers Medal, Bronze Star, Air Medal)	1 x 5=5
c. Number of wounds	5 points per wound as recognised by award of Purple Heart	1 x 5=5
4. Parenthood Credit	12 points per child under 18 years up to a limit of three children	0
TOTAL		**=140**

The 27th Infantry Division cemetery on Saipan.

most soldiers and the vast majority of unit leaders had more than enough points to go home. To ensure everyone was treated fairly, those with the highest points and most overseas time departed first. This included most of the men who arrived in Hawaii in March 1942, and Michael and 17 other members of his company numbered among them. Michael celebrated his seventh year of service and his 24th birthday on the ship heading home. He had almost five years of active service when he was discharged in August 1945.

The next groups to leave were those soldiers with 105 points, and then 85 points. By September, the vast majority of members of Michael's old company and regiment were replacements fresh from the US.

On September 2 Michael sat at a bar in New York City and listened to President Truman's address to the nation. "We shall not forget Pearl Harbor … We think of those whom death in this war has hurt, taking from them fathers, husbands, sons, brothers, and sisters whom they loved. No victory can bring back the faces they longed to see. Only the knowledge that the victory, which these sacrifices have made possible, will be wisely used, can give them any comfort. It is our responsibility – ours, the living – to see to it that this victory shall be a monument worthy of the dead who died to win it."

Michael remembered with fondness and regret those buried in the island cemeteries on Makin, Saipan and Okinawa, and tipped his Jameson's in respect to his fallen comrades.

The 165th Infantry Regiment deployed overseas in February 1942 had entered combat on November 21, 1943, and had suffered casualties commensurate with other regiments deployed to the Pacific. It came home in December 1945 and furled its colors at least temporarily on December 26. Not even a handful of the men present in October 1940 came home with the regiment's colors.

165th Infantry Regiment battle casualties in the Pacific Theaters of Operation							
	OFF KIA	EM KIA	OFF MIA	EM MIA	OFF WIA	EM WIA	Total battle casualties
Makin 20–22 Nov, 1943	5	27	0	0	7	74	113
Saipan Jun–Jul, 1944	15	168	0	2	31	667	996
Okinawa Apr–Aug, 1945	11	194	0	4	27	671	1903

The remainder were earlier evacuated because of wounds or injuries, or were high-pointers shipped home on furlough in May and June 1945.

The average infantry regiment in the Pacific Theater of Operations lost 25 officers and 365 enlisted men killed and 57 officers and 1,091 enlisted wounded. In approximately six months of combat, the 165th Infantry Regiment suffered 31 officers and 409 enlisted men killed, and 65 officer and 1,412 enlisted wounded, the majority being lost in June 1944 (Saipan) and April 1945 (Okinawa).

KEY
KIA = killed in action
MIA = missing in action
WIA = wounded in action
OFF = officers
EM = enlisted men

Michael's dress, equipment, and demeanor have changed dramatically since 1940. Although only 24 years old, he is by now a combat-hardened veteran, on whom the stress of combat has taken a heavy toll (1 and 2). He wears late war HBTs, and 1943 buckle-top combat boots. He carries the M1 Thompson submachine gun with 30-round stick magazine. Attached to his M1936 pistol belt are three-pocket submachine gun pouches, two canteens with covers, and the jungle first aid kit. A Mk II A1 fragmentation grenade is hooked into his shirt pocket. Across his chest he bears an ammunition bag for additional magazines. On his back, he carries the M1936 musette bag strapped over his shoulders like a haversack.

The M1 Thompson, Michael's weapon of choice, is shown in exploded detail (3). Also shown is one round of .45 cal. ammunition (4). The "sniperscope" rifle is also shown (5). This comprised a US carbine with suitable mountings to take various models of infrared night-sighting devices. No open or conventional sights were provided. Developed in 1943 to defeat the infiltration tactics of the Japanese, it accounted for c.30 percent of total Japanese casualties suffered by small arms fire during the first week of the Okinawa campaign.

A detail shows the infrared screen on the front of the sniperscope (6). The correct firing position is shown too (7). The M2-2 flamethrower (8), an improved version of the M1A1 introduced in 1944, was powered by compressed air and fueled by a mixture of gasoline and naphtha. It was very effective in neutralizing pillboxes, bunkers and caves. The satchel charge (9) consisted of a non-electric blasting cap inserted into one of eight blocks of Demolition block C-2, each of which was equivalent to 3lbs (1.36kg) of TNT: also shown is a time fuze and fuze igniter (11). These were placed inside a satchel or bag (various types are shown), secured and projected. A sketch shows how it could be thrown at the enemy (10).

CHAPTER 5

MEDITERRANEAN THEATER OF OPERATIONS, 1942–45

"What was astonishing was the speed with which the Americans adapted themselves to modern warfare. In this, they were assisted by their extraordinary sense for the practical and material and by their complete lack of regard for tradition and worthless theories."
Field Marshal Erwin Rommel, Armeegruppe Afrika

The US Army entered combat in the MTO on November 8, 1942 with ten regiments. Between that date and May 1945, US Army infantry units fought in eight named campaigns in North Africa and Italy.

US Army strength in the Mediterranean Theater of Operation, 1942–45

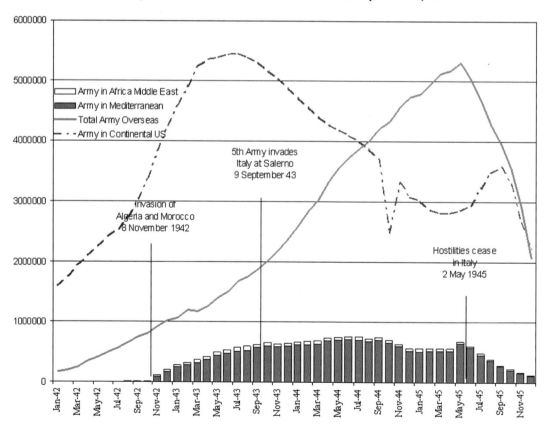

US Infantry regiments in combat in the Mediterranean Theater of Operations

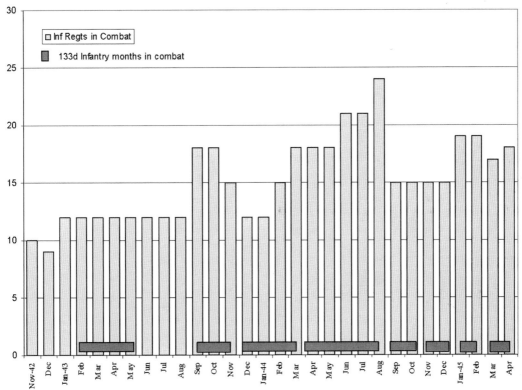

Although this was the US Army's first major area for offensive operations, it rapidly became a secondary theater for US troops, and strength in the Mediterranean never reached the level of the buildup in Europe or the Pacific.

There were never more than 24 US infantry regiments serving at one time in the MTO. They accumulated 500 months in theater, and 446 combat months between Pearl Harbor on December 7, 1941, and May 2, 1945 – the day the last German forces surrendered in Italy. Strength rose to 18 regiments then dropped to 12 by December 1943, increased to 24 in August 1944, and then fell to 15 in September 1944 with the invasion of southern France.

Units remained in the line for extended periods and were subjected to daily losses, if not directly due to combat, then to the terrible weather. As with the PTO, units were short of strength due to a replacement policy which kept soldiers in hospital assigned to their former units and fewer replacements than needed actually reaching units requiring them.

For every soldier felled through combat in the MTO, two others were stricken with disease or non-battle injuries, and 63 men out of every thousand were hospitalized every day of the campaign. The average daily casualty rate for the US Army was one battle casualty for every four and a half rendered ineffective through disease or non-battle injury.

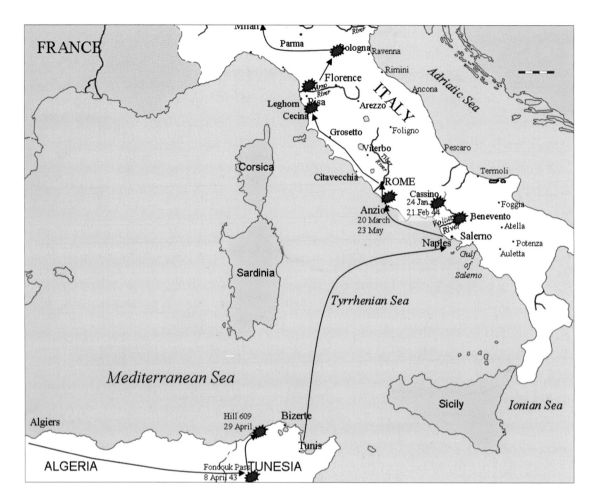

The route of the 133d Infantry Regiment in the Mediterranean Theater of Operations.

The Fifth and Seventh Armies' veteran divisions were deployed to fight in France; with two departing in November/ December 1943 and three in August 1944, and were in turn replaced by OR and AUS divisions arriving from America. Only the 34th Infantry Division (NG) remained in the MTO from beginning to end.

THE 133D INFANTRY REGIMENT

The 133d Infantry Regiment (Iowa Army National Guard) was federalized along with its parent 34th Infantry Division on February 10, 1941. Its first battalion arrived in Northern Ireland on January 26, 1942, less than a month and a half after Pearl Harbor. The 34th Infantry Division was the only original US division landing in North Africa to spend its entire war in the MTO, with one of its regiments beginning active combat on November 8, 1942 when it landed west of Algiers. The remainder of the division landed in North Africa on January 2, 1943. Major engagements at Fondouk and Hill 609 followed, and after a period of retraining, they landed at Salerno, Italy, on September 21, 1943. The 133d Infantry Regiment spent the next 19 months fighting up the "boot" of Italy, which included crossing the Volturno River three times, San Angelo D'Alife, Cassino, Anzio, Rome, Cecina, the Arno River, the Gothic Line, and the final battles in the Po Valley in spring 1945.

The 133d Infantry Regiment remained in Europe throughout the summer of 1945 and returned to the US with its parent division in October that year where it inactivated on November 3, 1945, after serving overseas for 45 months.

JOHN'S STORY

Our soldier, John Smith, was born in northern Georgia and enlisted at age 19 in January 1942. John's father was a hard-scrabble dirt farmer, like many in the triangular area where the states of Georgia, Alabama, and Tennessee touched. His mother probably died birthing the youngest of the children, now a six-year-old girl. John had an eighth grade education, a little higher than normal for a boy growing up on a farm during the 1930s. Like many during the Great Depression, he had left school to help his father and brothers work the farm. In 1940 and 1941, John's brothers left to find work in defense plants. With his brothers gone it was difficult for him and his father to work the plot of land with the few farm implements they had. There was seldom enough to eat and their diet was poor. After Pearl Harbor, John decided to join the Army but since he was only 19 he had to get his father's permission.

John trained at an RTC and was initially assigned to the newly formed 76th Infantry Division (OR). He was later assigned overseas to North Africa as a replacement to the 1st Battalion 133d Infantry Regiment, 34th Infantry Division ("Red Bull") after one of the battalion's companies suffered heavy losses recapturing Kef-al-Ahmar Pass.

Enlistment, reception, and initial training

John's family didn't read much besides the Bible, and they received most news from a neighbor who had a radio. They heard of the attack on Pearl Harbor and the US' entry into the war in this way. The more John heard, the more he wanted to enlist. He was too young to register for the draft, and was afraid the war would be over before he was drafted. Moreover, he wanted to earn money for his family to tide them over until things improved. With the draft and many people leaving to work in defense factories, there were few hands to help in the fields come planting season, which meant that fewer acres would be planted and the next year would be a hungry one for his family.

The small town John lived near didn't have a recruiting station, or any other military presence for that matter, so in January 1942 he walked and hitchhiked to the nearest town with a recruiting station to enlist. There he found that, since he was under 21, his father had to sign a waiver for him to enlist and there was no enlistment bonus. The recruiter gave him a round trip bus ticket to travel home and back.

In February, John returned to the station with his birth certificate and his father's very carefully block-printed letter. He then took a preliminary physical, which he almost failed because he weighed only 120lbs (54.4kg), low for a 5ft 10in. (1.8m) frame, and did fail because his teeth were in poor shape – enough so that he was deferred from enlisting until the worst teeth were fixed. After a note from the recruiter to a local dentist, three teeth were pulled and John was ready to proceed.

Having met the basic physical qualifications to be a soldier, he boarded a bus along with other enlistees and inductees from the area for the trip to Fort McPherson, Georgia.

The men were put into formation as soon as they got off the bus, and had to quickly learn the position of the soldier: head erect, chin in, eyes looking straight to the front; body erect, chest lifted and arched, shoulders squared, arms hanging with palms in and thumbs along the seams of the trousers; heels together, and feet turned out at 45 degrees. From the bus they gaggle-marched to the mess hall for their first US Army meal of fried chicken, mashed potatoes, beans, coleslaw, milk, coffee, and apple pie.

The sign in the mess hall stated: TAKE ALL YOU WANT, EAT ALL YOU TAKE. At the time soldiers received about 4,500 calories a day, or about 1,000 to 2,500 calories more than most well-fed civilians, and it was much more than John had enjoyed as a civilian.

After "chow," the men filed into brand-new barracks of unfinished wood for the night, where the beds were single bunked, head to foot to prevent the spread of meningitis.

They received their first lesson in making a bed US Army style. The corporal demonstrated by first tucking in the head sheet, then making hospital (45 degree) corners by pulling up the edge of the sheet about 15 in. from the end of the bed and lifting it up so it made a diagonal fold, laying the fold onto the mattress and tucking the hanging part of the sheet under the mattress. He then dropped the fold, pulling it smooth and tucking it under the mattress, following at the foot with the same procedure for the top sheet and blanket, except beginning at the foot.

The next day, John underwent another, more thorough physical. Some who had passed the physical in their hometown were disqualified and sent home by the Army doctors. An officer administered a literacy test that tested to fourth grade level those who had not completed high school. Some of the boys who arrived with John could not read, so they were given a verbal test to determine whether they could follow instructions. Those who failed all the tests were interviewed, and if found not to be malingering, they were sent home.

After passing the medical and literacy tests, those remaining received their serial numbers which identified them from other soldiers of the same name, and which would stay with them the remainder of their service. There were two lines, both in alphabetical order but with brothers separated, one for draftees and one for enlistees. As an enlistee, John's number began with a 14, the first number signifying he had enlisted, the second designating the corps area in which he had enlisted. The other six numbers were corps numbers generally indicating when a soldier enlisted; the lower the number the earlier in the war a soldier had signed up.

John then – with several hundred other boys and men, draftees, and enlistees alike – raised his right hand to swear the Oath of Enlistment. John noticed that most of the men were in their twenties. He raised his right hand and swore the following oath:

> *"I _____ do solemnly swear (or affirm) that I will bear true faith and allegiance to the United States of America; that I will serve them honestly and faithfully against all their enemies whomsoever; and that I will obey the President of the United States and the orders of the officers appointed over me according to the rules and Articles of War."*

The next few days passed rapidly, transforming civilians into recruits, with continuous testing to determine what the men were best suited for; they were read the Articles of War, issued with uniforms, and taught the rudiments of drill; all before they were shipped to their training location.

The classification tests determined mechanical aptitude and general IQ – after which the new soldiers were interviewed for job qualifications. John scored an 80 of a possible 160 on his test, which placed him mid-range in Class IV and about average for someone with eighth grade schooling; those with better education and reading ability normally scored higher, although this was not always the case. The different classes were Class I (over 130) very superior; ; Class II (110 and over) superior; Class III (109 to 90) average; Class IV (89 to 70) inferior; and Class V (69 and below) very inferior.

Soldiers display their newly issued clothing, as the NCO calls off each item.

As an enlistee in January 1942, John could volunteer for any skill the Army contained if he were qualified. However, after taking the tests and being interviewed by a classification specialist, he opted for the Infantry over the other branches he was offered – Quartermaster and Engineers – as the Infantry Branch seemed more exciting than the other two.

Next came clothing issue and John and his fellow enlistees formed a line going into a long building. It was like an extended assembly line. The soldiers slowly walked down a long counter where the clerks, after a quick glance as to build, piled the new soldiers' arms with uniforms of all sorts: two-piece herringbone twill (HBT) work clothes, khakis, raincoat, overcoat, caps, underclothes, socks, dress shoes, service shoes, and canvas leggings. John now had more clothing than he had ever owned at one time in his life. He was especially impressed with his service shoes: a clerk had measured them to fit his feet while he wore army socks and held a bucket of sand in each hand. A soldier in 1942 walked much more than he rode, and a soldier falling by the wayside due to a foot injury was as serious a loss to his unit as a soldier who was wounded.

John and his comrades then stood in line for a series of inoculations: smallpox, typhoid fever, and tetanus. They were all read the Articles of War, which, the officer explained, were no more than commonsense rules necessary for good order and discipline. John especially remembered the articles concerning company punishment where a commander could withhold privileges and administer extra duty for one week for offenses not warranting a court-martial: absent without leave, for being away from his assigned place of duty without permission; desertion, for leaving one's post without intention of returning; neglecting equipment, for losing, selling, or neglecting to take care of his equipment; misconduct, for being drunk and disorderly, writing bad checks, lending money for interest, and a host of other minor offenses. John realized the seriousness of the Articles when he learned that the strongest penalties were for desertion and divulging military secrets, both of which were death.

The next morning everyone fell out for their first taste of calisthenics, and then watched movies on venereal disease. That afternoon, John found his name on the company bulletin board for shipment to the Infantry RTC at Camp Wheeler, Georgia. Before they departed on the train there was yet another physical inspection, this time to catch any cases of gonorrhoea that might have escaped detection so far.

Camp Wheeler

On arrival at Camp Wheeler, John and his comrades were quarantined for 72 hours to ensure there was no infectious meningitis in the group. John and his comrades received their issue of infantry equipment that included an M1903 Springfield rifle, pack, cartridge belt, canteen, tent-half, mess kit, and gas

John is shown here in front and rear views age 20: he has recently arrived in North Africa and is about to enter first combat. He wears the Parson's jacket, with the "Red Bull" 34th Infantry Division patch (1) on his left shoulder (the 133d Infantry Regiment crest is also shown (2), and the First Pattern Herringbone Twill (HBT) trousers: to keep warm, he wears his woolen brown trousers under these, as well as a thick woolen brown shirt under his jacket. He wears standard issue boots and canvas leggings, and the M1 helmet. John carries the M2A2 gas mask (3) and bag (4), and is armed with the M1 Garand rifle (5): a detail of one 8-round clip (6), one .30 cal. bullet (7), and how to load the clip into the rifle (8) are also shown. John's M1 helmet (9) is shown in full detail, comprising the inner composite liner (10) and strap (11), the outer steel shell (12) and chinstrap (13), with an exploded view of the buckle (14), and the lining headband (15). John also bears the M1928 haversack (16), with the M1910 entrenching tool (17) and a bayonet attached. John is also equipped with the five-pocket M1928 cartridge belt (18), with a canteen (19) and the M1910 first aid pouch (20) attached. Also shown are the M1936 suspenders (21): these were attached to the belt to give support for heavier items carried.

Spartan World War II era barracks. The beds are arranged head-to-toe, and beneath them are soldiers' shoes: foot lockers are placed along the center isle. Field gear and clothing were placed on shelves and pegs mounted on the walls.

mask. The individual equipment was stored on pegs near his bunk and his rifle was in one of the circular gun racks placed down the center aisle of the barracks.

Everyone received a short haircut during the first week of training. Each day except Sunday began with First Call at 0630hrs and Reveille at 0645hrs. A daily schedule was busy from the start. Make up bunk, wash, dress, fall out to the barracks, across the road to the mess hall at 0700hrs, sit at the table until whistle is blown, turn over plate, fill plate, start eating. Then calisthenics in undershirts, back to the barracks to sweep and mop. Out into the street at 0845hrs for manual of arms, close-order drill, or weapons training. Back to the company area for lunch; out into the field for afternoon training. Back to the barracks at 1745hrs, dress in khaki uniform for retreat. Supper at 1845 hrs after retreat, and evenings free until 2400hrs, but lights out and Taps played at 2200hrs. Saturdays were different; everyone prepared for and stood a parade and then inspection, and if everything was shipshape, they were allowed on pass beginning at noon.

John was surprised at the different kinds of people in his training company. His company was principally from the East Coast and South, although some were from as far away as Maine, and like him, many were farmers. Some were mill workers, others had been clerks or salesmen, and there were a few professional musicians and educated white-collar professionals. Education ranged from almost none to post-graduate level. The more technical branches had little need for the men steeped in the humanities or salesmen, and many ended up in the different combat arms branches. It appeared that only those with technical skills or craftsmen were not represented – they were more likely to be in the Ordnance Corps, the Engineers, or one of the other technical branches. Many of those from small southern farms, including John, had never driven a car and, unlike the men from the cities and towns, were mechanically illiterate. All of the recruits were single.

As one of the younger men, John listened to the talk of those who were older. "If a bullet has my name on it, it'll get me" was a popular philosophy. Most, including John, did not want to lie around camps for two or three years; they wanted to see immediate action, and if they were destined to die, they did not want to languish in boredom until it happened. It seemed as if everything was happening in the Pacific. Thirteen weeks seemed long enough to prepare for combat.

John and the other recruits saw their officers only during training. In 1942, most officers at the training centers were either too old for front-line duty or brand-new second lieutenants. The recruits all felt a certain air about the "90-day wonders" who were present at much of their training. Many preferred the older, gray, mustachioed lieutenants who appeared to have an inordinate amount of patience and who didn't seem to rely so much on threats to get things done. But it was the noncommissioned officers, living in the NCO rooms at the end of their barracks, that kept them in line and focused on learning to be a soldier and who, if crossed, could make life miserable for a young soldier. Anyone thought to be "goldbricking" or trying to pull the wool over one of the NCOs' eyes was in for a very long day, although most probably these same NCOs attempted the same tricks when they were young privates. It was all a matter of learning the ropes.

Later, when the new recruits were allowed on pass into nearby Macon, they had to show the pack of prophylactics they were carrying before signing out. The Army considered those who did not return from pass AWOL, and after payday, there were usually several men from each company absent. The penalty at Camp Wheeler was a summary court-martial, which usually adjudged three days' guardhouse for every day AWOL.

In the beginning, it seemed the recruits watched training films almost every day. The first film featured graphic pictures of advanced cases of venereal disease and the Army's preventative instructions. Others were on customs, courtesies, and Army regulations; the reason the US was fighting; plus myriad other classroom-type instructions. Frequently, practical application followed what they had learned on the screen.

By the second week of basic training, the men began learning about their areas of specialty; specialties that were assigned to the men based on the interviews. John found himself training to be a heavy machine gunner, MOS 605. His training company contained soldiers training to be heavy machine gunners, and mortar men. Other companies trained soldiers to be infantrymen in rifle companies. Most of the training was similar, only diverging with weapons training. John's company only familiarized with the M1, M1903 rifles, and the BAR, while qualifying on the machine gun or

TRAINING AT CAMP WHEELER, GEORGIA, MARCH 1942
This illustration shows a standard speed-type obstacle course, which John completed in March 1942 during training at Camp Wheeler, Georgia. The course measured a soldier's endurance and agility, and the 100yd (91m) course (shown in shortened perspective at the top of the illustration) was run during the third week. The soldiers shown carry M1903 Springfield rifles with affixed M1905 bayonet and bear M1928 haversacks. The men had to hurdle two fences, run through a maze (1), scale a 7ft (2.1m) high wall (2), crawl under a trestle (3), leap across a ditch, run across elevated wood beams (4), and then sprint to the finish line. The course developed stamina, fitness, and coordination, and the soldiers would compete against each other to see who could record the fastest time.

2½ft (0.76m) hurdle

Vault 4ft fence (1.2m)

Dodge through maze

Climb over
7ft (2.1m) wall

Crawl under
trestle

Jump
6ft (1.8m) ditch

Cross
elevated beams

1

4

mortar, and familiarizing with the other weapons. Those in the training rifle companies, dependent upon MOS, qualified with the weapon of their duty description, and more of them got to throw the hand grenade. During this period of the war, there was not enough training ammunition to qualify every man on every weapon. Later, in 1943, recruits had more than enough ammunition to fire.

John's company practiced throwing blue-painted practice grenades into windows and trenches on a grenade course during the second week. John and his comrades all wanted to throw a live grenade but the sergeant selected only one to do so. Everyone got down behind a berm while the recruit went alone to the grenade pit. They watched him take the grenade in his right hand, pull the pin with his left, and heave the grenade "in a graceful arching motion". A wait of a few seconds, then a cascade of dirt, and the boom of the explosion.

Next came pistol familiarization. The recruits were handed an M1917 .45 cal. Smith & Wesson revolver, shown how to aim, and with the admonition not to flinch because "it was nothing but a gun" they fired their 20 rounds at targets positioned 15 and 25 yards (14 and 23m) away. John scored a 110 of a possible 200 points, just a bit above average for his platoon.

Soon thereafter, John's company fell out with gas masks and marched down the dusty road to the gas chamber. There they lined up, put on and cleared their masks, buttoned the top button on their HBTs, and walked into the chamber. Once inside, John noticed that his skin burned a bit, but he was able to breathe without difficulty. When ordered to remove his mask, his eyes, nose, and throat began burning; he, along with the others, rushed out the door and into the fresh air. After everyone had experienced the sulfur trioxide (FS), the men filed in again to practice donning their masks in a chemical environment. The instructor released the chloracetophenone (CN), which John noticed had an odor of apple blossoms and made his eyes burn, immediately producing tears; he and his comrades held their breath until the instructor announced "Mask!" Everyone rapidly donned and cleared their masks, and then stood steady in the gas-filled room. It was quickly apparent which soldiers had not properly put on and cleared their masks when they ran for the door. The remainder filed out.

Lungs still burning a bit, they spent the remainder of the day sniffing cloths containing the scents of the different gases. Any hesitation or uncertainty in a gas environment meant death or debilitating injury. Lewisite (M1) smelled of geraniums, and blistered skin and lungs; chlorpicrin (PS) had a strong odor of licorice or fly paper and was a skin, eye, and respiratory irritant; mustard gas (H) smelled like garlic, attacked the eyes and lungs, and caused blisters on the skin; phosgene (CG) smelled of new-mown hay and caused severe nausea, vomiting, chest pain, shortness of breath, and headaches. At the end of the long day, the

Enlisted Military Specialties within an Infantry Regiment

Enlisted men MOS	Description	Location	Enlisted men MOS	Description	Location
60	Cook	All	657	Litter Bearer	Med Det
501	Admin and Tech clerk	HQ	666	First Aid man	Med Det
55	Clerk General	HQ	667	Message Center Clerk	HQ
56	Mail Clerk	All	673	Medical NCO	Med Det
345	Truck Driver, Light	All	674	Message Center Chief	HQ
502	Administration NCO	HQ	675	Messenger	All
504	Ammo handler	HQ and Sep Co	676	Message Dispatcher	HQ
505	Ammunition NCO	HQ and Sep Co	729	Pioneer	HQ
511	Armorer	All	734	Halftrack driver	HQ and AT
521	Basic	All	744	Reconnaissance NCO	HQ and AT
531	Cannoneer	Cannon Co	745	Rifleman	Rifle Co
585	First Sergeant	All	746	Automatic Rifleman	Rifle Co
604	Light MG gunner	Rifle Co	760	Scout	HQ
605	Heavy MG gunner	Hvy Wpns	811	Antitank NCO	Bn, HQ, and AT
607	Mortar Gunner	Rifle and Hvy Wpns	812	Heavy Weapons NCO	Hvy Wpns Cos
608	Gun Pointer	Cannon Co	814	Operations NCO	HQ
609	Antitank Gunner	Bn, Hq and At	815	Ordnance NCO	HQ
631	Intelligence NCO	HQ	816	Personnel NCO	HQ
651	Platoon Sergeant	All	821	Supply NCO	All
652	Section Leader	All	824	Mess Sergeant	All
653	Squad Leader	All	835	Supply Clerk	All

instructors made John and his comrades don their masks and march the six miles back to barracks in them.

They ran the 100yd (91m) obstacle course during the third week. The men competed against one another in a contest to finish first. The course involved hurdling two fences, running through a maze, scaling an 7ft (2.1m) high wall, crawling under a trestle, leaping across a ditch, running across elevated wood beams, and then sprinting to the finish line. Lanky as he was – but weighing about 15lbs (6.8kg) more than he had a little over a month previous – John was able to finish in the top ten of his platoon.

Later, in the ninth week, John and his company negotiated another much more grueling course. This time it was using a rope to climb up and over a 12ft (3.6m) wall and dropping to the other side. Next, up a slanting ladder; across a log; jumping through a framework of logs; running, grabbing a rope, and swinging over a water-filled ditch; crossing another ditch using hand-over-hand along parallel bars about 10ft (3m) above the water. Then through a small tunnel; over a series of log obstacles, and through wire entanglements; this all run at full speed with officers encouraging them at each obstacle. After a quick breather the recruits ran it a second time.

With gas rationing in effect, the men marched everywhere. While training on the machine gun range, they marched three miles (4.8km) out after breakfast, hand-carrying the machine guns; three miles back for lunch, three miles out again after lunch; and when the day was done three miles back again carrying the machine guns.

John was in good shape, so the marches really did not affect him, although he got his share of blisters while breaking in his shoes.

During the third week, the men began to march with fully loaded haversacks. One day they began marching at 0830hrs with full equipment and had covered 10miles (16km) by 1030hrs. They marched another five miles (8km) after lunch, and then double-timed for 24 minutes. When they returned from this speed march, the soldiers stretched out on their bunks with bare feet for the medics to check their blisters.

John's real problem was refolding his tent-half and blanket into an envelope roll within the time specified. He was not alone, however. For the life of him, he could not make head or tail of the instructions in the *Soldier's Handbook*, and neither could some of the educated types. It was down to practice, with the first few tries looking like overstuffed sausage rolls.

Although John's primary weapon later would be a heavy machine gun and pistol, during training he carried an M1903 Springfield rifle, as all infantrymen were riflemen first. He and his comrades trained in the intricacies of the Springfield rifle in their section of the parade field, learning the names and descriptions of each part, disassembly, assembly, then sighting exercises and dry-fire practice from the prone position. Like many of the other men from the farm, John had grown up around rifles and considered himself a crack shot. He found the Army way of firing rifles to be quite different and difficult, especially the way he had to twist his body and wrap the weapon's sling around his arm to achieve the required firing position.

Soldiers check the fitting and seal of their M1A1 service gas mask prior to entering the gas chamber.

John's company fired the M1903 Springfield, the M1 rifle and the M1918A1 BAR during the fourth week of training. His first rounds with the M1903 were at every quadrant of the target as he tried to adjust his body to his rifle. An officer observed his problem and let him fire without the sling, and John hit the target every time. However, for all the time on the rifle range, John fired fewer than 50 rounds in total. Much of the remaining time he spent in the rifle pits, pulling and marking targets while others fired. He heard that the recruits training as riflemen fired many more rounds from the M1 and BAR, qualifying with each. John's firing was just for familiarization. He would have to qualify on the machine gun.

John found to his relief that his machine gun training was more by practice than by lecture. They watched a training film on assembly and disassembly of the M1917A1 Browning heavy machine gun, then they took one apart, naming each piece, and reassembled it. This progressed to the point where the recruits could take the M1917A1 apart and put it back together blindfolded. They also learned to set the weapon's headspace and timing by feel, while their instructors told them they might have to change barrels during the night in the heat of combat.

Next came crew drill, or putting the machine gun into operation. After a five-minute demonstration by the cadre, the corporal instructor broke the recruits into groups of three for crew drill, numbering the men in the groups from one to three. The corporal gave the commands, the number one man snapped the tripod in place, the number two brought up the gun and placed it into position on the tripod, and the number three hurried forward with the water container and ammunition box. Then they rotated positions until every man had practiced each position.

Two M1917A1 heavy machine gun platoons practice timed crew drill.

Unfortunately for some, it was not just hands-on learning. Besides the practical work, they had to learn to use the traversing and elevating (T&E) mechanism in precision firing, studying the firing tables when planning the use of the machine gun in both indirect role and when firing over the heads of friendly troops.

John quickly learned what a mil represented – one mil at 1,000 yards (914m) equaled one yard of deviation, and that there were 6,400 mils in 360 degrees. The M18A1 tripod had a 6,400-mil traversing dial, scribed in 20-mil increments, that the machine gun cradle rested on. The traversing and elevating mechanism was located at the rear of the cradle. Using the mechanism, John found he could traverse left and right in 50-mil increments and fine tune direction one mil at a time; thus he could elevate the weapon up to 65 degrees, or 1,156 mils, in 50- and one-mil increments.

Like many of his comrades, John had to visualize the movement of the barrel when zeroing and setting preplanned targets on the T&E mechanism, so that he did not lay the gun in the direction opposite to the direction he wanted the rounds to strike. Another of John's concerns was understanding the firing tables for the ammunition the machine gun fired, the calculations necessary for computing the gunner's rule for firing over the heads of friendly troops.

The machine gun range, to which they normally marched four times a day was three miles from camp: out and back for lunch, and out and back for supper. Sometimes the mess sergeant brought their chow out, and they ate out of mess kits, but that was not often. They spent days on machine guns, dry shooting and learning to coordinate the multiple actions needed to handle the guns while firing. John found the instructors were competent, and very patient with those to whom the mechanical training did not come easily. When they returned to barracks after dinner, many times the machine guns were set up so the men could practice. The large influx of draftees had not yet arrived at the training centers and the onus was on properly training soldiers.

While they practiced manipulating the T&E, they also practiced the machine gun fire commands. The corporal would call out the six elements of the initial fire command: the alert (fire mission), direction (front, front right, etc.), description (dismounted troops), range (700), method of fire (traverse, search, traverse and search; engagement: slow-, rapid-, or quick-fire), and the command to open fire (fire, or, at my command) with the gun crews repeating each element as it was given.

Then they fired for record on the 1,000in. range with the silhouettes scaled so that they represented men at 441 yards (403m). John had to traverse and search the different targets designated on the paster; some series of targets ran horizontally across the target, others diagonally, and still others vertically. He was just able to make out the strike of the rounds on the target and adjusted accordingly using the T&E. His final score, a 95 out of a possible 200, was not good enough for a marksmanship badge, although his score was about average for the machine gun platoons.

They progressed from the record 1,000-in. range to field firing where they put the theories they had learned to use. They practiced machine gun manipulation in the morning, ate their lunch out of mess kits, and in the afternoon sandbagged the guns and fired on targets from 200 out to 1,000 yards (182 to 914m). Each man had to be sparing with his ammunition, though, as only 100 rounds were available to each. The practice of firing short bursts on the 1,000in. range paid rich dividends.

John learned to adjust moving the burst into the target. Using the T&E, he had to calculate how many clicks of traverse it took to move the strike of the round from the initial burst to the target. For example, when he fired on a target at 750 yards (686m), he observed the strike 10 yards (9m) to the right and about 50 yards (46m) short of the target, so he would traverse the gun to the left 15 clicks (mils) and add one or more clicks (mils), depending on the slope. Once on target this was a great method to remain there; however, it took some time adjusting to the target.

The technique John most liked, and was best at, was the adjusted aiming point method where he walked the rounds to the target by estimating the distance to the target from the strike of tracers and dust. For example, when he fired on a target at 500 yards (457m) and estimated that the rounds impacted 30 yards (27m) short and 15 yards (14m) to the right, he moved his aiming point about 30 yards beyond the target and 15 yards to its left and fired again, usually hitting the target with his second burst.

The last day of the month, unless it was a Sunday, was payday. Pay for a private was $21 a month, less allotments. John stood at parade rest near the end of the alphabetically ordered line, waiting his turn with the pay officer. When he was the next man to be paid, he rapped sharply on the door and waited for the word "Enter". He marched to within two steps of the pay table, halted, saluted, and said: "Sir, Private Smith reports for pay." The lieutenant looked him up and down, looked at his pay record, and counted out 11 crisp one-dollar bills. John had received the other $10 as a partial pay for incidentals when he first reported to Fort McPherson. John bent at the waist and scrawled his name on an entry line next to his name. He re-assumed the position of the soldier, stepped back one pace, halted, saluted, executed an about face, and left the room. Outside he passed a line of pay tables for the company fund, barber shop, war bonds, PX (Post Exchange), and other entities wanting soldiers' money.

Guard duty was also a fixture of John's training. Before guard mount, everyone prepared by memorizing the 11 General Orders as well as the names of the different commanders in the chain of command, and anything else they thought the officer of the guard would ask as he inspected the three files of guard shifts. Guard mount over, the men went to their anti-aircraft alert duty posts, where each sentinel pulled guard one in three: with two hours on, and four hours off.

One of the last experiences of his basic training was the Dismounted Full Field Inspection as portrayed on page 78 of the *Soldier's Handbook*. The entire battalion arrayed on the parade field and at the commands "Unsling equipment", "Display equipment" they lined up, covered off to the front and sides, pitched tents, and laid out equipment for display precisely as prescribed: mess kit knife with cutting edge to the right, gas mask with strap vertical, shaving brush with bristles down. When the inspecting officers began their inspection, the soldiers stood between their tents in ranks as straight and orderly as rows of corn. Inspection complete, a bugle sounded and the soldiers pulled out the tent pegs on the right side while holding the tents erect. At the next bugle call they folded the tents to the left in one mass motion: each platoon vied with the others to see which would be repacked first and ready to leave.

During the last day they turned in their bedding and working equipment but kept their gas masks and mess kits, which they packed among their other items in their two barracks bags. Officers and NCOs double-checked their equipment and their records before allowing them to supper, which was a celebration with pitchers of 3.2 beer on the tables. Later that night, orders came sending the newly minted infantrymen to different camps and divisions. In groups of 50 or so, including a lieutenant and a sergeant, the men boarded trains at the station throughout the night and next day.

Replacement

After several days of riding the train and sitting at sidings, John and his comrades arrived at Fort Meade, Maryland, where the 76th Infantry Division was forming. They had arrived just before the majority of the enlisted men who were coming straight from the reception stations and who were to take their basic training with the unit.

John immediately noticed the disorganization of the newly forming unit. There was too little equipment and most of the

Guard Duty General Orders
1. To take charge of this post and all Government property in view.
2. To walk my post in a military manner, keeping always on the alert and observing everything that takes place within sight or hearing.
3. To report all violations of orders I am instructed to enforce.
4. To repeat all calls from posts more distant from the guardhouse than my own.
5. To quit my post only when properly relieved.
6. To receive, obey, and pass on to the sentinel who relieves me all orders from the commanding officer, officer of the day, and officers and noncommissioned officers of the guard only.
7. To talk to no one except in the line of duty.
8. To give the alarm in case of fire or disorder.
9. To call the corporal of the guard in any case not covered by instructions.
10. To salute all officers and all colors and standards not cased.
11. To be especially watchful at night and, during the time for challenging, to challenge all persons on or near my post and to allow no one to pass without proper authority.

company officers and NCOs were newly promoted; many had only been in service since 1941. From what he could tell, there were four RA NCOs and no RA officers in his company. He could tell the 76th was a low-priority unit by the equipment they trained with, much of which was older than the gear with which he had recently trained. They wore the old M1918A1 helmet and carried the old Springfield, as opposed to the new M1 helmet and M1 rifle, and machine guns were almost nonexistent.

Since John was a trained soldier, his commander promoted him to private first class and made him a heavy machine gun squad leader, responsible for a seven-man squad although he continued to bunk in the same barracks they did. John had little idea of what to do, so he imitated the NCOs who had trained him as an infantryman: their standards and expectations had been clear. In the steadily forming 76th everyone was too new to have any experience to draw from. John noticed that field grade officers frequently inspected training, and that they often pulled the officers training the recruits to the side to confer with them, after which they usually changed the training, which didn't impress the soldiers they were trying to train.

John also noticed more "nickel and dime" infractions that his old instructors had corrected with an "ass chewing" or summary court-martial; here the same breaches saw soldiers digging 6ft x 6ft x 6ft (1.8 x 1.8 x 1.8m) pits, standing at attention and saluting passing officers for one or two hours, or cleaning steps with a toothbrush.

In September, John heard that all the soldiers in the division were going to be shipped out as replacements, with more soldiers coming in to replace them. John felt his basic training had been adequate, but he knew that the training these soldiers had received in such a short time did not compare. They had not progressed very far with the weapons training because of the shortage of weapons, and those who were designated cooks or mechanics got even less weapons training. Although they were infantrymen, they trained solely in their "specialty" almost as soon as they had arrived from the reception station. Other RTC graduates designated as replacements like John began arriving soon after.

John received a ten-day furlough home before shipping out in late October. It was not easy to hitchhike with gas rationing, but John made it home by train and bus in two days. He stayed for seven days saying good-byes, and then headed back to Fort Meade, arriving two days late. His thought at home was "What are they going to do, send me overseas?" Later, after demotion to private and a stay in the brig, he thought differently.

Pay for a private increased from $21 to $50 per month in September 1942. Anticipating combat, John signed up for $10,000 worth of the government's National Service Life Insurance at $6.40 per month and made out an allotment to his family for $30, figuring that he could live on just over $10 per month until he was promoted again.

After leaving Fort Meade, John and his comrades passed from one organization to another, with little time in any to get their bearings. Many were RTC graduates, but there were also some who had received all their training in the 76th or 78th Infantry Divisions.

Once at Camp Kilmer, New Jersey, John and his comrades underwent another medical screening, were issued a dismounted cartridge belt, a new M1 helmet, and pins and poles to go with the already issued shelter half, a gas mask, and a mess kit. Officers informed them the equipment they were missing would be issued once they arrived overseas. They boarded a darkened troop transport and filed into cramped holds with bunk beds stacked five high. Here they stayed for almost the entire voyage, except when they were standing in line for one of the two daily meals which they took standing up.

On arrival in Oran, Algiers, all of the replacements debarked and assisted in setting up tents in the replacement camp. Soldiers of every MOS imaginable bunked together. There was little to no training, and while the men waited for orders to the front they did little except serve as details unloading ships. Soon it was 1943 and, because of the battle of Kasserine Pass and other engagements, the demand for replacements at the front increased. John noticed that riflemen left first. By the time it was his turn, the camp consisted mostly of heavy weapons and infantry rear-echelon men (cooks, clerks, and mechanics).

One day in early March, the camp cadre assembled John along with hundreds of other soldiers. They were issued with M1 rifles, plus what little other equipment there was available to cover what had not been issued in the US. Loaded in the back of open $2^{1}/_{2}$ton trucks, they were driven the several hundred miles to the front in Tunisia. John didn't realize just how cold North Africa was until they drove through some of the high mountain passes. He was happy finally to be going to a unit, but many of the soldiers in the truck with him were not infantrymen, and some told him they had never even fired their rifles.

Replacements wait to board a train. All of them carry the gas mask, some an M1936 musette bag, and are dressed in various patterns of HBTs. It is summer, and some have partially rolled up their sleeves.

North Africa
Reception and integration

John and his truckload arrived at their new regiment, the 133d Infantry of the 34th Infantry Division, during the last days of March 1943. Before shipping to a company, NCOs inspected their equipment, and each soldier was interviewed by the personnel section. The personnel clerk asked John what type of training he had had, what weapons he had qualified with, and other pertinent questions.

Since only a few of the replacements were riflemen, John found himself assigned to a rifle company in the 1st Battalion which had suffered heavy losses in the recapture of Kef-el-Amar Pass on March 11. Only six enlisted replacements besides John's shipment had arrived for the 133d since February 9, and every rifle company was short of men. When John complained that he was a heavy machine gunner, the personnel sergeant told him the heavy weapons companies were up to strength and that the rifle companies had priority on the replacements. Other heavy weapons soldiers, clerks, cooks, and mechanics also found themselves serving in rifle companies.

The men selected for the 1st Battalion loaded the trucks and headed for its companies guarding Sbeitla airport. At each stop the sergeant got out of the cab, walked to the back, and called surnames off his nearly alphabetical list. At John's company, the sergeant called out surnames from M through S, and then gave the list to the company first sergeant who assigned the men to the platoons. John found himself a rifleman in a rifle platoon. The first sergeant assured him, however, that if he lived, and if there was an opening

Soldiers wait in foxholes, their M1 rifles at the ready. Those with helmets (one of whom is a Private First Class) have their chinstraps buckled, but the soldier in the background has opted for a woolen hat.

Infantrymen move forward. Each soldier has his raincoat and overcoat attached in a horseshoe roll around his M1928 haversack, and two canteens hang from each man's cartridge belt. Among the identifiable weapons are the M1 rifle and M1918A2 BAR.

in the weapons platoon, and if the company received more replacements, he might later be assigned to the weapons platoon.

John's next stop was his platoon leader, who assigned him to a squad after asking him when he had last qualified with his M1. He was surprised and angered when John told him he had only familiarized with it, and that more than six months ago. John didn't even know how to break the weapon down to clean it. During the next few days those unfamiliar with the M1 fired hundreds of rounds apiece at targets in the desert and practiced squad and platoon tactics. It was all the company could do to prepare them as riflemen.

John found that his regiment was a National Guard outfit from Idaho, overseas since February 1942, the same month he had entered service. They had landed from the UK in North Africa on January 3, 1943, and been in the front lines since the middle of February. About two-thirds were high school graduates and a third of them had attended college. His company commander appeared to be in his late thirties, as did many of the NCOs. The men in the company were friendly enough to the replacements, but they spent most of their time with one another, leaving the new men by themselves.

First combat

On April 7, John's battalion moved forward toward Fondouk with the regiment's other battalion. He discovered one of the reasons his regiment was often held back in reserve and not on the front line was because its 2d Battalion was the "Palace Guard" for General Eisenhower's headquarters.

The hill masses of Fondouk loomed high over the desert sand, enabling the Germans to observe every move on the desert floor. John's regiment attacked at 0500hrs in column of companies, with his company last to move out of the protecting cover. Their objective was a hill barely discernible though the haze, about five miles (8km) away.

John followed as the next-to-last man in his squad of ten, two short of authorization. He felt more comfortable with his M1, but he was still unsure of what to do other than follow the leader. They advanced across a field of poppies by squad bounds. As they moved, the platoon leader picked out locations for the base squad to move to, with the remainder of the platoon following. With the haze burning off, the men felt the Germans watching their every move. Just as they began crossing the wadi (a dry riverbed) that lay in their path, artillery, mortar, and then machine gun fire began landing among the soldiers. Everyone went to ground and tried to find even the smallest bit of cover.

When the company commander was wounded, John's platoon leader yelled to his platoon sergeant that he had assumed command of the company, and for the sergeant to take control of the platoon. The attack continued in fits and starts across the open desert. The men could see no one to shoot at; all they could do was move forward toward a cactus patch at the nose of their objective, hoping that it might offer some concealment from the German observers.

They were still advancing slowly when M3 Lee and the new M4 Sherman tanks of the 751st Tank Battalion drove through their lines. John felt a quick thrill as he watched the tanks move forward in clouds of dust. The German fire shifted from the infantry to the tanks, and soon tanks were burning on the desert floor; those not knocked out pulled back behind the helpless infantry.

The next day was much the same. Whenever they moved, German artillery and mortar fire rained down on the men. By the afternoon of April 9, one of the companies was near the road that ran diagonally across their front. The enemy fire was too intense to move much closer, and casualties were creeping higher.

After dusk fell, John's company followed the company ahead as it circled to the right behind the company near the road, and then John's company passed behind it, until the three companies were on line along the road. Word passed to the men to drop everything except their cartridge belts, bayonets, entrenching tools, water, and grenades, and prepare to attack that night. This way the German's would not see them until it was too late.

Word passed that John's company was to take the far right side of the hill. The highest point on the top of the hill was the dividing point between the companies, with the area on the left assigned to the left-most company, and the portion on the right assigned to the remaining two rifle companies. Weapons remained on safe, and orders were that they were not to fire unless fired upon.

The battalion attacked at 2200hrs, just as the waxing crescent moon dropped below the mountains to the right rear. With just the stars for light, John's company advanced on a compass bearing, in column of platoons, with soldiers within 1 or 2 yards (0.9 or 1.8m) of another. Every so often, someone kicked a rock; otherwise, it was deathly quiet. They passed quietly between what they believed were the German listening posts and began climbing the hill's steep slopes. John was sure the Germans could hear his heart beat. About

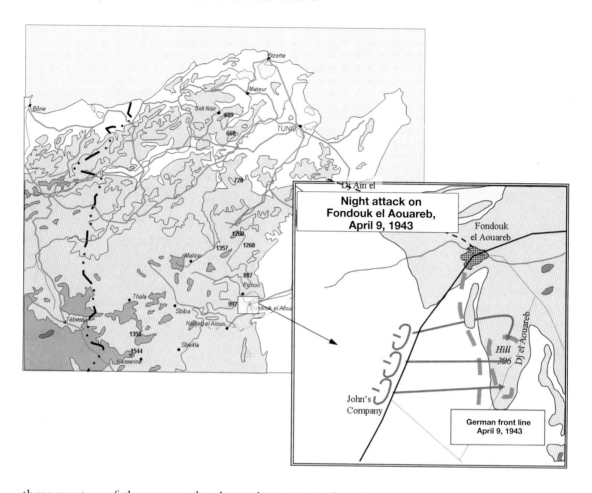

Night attack on
Fondouk el Aouareb,
April 9, 1943

German front line
April 9, 1943

three-quarters of the way up the slope, there was a whoosh as a
green flare from one of the German positions on the hill shot into
the air, illuminating John and his comrades. Machine guns and
grenades quickly followed, but the Americans were too close;
firefights began and ended at less than 10 yards (9m). The gap in
the German line widened as men still on the slope made it to the
top and split off to the right and left, overrunning the enemy
positions before them. John found himself on his company's left
flank, with heavy firing from what he thought was another
company off to his left. It was all confusion. Weapons fire lit the sky
like lightning. John instinctively fired at men wearing "coalscuttle"
helmets highlighted in the muzzle flashes. Too many soldiers were
randomly firing in the dark and rounds were going everywhere.

By 0100hrs, the battle was over, and leaders tried to find their
soldiers in the pitch black to put together some semblance of a
perimeter before the Germans launched a counterattack. But no
attack came. After the battle, an intense fatigue washed over John,
and it was all he could do to scratch a position in the hard earth; he
kept nodding off while sitting up, awakening when his head
bounced forward on his chest. The only way to stay awake was to
work. It was the same in all the single-man foxholes.

Fondouk Pass fell the next day to the 133d in conjunction with the 135th Infantry and British tanks. Total casualties in John's company averaged 18 percent. Four of the five officers were wounded as were four NCOs and 16 other ranks. Only one soldier died during the two-day battle.

They stayed at Fondouk, training with tanks and artillery the next few days because the coordination between the infantry, tanks, and artillery was poor. John noticed that everyone was more attentive than they had been before the battalion's first big battle. Later, after returning to the Maktar area for rest and recuperation, the men spent more time on night operations. All had a new respect for night attacks that allowed them to draw close to enemy positions, instead of trying to attack in the daylight when every move was watched.

Before the battle, officers and NCOs had removed their rank so they would not be ready targets for snipers. General George Patton visited the battalion at Maktar and found he couldn't tell the leaders from the privates, so he ordered the men to have their ranks pinned or sewn on by the next morning.

In late April, John's regiment was again in the front lines for the 34th Division's assault against the fortified hill positions near Sidi Nsir. John's company was in reserve and played little part in the battalion's capture of Hill 609. John remembered his reaction to the atabrine pills and the six-hour march in darkness to the jump-off point more than anything else.

In the rear areas, medics handed out a yellow pill known as atabrine to combat malaria. The pill itself was very bitter, and its

A patrol moves through a platoon position in Tunisia.

prolonged use imparted a yellow hue to the skin. Its side effects were headaches, nausea, diarrhea, vomiting, and in some cases, temporary psychosis. The rumor quickly spread that the Army was issuing the pill to decrease their sex drive. What had not been determined was the amount of atabrine needed to combat malaria, so to be safe rather than sorry, medics issued soldiers larger doses than required.

Ordered to attack early the next morning, John's battalion began to move to its attack positions at 2130hrs on the night of April 29. His company began the march forward about 2200hrs after the battalion's other companies had moved out. As at Fondouk, the soldiers walked so close together in the darkness they were almost touching one another. They followed a narrow, rocky, and winding trail, part of it below the cliffs along the Sidi Nsir River. There were numerous breaks between the lead and trail elements when soldiers negotiating difficult parts of the trail halted the column behind them while those ahead kept walking. It was shuffle forward, stop; wait to cross the obstacle, cross; then hurry to catch up with the lead element. At the next obstacle, the process repeated itself.

John was unhappy that his company was last in order of movement, standing and waiting for the men ahead to move, marching two or three paces and then waiting again, all the while his bowels churning from the large dose of atabrine. He was not the only victim, as many of the men experienced acute attacks of diarrhea and nausea while moving to the assembly area.

The nighttime movement ended at 0400hrs, and men fell asleep where they sat, while commanders reconnoitered and received the final assault orders. At 0515hrs, the assault companies moved forward with the tanks that had moved up during the early morning. John's company followed as reserve some 500 yards behind.

Unlike Fondouk, infantry and armor worked well together. John watched infantrymen walk alongside the tanks and point out targets for them to engage, while the infantrymen nearby protected the tanks. By 0645hrs, Hill 609 was won, and the soldiers began digging-in against German long-range artillery. Not a soldier in John's company was killed or wounded but other companies were not as fortunate.

After two days in position, John's battalion pulled back to an assembly area. For the next six days, John and his fellow soldiers walked the hills and mountains, clearing the Eddekhila and Chougui Passes.

Hill 609.

On the morning of May 8, word passed that, for the 34th Infantry Division, the war in North Africa was over.

For the next three months the men policed the battlefields of German and Allied equipment, building and running staging areas for divisions preparing for the invasion of Sicily. In August, they returned to the Oran area for mountain training and the Fifth Army Battle School, where they participated in extremely realistic live fire exercises; several men were killed or wounded in the training.

In early September John and his comrades received word to begin packing for overseas movement. With Sicily fallen, there was only one destination: Italy. The 100th (Nisei) Battalion joined the 133d Regiment as its 2d Battalion for the coming operation. John and his comrades wondered how this new battalion would fight.

Italy, 1943–45
Salerno to Cassino

With the attached 100th (Nisei) Battalion in place of the regiment's 2d Battalion, the 133d Infantry numbered 3,981 men, almost 600 over its authorized strength when it landed on September 22. The 1,432-man Nisei Battalion was almost as large as two standard infantry battalions, and was organized around five rifle companies (A–E), with heavy weapons, service, and headquarters companies.

Soldiers on route march during training near Oran, Algeria.

All the enlisted men were Nisei (Americans of Japanese descent), and the battalion could not draw replacements from the normal pool. It was not until after the bloodletting at Cassino that replacements arrived from the US. In the interim, as casualties ate away at rifle company strength, the five companies became three, and by February 1944, battalion strength stood at 521.

On September 22, 1943, when assault craft landed the 133d Infantry under fire at Salerno, Italy, John was no longer a "rookie". There was still much for him and the other members of his company to learn about the art of soldiering, however. He and the other replacements were still a minority in the company, most members having come overseas with it.

During the following six weeks, John's 133d Infantry Regiment fought up through the rough, mountainous terrain to its first real action near Benevento, across the Calore River and up to make its first crossing of the Volturno River, learning as it went. A second nighttime crossing of the river brought them out on to open terrain near San Angelo D'Alife, and then they crossed the Volturno a third time: they never seemed to dry out.

During the early days of the campaign, much was learned. Although John and his comrades had seen combat, many of the lessons in the books were relearned the hard way. One of the quickly validated lessons from the field manuals was the use of binoculars and observation positions. After entering a town, John's sergeant climbed to the second story in a building to observe the terrain in front. Instead of remaining in the shade and away from the window, he became too interested in observing and moved close to the window opening. A sniper saw the glint from his binoculars and shot him. John, now the most senior man, acted as squad leader until they left the line.

Later they moved into a quiet sector. Since their position was visible to the Germans, they kept everything under cover. After about a week, a soldier hung a towel and his underwear out the window to dry: the result was an enemy barrage, casualties, and a now active sector.

John and his comrades found that the Germans were fond of planting mines, and they were almost more afraid of them than facing machine guns. They also noticed the Germans were very neat. In some of the fully marked minefields that the Germans had

Soldiers of the 34th Infantry Division move through an Italian town. The two men to the fore carry the M1903 Springfield sniper rifle and the others the M1 rifle. The man on the left carries what appears to be his raincoat folded over his cartridge belt. They have the "Red Bull" stenciled on their helmets.

left with signs and wire, tall clover grew over buried mines, and in the mine-free lanes, the grass was mowed.

After a night attack that completely surprised the Germans, John's company dug in, and prepared for the coming day. At first light, a single German, about 300 yards (275m) distant, jumped up and ran back toward his lines. One rifleman fired and missed, then another and another. Soon everyone was firing at the moving target, giving away the company positions. What seemed like the whole German army responded with heavy small arms and artillery fire, killing or wounding many in the company and forcing John's comrades deep into their holes for the remainder of the day. Another lesson learned.

It was fall; a chill was in the air and the water cold as the men fought their way up Italy's "boot" through grape arbors and villages until they reached the lower range of the Volturno River and crossed it again.

Night attack across the Volturno

John walked down the chow line with his helmet in one hand and mess kit in the other. The mess sergeant put five K rations and a D ration bar in the helmet, while the cook's helpers filled his mess kit with a steaming stew of meat and potatoes. After chow, platoon sergeants sent details to draw ammunition from the supply sergeant: a bandoleer of 96 rounds for each rifleman, 500 rounds for each BAR, two grenades a man, rounds for the carbines, and signaling flares. Now extremely practiced, John rolled his blanket into his shelter half and attached the roll to his haversack in almost total darkness, knowing instinctively where every strap was. Then it began raining and John sought shelter under some low bushes, keeping his haversack on his shoulders as a backrest and leaning

Soldiers clear an Italian farmhouse of snipers. Several men watch the windows, while others approach the house from its blind side.

into it. His head soon rested on his chest, eyes closed, while the rain dripped on his helmet.

Sometime later he awoke, shivering and stiff. The night was pitch black with low cloud overhead. Soldiers around him were stirring and standing. One of his buddies helped pull him to his feet and he did the same for the man next to him. The column wound its way up the muddy trail, with men sliding or falling at almost every step.

John followed the dirty piece of white engineer tape tied to the haversack of the man in front. It was a lesson learned some time back that helped prevent men from losing contact with one another while walking in the darkness. It also told John what was up ahead: if the tape went down, the man in front had stepped in a hole; up and the man was climbing; down fast meant he was on a slope and if it slid sideways it meant the man was sliding down the slope. Whenever someone slipped, the line behind him waited while he got back up, but the line in front kept moving forward, threatening to leave the waiting men in the rear. It was almost midnight when the company reached the attack position, and the men began digging hasty positions in the mud.

When it was time to move, the soldiers formed in squad columns with men dispersed just far enough apart that they had the next man in sight. The communications man walking with the commander had a roll of assault telephone wire that he paid out as they shuffled forward. The commander had radios also, but chances were they wouldn't be functioning when they arrived at the other side. At 2400hrs the artillery started and the soldiers crossed the river. Once on the other side, they assumed attack formation.

John's company led the assault with his platoon third in line. The lead platoon angled right toward an orchard to conceal their movement. Not long after entering, John heard a series of blasts followed by screams and then silence. Someone had detonated a series of mines, wounding the platoon leader and all the NCOs. The eight men remaining in the lead platoon walked back along the formation and fell in behind the trailing platoon. The second platoon in line then took the lead, veering to the left of the orchard. Another series of explosions, whispers for a medic passing the word that the lieutenant and some others were down and needed help. Now it was the third platoon's turn to lead. John's squad followed their platoon leader as he backtracked a section and steered a large arc around the mined areas. They walked in the dark for about an hour when with a flash and crack, an explosion blew the lieutenant into the air, and injured those directly behind him. Those not wounded stood still, hearts beating, not wanting to put a foot wrong. They heard the company commander moving forward to see what was going on when another blast killed the commander and wounded still more. As his squad leader was wounded, John took command and had his men begin probing for mines with their bayonets while they slowly turned around and retraced their steps to safety. With all the officers down as well as

JOHN, STAFF SERGEANT, ITALY, EARLY 1945
John is now 22 years old, and his equipment and demeanor have changed dramatically since 1942. A combat-hardened and weary veteran, he is bearded and has a grimy face from huddling around oil stoves on an Italian mountainside. He wears the M1943 field jacket (1) with M1943 pile liner (2). His jacket displays the 34th Infantry Division patch on the left shoulder, Staff Sergeant stripes on his left sleeve, and the blue Combat Infantryman's Badge above his left breast pocket. He wears the woolen Enlisted Men's trousers, tucked into his M1944 Shoepac boots (3). He also wears brown woolen gloves and the M1 helmet, which has a small "Red Bull" painted on its front. Under his helmet he wears the wool knit cap (4). John is armed with the M1 .30 cal. carbine, and wears the M1936 belt, with M1 carbine ammunition pouches attached. Also hooked on are a canteen and first aid kit pouch.

several of the enlisted men – mainly NCOs – John's company fell back to the rear of the battalion to become the reserve, while another company took the lead.

No longer up in front, John and his comrades listened as more mines exploded. They'd been walking almost five hours as dawn colored the sky, when they heard German machine gun fire to their front. Everyone heaved a collective sigh of relief because they knew then that they had cleared the mined area. John, along with his comrades, knew that the only place sure not to be mined was the enemy position, so they surged forward through machine gun and mortar fire to seize the objective.

Winter 1943

During the winter months of 1943, John's regiment held its forward positions in the same manner as the Germans. Only a few soldiers occupied positions on the forward slope, while support positions were located on the reverse slope, out of enemy sight. Battalions rotated up and down the mountains to provide short intervals of rest, although they provided the carrying parties for the men on top. The constant rain turned the dirt roads to quagmires and the ever-present fog hid the mountain peaks from the valleys. Once wet, nothing dried without fire, and there was no fire in the forward positions. On the reverse side of the hill, John and his comrades searched for dry leaves, straw, long grass or cardboard to put some distance between them and the cold ground. One man placed his blanket on top of the long grass to keep at least some of the cold from penetrating and they used John's blanket as a cover.

Mules carried supplies up the winding trails as far as they could into the mountains. When the trails became too treacherous, men took over and backpacked the supplies the remaining two miles (3km). Soldiers from battalions in reserve climbed the mountain every night, packing on average 85 five-gallon (23l) cans of water each weighing 40lbs (18kg); 100 cardboard cases containing 12 K rations of three meals each and weighing about 44lbs (20kg); ten cases of 100 D ration bars (four-ounce bars of 600 calories each); 10 miles (16km) of telephone wire, 25 cases of grenades, plus rifle and machine gun ammunition, about 100 81mm (3.18in.) mortar rounds, one radio, two telephones, and four cases of first aid packets and sulfa drugs. The backpackers also brought mail, additional cigarettes, and cans of Sterno so the men on top could heat coffee.

Ernie Pyle in *Brave Men* noted one 5ft 7in. (1.7m) 135lbs (61kg) 18-year-old backpacker who made four trips to the top of a mountain in one day. Each trip took an unencumbered walker three hours; yet his climbs were with heavy load.

On one occasion, John and his comrades were relieved from their position and, as they hobbled down the trail, were stopped and pressed into service as guides along the trail because there was no one else to do it. Finally relieved, it took John almost an entire day to climb down the rest of the mountain because he could

A soldier removes a German "Bouncing Betty" S-mine with an M1918 "knuckle buster" trench knife. Once triggered, and after a slight pause, an ejector charge blew the mine into the air where it exploded, sending hundreds of small steel balls out to a radius of about 5 yards (4$\frac{1}{2}$m).

hardly walk. His feet swelled as soon as his wet boots and socks came off: they were mottled and numb. He'd gone almost two weeks without taking his boots off, leaving the laces loose for circulation. He massaged his feet and as they thawed, John felt first a tingling pain, then burning pain, and finally an intense itching. However, they did not discolor, and John was back for duty, and back up the mountain, within a week.

Sometime in November, the men packing supplies up the mountain arrived with heavy winter combat trousers and jackets to augment the HBTs, trench coats, and long underwear the men had been wearing. They also brought up cellophane gas capes, normally used to protect against blister gases, from which the men fashioned impromptu sleeping covers.

One of the officers brought up a translation of an article, published in *Die Suedfront*, a German magazine for soldiers fighting in southern Italy, that described American infiltration tactics of 1943:

The Americans use quasi-Indian tactics. They search for the boundary lines between battalions or regiments, they look for gaps between our strongpoints, they look for the steepest mountain passages (guided by treacherous civilians … They infiltrate through these passages with a patrol, a platoon at first, mostly at dusk. At night, they reinforce the infiltrated units, and in the morning they are often in the rear of a German unit, which is being attacked from behind, or also from the flanks simultaneously.

The battalion was scattered across a series of pinnacles at about the 2,700ft (823m) level. It was always freezing or nearly so, and the water froze nightly in canteen necks. Supplies had to be hauled great distances over rough terrain by mule trains and carrying

Soldiers carry a litter patient down a steep slope in Italy.

parties. It took litter bearers 12 hours to make a three-mile (4.8km) round trip carrying a single patient. During the winter months the Germans on the next mountain over were of secondary importance: they were probably suffering as much as John and his comrades. There were no truces and patrols still went out, but other than that it was "live and let live"; unless the other side became too complacent and walked around in the open on the forward slope.

Finally, after what seemed a lifetime of cold, the 133d Infantry pulled back to a rest area near Alife, Italy, for almost three weeks. John and his comrades took their first hot showers in months, exchanged their grimy and torn uniforms, cleaned equipment, and trained the many new replacements who were arriving. After about ten days of slacking, training began again, emphasizing physical hardening with marches, scouting, and patrolling. The marches were nothing for John and others who had spent much of their recent time hauling rations and ammunition up steep mountain trails. However, some soldiers discovered they'd been marching with collapsed arches or other lameness. In the warm, stress-free environment many men discovered they had been living with arthritis, hernia, or heart problems up on the mountain. All it took was less stress and proper rest for their bodies to signal they were broken. Some spent time in hospital and returned; others went back home to the US.

Cassino

They moved forward again early in January 1944, taking hills leading to the Rapido River, crossing it on the night of January 24, in an effort to seize Cassino. John remembered little of the three weeks that followed.

One man called it a "little Stalingrad", with back and forth, see-saw, close-range, house-to-house fighting. Tanks trundling down blocked and rubbled streets with infantry on both sides, advancing until the tanks ran out of ammunition or were destroyed, and the infantry pushed back. The constant cold and wet, the tiredness from continual shaking and ever-present fear, only getting catnaps for sleep, watching friends be killed or wounded, and wondering who was next: it was debilitating and demoralizing.

Each of the Italian houses was a fortress with walls several feet thick. In some, the Germans had built pillboxes containing antitank and machine guns that covered the critical intersections. John's unit developed several techniques to reduce the German positions. Since doors and windows were usually covered by defensive fire, the infantrymen used tanks or bazookas to blast entry points through walls. They found the pillboxes took fewer rounds to penetrate than the houses. When available, they used 8in. howitzers to fire directly into the houses.

Soldiers fire an 81mm (3.18in.) mortar into Cassino. The soldier on the left is the gunner, who sets the elevation and deflection on the mortar and keeps the bubbles on the sight level. The next man over is the assistant gunner, the next an ammunition bearer, and the man on the right is the mortar squad leader.

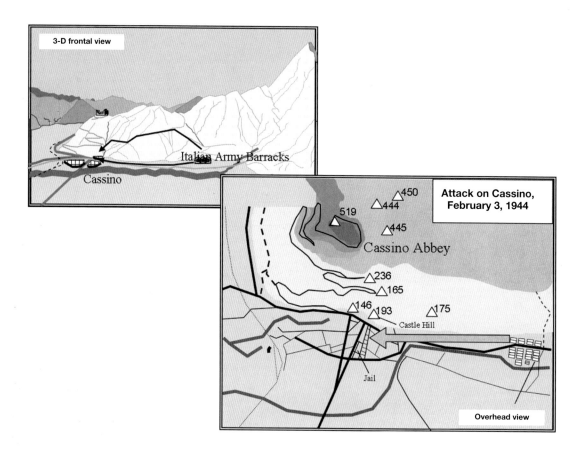

One afternoon in early February, about the tenth day of the battle, John's company, supported by a platoon of tanks, attacked into the smoke-blanketed northern sector of Cassino proper. A squad walked in front of the lead tank, the remaining two squads of the platoon behind. The company headquarters followed the second tank, one platoon the third tank, and John's platoon split into two groups; John's squad with the platoon headquarters following the fourth tank, while the remaining two squads brought up the rear. The company stood at fewer than 80 men, the preceding ten days of combat having sapped almost half the company's strength through both battle and non-battle casualties.

Once they reached the outlying buildings, most two stories high, John watched as the lead elements began clearing each house individually, five or six men working against each. First a tank fired into the house, creating smoke and dust, and suppressing those inside; after which three men rushed forward, tossed in a grenade, waited for the blast, and then rushed through the door. The covering group fired rifle grenades through the upper windows, driving any Germans on the second floor down the stairs to be killed or captured by the men inside.

Then the next group would leapfrog the first and repeat the process. Two men remained in each cleared house to ensure the

Germans did not reoccupy and the remainder continued down the street with the tanks.

As the band reached the first crossroad, a hidden antitank gun knocked out the third tank in the column while machine gun fire drove the remaining infantrymen into the doorways of houses alongside the street. The two leading tanks couldn't pull back past the burning tank, so they stayed and fired their cannon and machine guns at every doorway and window nearby. John, his company commander, and about five other infantrymen rushed across a small square and seized two big buildings. They spent the rest of the night holding the buildings, waiting for reinforcements. Unfortunately, during the night, the two tanks found a way around the disabled third, and pulled back. With no radio communications, the commander relied on runners to get through to battalion: but none ever returned. When the sun rose in the morning, and with no relief in sight, he pulled the company back out of the town, picking up the riflemen who had remained in each house as they retreated. John wished that support had come, as he hated seeing good men wasted in a successful attack that had to be abandoned.

During the third week of February there wasn't much forward movement. John's company had captured the jail sometime during the second week, and had held on, too exhausted and too battered by the German fire to do more than await relief. Some of the fights had degenerated to rock throwing after both sides had run out of grenades, playing toss between houses just 10 yards (9m) apart.

Unable to dig in the frozen ground, John and his comrades resorted to piling rubble around them for protection. The cold, wet weather caused more casualties than the Germans did, with trench foot and respiratory diseases affecting almost everyone. The only replacements to make it to the front lines were men from headquarters, motor pools, and kitchens. Soldiers remained pinned in these positions during the day because of the closeness of the enemy, and didn't move at night lest they be caught in the open by German shelling.

A general from outside the division visited once, and received an earful from officers and enlisted men alike on how the battle was

A position built of rocks in the Cassino area.

1. M4A2 Sherman tank blasts house at close range

2. First group of infantrymen move from cover, and toss grenades through ground-floor door and windows

ABOVE AND OPPOSITE
Monte Cassino house
clearing, 1944.

progressing. When General Lemnitzer returned to 15th Army Group, he said the men around Cassino were dispirited and almost mutinous, and he recommended they be pulled out of the line for rest.

In the three weeks between its first attack to take the Italian barracks area and the final effort in the northeastern corner of Cassino, the 133d Infantry had captured 138 prisoners but had 132 killed, 492 wounded, and 115 missing; most were lost from rifle companies. Non-battle casualties probably reached over 1,000, again primarily in the companies on the front lines. John's rifle company, like most of the others, averaged fewer than 50 men present when they pulled off the line.

The nature of combat

Combat against the Germans was not continuous: the infantryman's primal living conditions were. The constant rain and mud and never drying out; the unforgiving hard ground; the cold, almost indigestible, rations; everyone bearded and gray; the dirty, almost rotting feet, and unwashed bodies were combined with the unceasing movement forward, never catching up on the missed sleep of night movement or guard and patrolling. Men passed the point of being tired, and went on only because there was nothing else they could do. Days merged into other days, until dates and days didn't matter. Specific instances are remembered, but not within any context: "Do you remember …?" "Oh yes, that was the day Sam was killed." Emotions were hidden from all but the closest of friends, and when the friends were gone, feelings were locked away.

On the front line, there was a reduced military formality, with little difference between officers and men. The social divide was between veterans and replacements; in the rear areas it was different – it became again officer and enlisted men.

Only eight men of the original company that sailed from England in 1942, and about six, including John, who had arrived in Tunisia remained after Cassino. The brothers, uncles, and cousins who made up the old Guard company were gone: some killed, some captured, and others sent home, either invalided or rotated back. To some it seemed they had always been, and always would be, soldiers. They were all hard and wise in the animal ways of keeping themselves alive and knew they had survived initial combat only because they were lucky. They all wanted to go home, but they had been at it so long that they knew how to take care of themselves and how to lead others. Every company was built around these little cadres of veterans. By now, most of the men in John's rifle company, as in all the other rifle companies in his regiment, were replacements. Some had just arrived and some like John

3. Supporting troops launch rifle grenades into top floor, and watch for German soldiers

4. Enemy occupiers surrender: second group of infantry and the tank move on to the next house

had been there so long that they were just as wizened as the original eight, with little noticeable difference between them.

Anzio

After Cassino, John and his comrades spent a month resting, reorganizing, and receiving replacements near Alife. The 2d Battalion returned from its 18-month tour as "palace guards". Unlike the companies in John's battalion, almost three-quarters of each company had been together since Northern Ireland, with very few replacements. It was an interesting contrast with the other battalions within the regiment. Two battalions had suffered through nine months of combat: their companies contained, on average, eight to 15 men who had landed in Tunisia; the rest were replacements, and all the survivors were sick of war. The other, at full strength, had yet to see combat: while the men were probably not eager for combat, they did want to prove themselves to the men of the other battalions.

The new replacements that arrived from the US in 1944 had received different training to John. Their training was four weeks longer, included more field time, more time on the ranges firing their weapons, and almost unlimited ammunition. However, the centers weren't teaching the intricacies of the trade. Most replacements hadn't the slightest idea of what a rifle sounded like to a man shot at and missed, or the "crack and thump" method of target detection. A soldier would hear the crack of the round overhead, and then the thump of the firearm's discharge. The two pointed an invisible arrow toward the shooter's position. By multiplying the number of seconds between the crack and the thump by 360ft (109.7m) (the distance sound travels in one second at 50 degrees), a soldier could determine the approximate range to the firer. The lower the temperature, the nearer the target; the higher the temperature, the farther away. Moreover, it seemed dumb for the replacements to learn the sounds of the different German weapons by being shot at. The new replacements were concerned with the coming battle that would break the Allies out of Anzio and they listened very closely not only to their training but also to the old-timers' war stories. The newly arrived regiment's as yet unbloodied 2d Battalion listened just as closely.

To augment their near-range firepower, the veterans advised the replacement soldiers preparing to clear a town to trade their rifles for tankers' submachine guns, then trade back after the action. They also advised welding two 30-round M3 "grease gun" submachine gun magazines together, one up and one down, so that all they had to do to keep firing was to eject the empty magazine, reverse it, insert it, and fire again. The only problem was that the magazine pointed down tended to foul with dirt. Those listening also noticed that many of the veterans had paid Italian shoemakers to sew a leather extension band that fastened with a buckle attachment around the tops of their combat boots. These boots were very similar to those worn by British "Tommies", and similar to the M1943 combat boot just arriving in theater.

John's regiment arrived at Anzio beachhead in late March, in the midst of a giant cloud of thick, oily, pale gray smoke, continually dispersed by hundreds of smoke generators. In mid-April they moved forward to defensive positions along the Mussolini Canal and the Cisterna River.

While in the defense, every company received heavy augmentation in machine guns, 74 light and

The combat infantryman in Italy.

Overseas shipment of infantry replacements to the Mediterranean Theater of Operations

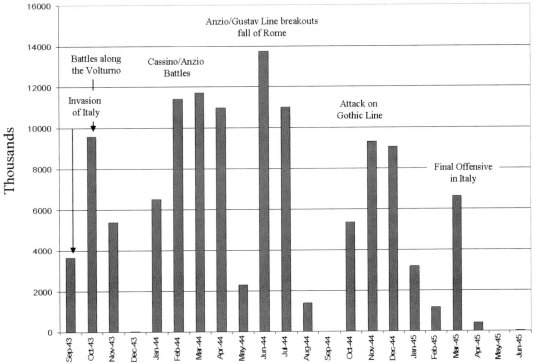

53 heavy guns being added to the regiment's normal authorization of 18 light and 24 heavies. It appeared that almost every position had some type of automatic weapon.

John touched a heavy machine gun for the first time since leaving the States and spent the next few days remembering the intricacies of the weapon before training soldiers in his platoon, and later company, in its use. His commander, impressed with this unknown machine gunner, fulfilled the departed first sergeant's promise of a year ago in Tunisia, and assigned John to the company's light machine gun section. John turned in his M1 rifle for an M1911 pistol and an M1919A4 air-cooled machine gun. He found the tripods different between the heavy and light machine guns, but the technique and theory were the same.

They dug two-man positions under the near side of the road passing through their sector; the heavy layers of asphalt provided excellent overhead cover from artillery and mortar fire. Those unfortunates who lacked such luxurious accommodation covered their abodes with ammunition boxes filled with sand, perforated steel planking, fence rails, and anything else that provided some support for the foot or so of dirt they piled on top. Usually there wasn't much artillery fire to speak of so John and his crew led a very quiet, inactive life. They even had hot rations or 10-and-1s (packaged rations suitable for ten men) instead of K and D rations.

60mm (2.36in.) mortar squad from the 133d Infantry in action. There are five soldiers in each mortar squad, as follows. The Squad Leader (1), a corporal, selects the firing position, and observes and adjusts fire. He has a pair of binoculars around his neck, and is shown communicating on a walkie-talkie. The gunner (2) carries the mortar, aims and sets its elevation, and ensures the sight levels are correct. The assistant gunner (3) feeds the ammunition. Both the gunner and assistant gunner are armed with the M1911 .45 cal. pistol. The two ammunition bearers (4 and 5) carry the mortar ammunition, normally six rounds each in containers. They are armed with M1 carbine rifles.

The 60mm (2.36in.) mortar is 726mm (28.6 in.) long, and weighs 42lbs (19.05kg) fully assembled. Two small diagrams show the maximum and minimum angles of elevation (6) and traverse (7) of the mortar. It is aimed using the M4 sight (8). This small instrument, weighing 1.16lbs (0.52 kg) uses a collimator instead of a telescope. The sight is mounted on the M2 mortar bipod (9), shown here without the mortar attached. Also shown is one shell (10): the range of each is approximately between 100 yards and 1,985 yds (91.44 and 1,815m).

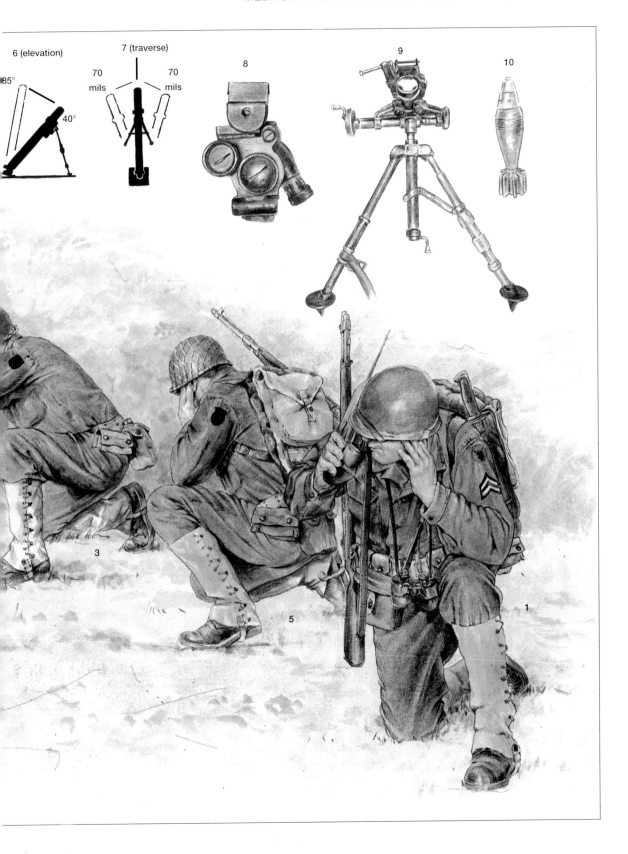

6 (elevation)

85° 40°

7 (traverse)

70 mils 70 mils

8

9

10

3

5

1

One man per position stayed awake while the other slept at night. Both Germans and Americans infiltrated patrols into each other's rear areas to capture prisoners and gain information. One night while on guard, John saw a shadow walking toward the platoon's position. He waited until it got within challenging distance and softly called out, "Red", expecting "Rover" in reply. Nothing. He called out "Red" again, waited a few seconds and then fired his borrowed M1. A man fell. Alerted, several men from the different foxholes moved to check the body, and then looked up at John. He had killed a new replacement who had become disoriented in the dark, and frozen when asked the password. Although his comrades consoled him, John felt terrible, but there was nothing else he could have done: he knew that it might have been a German.

The replacement was one of a group attached to the company for "battle inoculation". Normally during the Italian campaign, replacements arrived at units when they were out of the line. Just before the Anzio breakout, the 133d received 250 replacements to train in anticipation of predicted losses. Each battalion received about 80 men each, and John's company about 25. All would return to the newly formed regimental replacement company. This means of replacement continued in the 34th Division until the end of the war. Since this company was not TOE, its cadre was drawn from the regiment's different companies, drawing down company strengths, but providing a safe haven for battle-weary veterans nearing exhaustion.

An elderly Italian watches as American infantrymen move forward. The infantrymen no longer carry the M1928 haversacks: in their place are rolls more reminiscent of the American Civil War. This image also shows the men wearing the new M1943 combat boot.

A rifleman armed with an M1 rifle and scope watches over infantrymen as they move toward a house in a valley.

Machine gunner

At 0630hrs on May 23, 1944, the Anzio Offensive began. The US/Canadian 1st Special Service Force passed through the positions held by John's regiment. Later that day his battalion moved forward, with his company capturing Highway 7, and on May 26, they attacked for three days toward Lanuvio.

On the move forward John located, by sound and observation, a German machine gun that had a rifle platoon pinned down. His team watched the position until the Germans shifted to fire in a different direction. They quickly moved their gun to a good firing position, set it up, and John, using burst on target, walked the rounds over the gun crew and silenced the gun. Mission accomplished, they pulled back under cover. Later the same day, a German counterattack struck John's company while it was crossing another field. Instead of immediately engaging the Germans, John waited until most were in the field, and then began firing at those behind the leading echelons as if he were hunting turkeys. The fire demoralized the lead elements: cut off from support, he watched them first stop, then go to ground.

His machine gun crew's luck did not last. A German patrol surprised John and his crew as they supported his company's advance across a wheat field. His assistant gunner died almost immediately, and his ammunition bearers retreated over the hill.

Unable to bring his machine gun to bear, John lay flat on his stomach just under a hail of bullets. Every time he moved, a bit of him popped above his cover and provoked more firing. Knowing a grenade would soon be coming his way, he broke for the rear, but he was knocked to the ground by a blow to his chest. Every breath

Infantrymen fighting from a destroyed building. The soldier on the left is firing a BAR.

he took sucked air into the wound, threatening to collapse a lung, and causing him intense pain. John formed a seal by putting his hand over the bloody hole, and almost instantly felt his chest recompress; and although breathing was still painful, it was easier. He rolled over on his stomach to keep his hand pressed against the wound if he passed out, and hoped that help would soon come.

Wounded, recovery, and return

John fainted as soon as he saw helmets painted front and back with a red cross. He awoke in the division clearing station. The clearing station functioned as a small hospital. Above Anzio, the roads were relatively good and the clearing stations were close behind the regiments they supported. An ambulance holding four litter patients brought John in from the 133d's collecting company. The dirt, shock, and exhaustion on every casualty's face made them all look the same. As medics removed the men from the vehicle, they sorted them by severity of injury. The seriously wounded who needed lifesaving care were treated immediately, while those in less critical condition waited, and those who did not need immediate assistance were shipped without further care to a hospital farther back. Those who were beyond help were set aside and made comfortable until they died.

With his sucking chest wound, John was treated as one of the seriously wounded – one who was expected to live with treatment. Had he been less severely wounded, his injuries would have been dressed and rebandaged at the clearing station, and he would have been moved to an evacuation hospital for surgery.

A hospital platoon set up next to the clearing station removed the 9mm machine pistol bullet from John's chest. While waiting to be operated on, John lay in a central holding area, in a corner of which lay men with thin white gauze over their faces – dying men. One could only tell they were alive by the flutter of their breath on the gauze. The chaplain passed among them, performing last rites, leading those who were semiconscious through prayers.

John had been given one ampoule of morphine and was sleeping when time came for his surgery. His litter was his operating table: two medics lifted it up and laid it across two large trunks. After the operation was over, more medics took John to a postoperative tent. When he had recovered sufficiently to move, he was shipped to a field hospital at Anzio proper to regain his strength. Within a week, he loaded onto an LST for shipment to a convalescent hospital near Naples.

The convalescent hospital was a place where men who no longer needed constant medical or surgical care, but had not yet recovered, could rest and recuperate. Those whose expected recovery was longer than the theater's evacuation policy transferred to a hospital in the US (between 1943 and 1945, evacuation policy to the US varied between 30 and 120 days). The shorter the stay, the more bed spaces were freed for coming casualties, but the fewer men available in theater to go back to their units upon recovery.

An M17A1 Browning water-cooled machine gun concealed in the trees covering the open area across which the Germans might advance.

John didn't consider his wound a misfortune, but a blessing. He was happy that he was alive and not too seriously wounded; although his friends were still up on the front line, he was glad he wasn't there. He had volunteered to fight but he also felt he had paid his dues and it was now his turn to sleep on clean white sheets, look at pretty nurses, eat good food, and be able to wash regularly. He also hoped that his wound might get him home, or at least out of combat. In September, John was discharged from the convalescent hospital and reassigned to a conditioning company near Rome that prepared men mentally and physically to re-enter combat.

Many of the men returning for combat duty were battle fatigue (neuropsychiatric) cases. In Italy during 1943 and 1944, these cases ranged between 1,200 and 1,500 per year per 1,000-man strength in many rifle battalions. As the war progressed, more veteran officers and NCOs with extended time on the front lines fell victim to neuroses. One psychiatrist estimated that infantrymen had an aggregate of 200–240 days on the line before cracking up – and the number of men on duty after this period was small and of negligible value. Many men, once diagnosed with battle fatigue, spent the rest of their time in the war shuffling between unit and hospital.

The men lived in prefabricated huts and went through a month of intensive training and marching, supplemented by organized athletics. The commandant frequently held parades and awards ceremonies to develop pride and raise the men's morale. During one of these ceremonies, John received the Bronze Star for his performance outside Lanuvio.

Medics load a wounded soldier onto a jeep that is fixed with welded brackets to accept stretchers. The two soldiers to the right both have entrenching tools attached to their web gear. The medics are clearly identifiable by the large Red Cross symbols on their helmets.

John remained in the conditioning unit about four weeks. He trained for the first three weeks, and spent the additional week in the depot receiving company. Here, a board of officers, including the company surgeon, interviewed him to decide whether he should be returned to duty, retained for additional training, recommended for limited service and sent to the replacement

With the ground too hard to dig, infantrymen resorted to blowing holes in the ice and rock with satchel charges. Additional spade - work turned the holes into fighting positions for front-line infantry.

Life on the reverse slope. Here things were easier, with positions dug into the earth and buttressed by sandbags. These warrens soon turned into reasonably warm abodes after the occupants spread cardboard and other materials on the ground, and the soldiers huddled close on top of four blankets, with four more on top of them.

depot, or returned to hospital. John hoped for limited service but the board assigned him temporary light duty and reassigned him to the 133d Infantry. He also received a welcome ten-day furlough in Rome, his first extended period of leave since he left the US.

John returned to the 133d Infantry while his battalion was in the mountains overlooking the Po Valley. Since John had not yet fully recovered, the personnel officer assigned him as a cadre man in the regiment's replacement company.

War's end

While John was away at hospital, his regiment participated in some of the most severe fighting of the Italian campaign, through the Alban Hills and into Rome. They undertook a rapid pursuit of the Germans through Civitavecchia, Tarquinia, San Vincinza, and Cecina, and then into the mountains again to grind against the Gothic Line defenses, finally halting on Mount Belmonte about ten miles (16km) from the Po Valley.

In December John returned to his battalion, at the time based in Loiana. Between December 1944 and March 1945, he rotated with his battalion between rest camps, training and manning the line. Battle casualties were low: only 30 killed, 28 missing, and 109

A winter patrol: soldiers dressed in cold weather parkas and camouflaged white helmets walk along a well-worn route.

OPPOSITE Soldiers advance through Tuscany, Italy. Few wear the haversack and most have their sleeping gear rolled into tubes and slung across their shoulders.

wounded for the four months; this was fewer than a quarter of the casualties suffered in the three weeks at Cassino or in the days following the breakout at Anzio. In February, John celebrated 22 months in the regiment and three years in service.

By late 1944, the replacements from training centers in the US were better than those received previously, or even those trained in theater from anti-aircraft and other deactivated units.

By February 1945, few Guardsmen and initial draftees who had arrived overseas with the 133d Infantry remained in the rifle companies, and they had voluntarily decided to stay. Most of those who remained from its service in Northern Ireland were cooks, clerks, drivers, and some men in the Cannon Company. The last instance of a Guardsman wounded in a line company occurred in October 1944. The rotation policy and casualties had made John one of the oldest men serving in a rifle company, and his time to rotate was approaching.

Some due to rotate were offered promotions if they stayed with the regiment. Lieutenants were promoted to captain, and some enlisted men were battlefield appointed to lieutenant. Officers and enlisted saw these men as more competent than replacement officers from the US because of their experience. Others were

Soldiers, supported by an M10 tank destroyer, prepare to cross a berm. The nearest soldier carries the new M1943 entrenching tool attached to his M1945 field pack.

offered NCO rank. John decided to stay when offered the platoon sergeant's position in the weapons platoon.

His commander promoted him to staff sergeant because all the technical sergeant positions were filled by soldiers on furlough, in hospital, and as cadre in the replacement company. In fact, there was only one technical sergeant on the front lines. This was not abnormal, however; every company was like a breathing organism, with men flowing in and out, constantly back and forth between the front and rear.

One of the different things about belonging to a long-service combat outfit was that not many men were court-martialed or listed on morning reports as AWOL. Many veterans believed that since they spent so much time on the line with little complaint, their unit should disregard such minor infractions. What occurred in the rear areas was different from what happened on the line.

John knew and understood the silent agreement. His principal duty besides ammunition resupply was sending a daily status report to the first sergeant detailing how many men he had available for duty and the status of those who weren't. He covered for those "old timers" missing in the rear as well as some of the newcomers who had acquitted themselves well on the firing line.

Already familiar with machine guns, John spent some time with the mortar men learning their craft. John learned how to adjust

A weary member of a heavy machine gun platoon stays awake while men around him sleep. The four machine guns rest against the column, one with a bouquet of flowers in the muzzle.

the 60mm (2.36in.) mortar fire using the direct alignment method. By staying within 100 yards (91m) of the mortars, he could adjust the impact of the rounds using the same mil formula he learned as a machine gunner. Once he sighted a target, he gave the direction in mils and range to the guns. He then adjusted each round's impact using the bracketing method (one round over, one under, and continually splitting the bracket until range was correct) and adjusted the deviation by using the mil reticle in his binoculars until the target was within the bursting radius of the round. Although he enjoyed adjusting the mortars, he was not able to practice as much as he wanted, especially with the shortage of mortar ammunition in the MTO at the time

He found one of the benefits of being responsible for the platoon's resupply was that he had a jeep, and didn't have to walk everywhere, except of course when he did his daily climb up the mountain to his sections' positions. Patrolling was also in the past.

Not every day on the line involved fighting. Soldiers faced with monotony perfected cooking recipes using C and K rations, read and reread letters from home, newspapers, and magazines, and evaluated equipment as only an infantryman could. Life on the line was bad, but not as terrible as the year before had been.

Hot coffee and food, even if only K rations, were lifesavers in the cold. Those on the front lines facing the enemy used heating candles or the much-valued German Esbit stove that burned trioxane fuel.

On the reverse slopes, squads used one-burner Coleman stoves that were about the size of a quart thermos and burned anything from kerosene to gasoline. They were prized possessions and John's friends said they would rather attack without a helmet than leave their stove for the next guy. Soldiers had woolen sweaters, M1943 field jackets, woolen underwear, trigger finger mittens and cushioned woolen socks for the winter of 1944. Those on the front lines also received mountain sleeping bags, shoepacs, cold weather parkas, pile caps, and insulated sleeping pads. As a result of this additional clothing given to the soldier on the line, and the increased command emphasis on combating cold weather injuries, trench foot cases reduced by 70 percent.

John and his comrades were happy to wear woolen trousers and shirts. Many thought the herringbone twill uniforms too much the color of the German field uniform. The GI woolen sweater and heavy woolen socks were favorites. John and every other infantryman had two pair of socks, one to wear and one to keep dry inside their shirts, rotating when those worn got wet. The new M1943 field jacket was nice but everyone preferred the zippered combat jacket they wore the year before.

The men on the front lines disliked the sleeping bags because they felt trapped by the zipper and since they couldn't take their boots off, the inside of their bags were soon a muddy mess. After infantrymen throughout Italy complained, the sleeping bags were retrieved and reissued to rear echelon soldiers and the infantrymen received four blankets each. Two men sleeping in a

German prisoners stream to the rear as the war's end nears.

pup tent shared eight blankets. The shoepacs – winter boots with rubber lowers and leather waterproof uppers – were good when the soldiers weren't moving much (like John's mortar men), but they weren't good for sustained walking. The boots lacked arch support, so walking for any distance ruined the feet.

The final offensive in Italy began on April 14, and on the 15th II Corps joined the Fifth Army offensive after a massive bombing and artillery barrage. All of the artillery rounds that had not been fired during the winter months smothered the German defenses and rear areas.

The fighting was not heavy and casualties were light with six killed and 26 wounded for the month in John's company, about 20 percent of the company's authorized strength, but nothing in comparison to some of its past battles. His regiment suffered the loss of only about five percent of its strength. Once Bologna fell on the 21st, it seemed the German defense dissolved, and the GIs could not advance fast enough on foot. Men loaded onto regimental vehicles, vehicles from other units, and captured German vehicles as they sped from Modena to Reggio to Parma. Motorized patrols pushed to the Po River and Mantova, the gateway to the Brenner Pass and Austria. The 133d Infantry then turned westward to liberate Brescia, Bergamo, Milan, and Gallarate. On May 2, John and his company were at Avigniana, just west of Turin, when they heard the war in Italy was over.

Adjusted Service Rating		
Group	**Remarks**	**John's points**
1. Service credit	1 point per month in the service since September 16, 1940	40 x 1 = 40
2. Overseas credit	1 point per month overseas since September 16, 1940	31 x 1 = 31
3. a) Combat credits	5 points for every Bronze Service Star (battle participation stars)	5 x 6 = 30
b) Decorations	5 points for the first and each additional award of the following for service performed since September 16, 1940 (Distinguished Service Cross, Distinguished Service Medal, Legion of Merit, Silver Star, Distinguished Flying Cross, Soldier's Medal, Bronze Star, Air Medal)	1 x 5 = 5
c) Number of wounds	5 points per wound as recognized by award of Purple Heart	1 x 5 = 5
4. Parenthood credit	12 points per child under 18 years up to a limit of three children	0
TOTAL		**111**

Based on a number of factors including time in service, time overseas, combat service, and parenthood. (War Department Press Release May 10, 1945).

On May 9, John and his comrades listened over the radio to President Truman announce the end of the war against Germany:

"The Allied armies, through sacrifice and devotion and with God's help, have wrung from Germany a final and unconditional surrender. The western world has been freed of the evil forces which for five years and longer have imprisoned the bodies and broken the lives of millions upon millions of free-born men. They have violated their churches, destroyed their homes, corrupted their children, and murdered their loved ones. Our Armies of Liberation have restored freedom to these suffering peoples, whose spirit and will the oppressors could never enslave… For the triumph of spirit and of arms which we have won, and for its promise to peoples everywhere who join us in the love of freedom, it is fitting that we, as a nation, give thanks to Almighty God, who has strengthened us and given us victory."

The war in Europe was over. After fighting for almost three years in the Mediterranean, John thought of home.

Going home

In mid-May, John and his comrades read in the *Stars and Stripes* that men with more than 85 points were going home. Knowing he was leaving soon, John listened to some of his men just below the cut bemoan the fact that they weren't awarded a Purple Heart when they had been wounded without going to hospital. Purple Hearts and decorations weren't important while in combat but they meant a great deal with the war over and men wanting to go home. Many orders were cut that retroactively granted soldiers Purple Hearts for earlier wounds and other awards that had gone without action during combat.

Most of the soldiers who traveled overseas in January 1942 were long gone, as were most who had arrived in Tunisia. Every soldier who had traveled overseas in January 1942 had more than 80 points of service and overseas credit alone. Moreover, when campaigns, medals, wounds, and children were added, some had as many as 120 points. The high casualties in 1943 and 1944 and the rotation policy meant that most of the men in his company were recent arrivals, with the great majority arriving in the months after Cassino. Most had four campaigns, 13 months of overseas credit, and 18 months of service, giving them 51 points plus the points for wounds, decorations, and parenthood.

John left in May with other high-pointers from all the divisions. On the left breast of his Eisenhower jacket he proudly wore his Combat Infantryman's Badge, Bronze Star, Purple Heart, and the European, African, Middle Eastern Campaign Medal with six Bronze Service Stars, one for each campaign he participated in. On his left sleeve were the 34th Infantry Division patch, staff

A Mediterranean war cemetery.

sergeant stripes, five overseas service bars, each denoting six months, and one service stripe for three years of service.

New replacements and men from divisions returning to the US in the summer, themselves high-point men from other units, replaced those leaving. The War Department reduced the points required to go home to 80 points early in September, 70 on October 1, and 60 points on November 1.

The 133d Infantry Regiment deployed overseas in January 1942, entered combat in late March 1943, and suffered casualties higher than most other regiments deployed to the Mediterranean. The average infantry regiment in the MTO lost 41 officers and 668 enlisted men killed, 133 officers and 2,413 enlisted wounded. In approximately 27 months of combat, the 133d Infantry Regiment lost 47 officers and 998 enlisted men killed, 18 officers and 449 enlisted men missing or captured, and 188 officers and 4,060 enlisted men wounded, most of whom were lost at Cassino and after the Anzio breakout. This did not include the thousands of non-battle casualties due to trench foot, frostbite, combat fatigue or other illnesses.

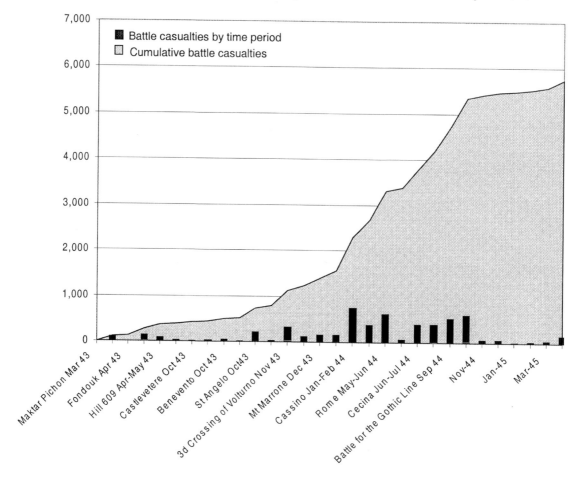

133d Infantry Regiment battle casualties, Mediterranean Theater of Operations

The 133d Infantry Regiment departed Italy aboard the USS *Monticello* on October 22, and arrived in Hampton Roads, Virginia, in November. Only a few of the men present when the regiment shipped overseas in January 1942 came home with the regiment's colors, and of those, most were in headquarters or support companies. The men in the rifle and weapons companies had been earlier evacuated for wounds or injuries, shipped home as high-pointers on furlough or discharge in May and June 1945, or buried in cemeteries in Tunisia and throughout Italy.

John sat at home on furlough awaiting his discharge. He was sure that his would be on white parchment, signifying an Honorable Discharge under excellent, very good, or good conduct. He was sure his few days of AWOL back in 1942 would not be enough to change the color of his discharge to blue, which represented a General Discharge for ineptness or misconduct. He knew of only one man to have received a yellow, or Dishonorable Discharge, which was after his general court-martial.

Once John was home, he sat in the quiet, not knowing what to do. He missed the camaraderie and adrenaline rush of active service. He surely would not be able to live as he had before the war; he had seen and done too much. So, rather than go back to farming, he re-enlisted: "I was with the 34th Division in Tunisia and Italy. First battalion of the One-Three-Three."

CHAPTER 6

EUROPEAN THEATER OF OPERATIONS, 1944–45

"Incentive is not ordinarily part of an infantryman's life … He fights without promise of either reward or relief. Behind every river there's another hill – and behind that hill, another river. After weeks or months in the line only a wound can offer him the comfort of safety, shelter and a bed. Those who are left to fight, fight on, evading death but knowing that with each day of evasion they have exhausted one more chance of survival. Sooner or later, unless victory comes, this chase must end on the litter or in the grave."
General Omar Bradley

US Army strength in the European Theater of Operations, 1942–45

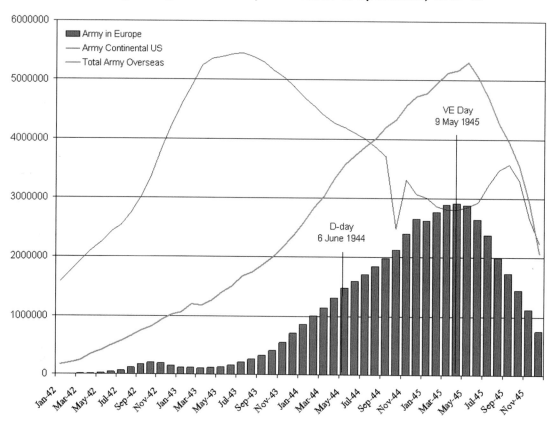

The European Theater of Operations – encompassing France, Belgium, The Netherlands, Luxembourg, Germany, Denmark, and Austria – is seen by many as the major theater of World War II with more infantry regiments serving there than in any other theater. Combat was sustained and brutal, with infantrymen seldom coming out of the line to rest and refit, and the endless stream of casualties and replacements reminded all of its intensity. It was here that armor played a large role in the sweeps across France and Germany. However, the infantry still had to take and hold the ground: at the Normandy beachhead, through the hedgerows, bloody Aachen, Metz, the Hürtgen Forest, the Ardennes, and thousands of other locations where men fought and died. The war in Europe ended just 11 months after combat was joined on June 6, 1944.

Unlike the first divisions in the Pacific or North Africa, the divisions landing on D-Day and in the following summer months had been training for combat for years. Most of their soldiers were draftees, many of whom had been in the Army more than three years.

The US Army entered ground combat in the European Theater on June 6, 1944, with 11 regiments; by the end of the war there were 129. Between that date and May 1945, US Army infantry units fought in six named campaigns in France, Belgium, Luxembourg, The Netherlands, and Germany.

Campaigns in the European Theater of Operations, 1942–45

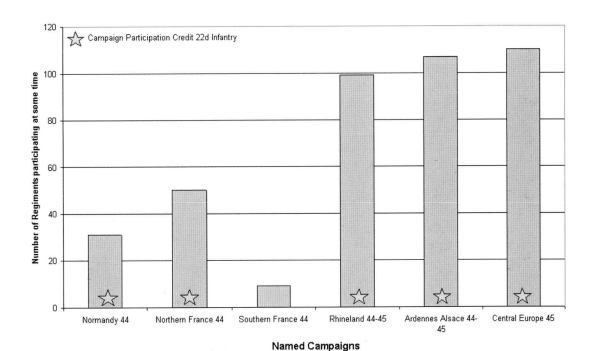

US Infantry regiments in combat in the European Theater of Operations 1942–45

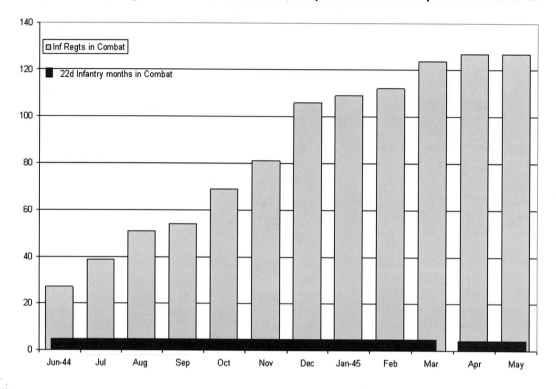

The greatest percentage of soldiers serving overseas served in the ETO, with the US Army increasing from 775 troops in January 1942 to 2,918,766 in April 1945. More infantry regiments served in the ETO than in any other theater, accumulating 1,408 months in theater and 1,026 months in combat during the period 6 June, 1944 through April 1945. Because of the large distances, and almost relentless combat along a continually moving front, there were very nearly too few divisions to man the line, resulting in units and their soldiers rarely receiving a respite from battle. Many times replacements were fed directly into units while they were in combat, because there was no other alternative.

Units remained in the line for extended periods and were subjected to daily losses, if not directly due to combat, then to the terrible weather. Unlike the Pacific and Mediterranean Theaters, replacement policies kept units at near full strength by removing soldiers in hospital from unit rolls, ensuring replacements arrived within two days of requisition and reassigning former recuperated soldiers back to their units.

For every soldier felled through combat in the ETO, one other was stricken with disease or non-battle injuries, and 69 men out of every 1,000 were hospitalized every day of the campaign. The average daily casualty rate for the Army was one battle casualty for every four and one half rendered ineffective through disease or non-battle injury.

1940 Regular Army maneuvers. Infantrymen in M1918 pattern helmets, puttees and M1903 Springfield rifles charge through dense smoke.

THE 22D INFANTRY REGIMENT

The 22d US Infantry is the regiment into which our composite soldier was drafted in February 1941. Joseph Stein was born in August 1918 in Brooklyn, New York. He was one of three children and had graduated high school in 1937. Since there were few jobs, Joseph's father insisted he go to university, and to make ends meet, Joseph worked as a night watchman. When Joseph was drafted, he became one of many from New York City, which during World War II supplied one of every nine men drafted; more draftees than any state except New York and Pennsylvania.

In 1939, the 22d US Infantry, a prewar component of the inactive 4th Division, consisted of two small battalions stationed at Fort McPherson, Georgia, and Fort McClellan, Alabama. In 1940, the 22d sent soldiers to the RA maneuvers in Louisiana, consolidated the regiment at Fort Benning, Georgia, conducted training, and performed garrison duties. When not on maneuvers, soldiers not on duty had all of Sunday, as well as Wednesday and Saturday afternoons free. Soldiers spent little time on tactical training outside the limited annual Regimental "Chief of Infantry's Combat Team" competition. It was only in October 1940 that the regiment's 1st Battalion was activated, and in February 1941 the regiment reached full strength with the arrival of thousands of draftees and reserve officers.

The regiment fought in the maneuvers of 1940 and 1941, trained as a motorized regiment at Forts Benning and Gordon, demotorized at Fort Dix, New Jersey, and went through amphibious training at Camp Gordon Johnston, Florida. The 22d sailed on the British ship *Capetown Castle*, arrived in Britain on January 18, 1944, and continued training there until June 6, 1944, when, along with the other regiments of the 4th, they assaulted Utah Beach, Normandy, France. From that period until March 14, 1945, the 22d was in almost continuous combat, fighting from the

Daily average non-effective rate (per 1,000 strength), European Theater				
	Disease	Non-battle injury	Battle injury or wound	Total Daily admissions per 1,000
Continental US	27.06	4.24	.01	31.31
Europe	26.52	9.77	32.44	68.73
Iceland and Alaska	19.91	5.65	.93	26.49

beaches to Cherbourg, the hedgerows, the St Lô breakout, Avranches, Paris, the Hürtgen Forest, the Ardennes Campaign, and Prüm. Returning to combat for the final month of the war, the 22d fought its final battles along the River Isar, south of Munich. The 22d departed Europe on July 3, 1944, for a short period of rest in the US and eventual shipment to the Pacific as part of the invasion scheduled for Japan. The Pacific War ended with the 22d still at Camp Butner, North Carolina, where it was inactivated on March 1, 1946, only to be reactivated on July 15, 1947.

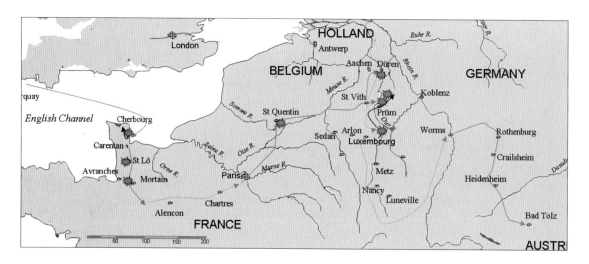

The route of the 22d Infantry in the ETO.

JOSEPH'S STORY

Induction, prewar, and post-Pearl Harbor training

Joseph listened throughout August and September 1940 as Congress debated the nation's first peacetime conscription law that called for able-bodied men to serve 12 months of active duty, followed by ten years in the reserves. Joseph was over 21 and, like many others his age, knew that being single, in good health, literate, and working only part-time, qualified him as a prime candidate for what might come. On October 16, with the law's passage, Joseph along with 16,000,000 other men aged 21–35 – including foreign nationals who desired to be citizens – formed long lines outside schools, government buildings and polling places to register for the draft. There was little discord, for although the US was not at war, most people, including those being drafted, supported the peacetime draft.

1941 maneuvers: a rifle squad defends a barn. They now wear M1938 leggings and carry the M1928 haversack.

After registration, each man received his draft number from his local draft board; each man's number was unique within his registration area. On October 29, Joseph listened as the radio broadcast the first National Lottery. Of the 9,000 numbers announced, the number 158 was the first number called; Joseph's number, 6685, was the fifth.

Within a few weeks, Joseph received an eight-page questionnaire; when it was completed it assisted the draft board in properly classifying him. Although he had been at City College in 1939 and 1940, Joseph did not re-register for 1941 because of his uncertainty of being drafted. There were no blanket deferments for school; however, college students registered for 1940–41 were deferred so they might finish the school year. Joseph passed all the tests and the initial physical screening given by his draft board, and received his draft card with the classification of I-A, which seemed quite an honor considering how many failed to meet prewar standards.

Class I meant the selectee was available for training and service after the physical examination; Class II, available for training and service but temporarily deferred; Class III, persons with dependents; Class IV, persons who were exempted by statute, non-declared aliens, conscientious objectors, were physically, mentally, or morally unfit for service, or had completed military service. The classes further subdivided with Class I-A for those found physically fit to Class IV-F for those found physically, mentally, or morally unfit for service.

When Joseph learned he was leaving for service in February 1941, his family and friends acted almost as if he were going back to college. This was still peacetime, and although his parents were a bit concerned, they felt it would be good for him to get the fresh air, and see the country outside New York.

On the day Joseph reported for induction, he dressed in suit and tie, packed his underclothes and shaving essentials and took the subway to the recruiting station. He noticed that most of the men standing in line waiting for the doors to open were his age or older. Later he found that all were single; the vast majority was literate, some were from the performing arts or in other professions not seen as contributing to the economy (see page 99 for a detailed description of the screening process). Some of the men had just arrived in the US from Europe. Joseph took yet another physical, this time by Army physicians, and a mental classification test. Of the 84 men standing in line, 70 were selected. Then they stood in a line in alphabetical order to receive their serial numbers: brothers were separated so their numbers were not sequential. As draftees, their numbers began with 3204 – the first 3 represented inductees of the AUS (when 1,000,000 men were drafted from the area it became a 4), then a 2 representing the 2d Corps Area composed of New York, New Jersey, and Delaware, and the 04 representing the fact that they were among the first 45,000 soldiers drafted from the area (see page 47 for National Guardsmen and page 99 for RA enlistees).

Joseph, and the others then raised their right hands to repeat the Oath of Enlistment:

> *"I_____ do solemnly swear (or affirm) that I will bear true faith and allegiance to the United States of America; that I will serve them honestly and faithfully against all their enemies whomsoever; and that I will obey the President of the United States and the orders of the officers appointed over me according to the rules and Articles of War."*

From the induction station, and others like it in New York City, Joseph and the other inductees traveled to Camp Upton on Long Island, where they were issued old musty World War I blouses, baggy pants, and wraparound puttees, and put into leaky pre-World War I eight-man Sibley tents, to await assignment to units. In February the ground was cold, but not cold enough to freeze the mud surrounding the tents. The food was plentiful but poorly cooked, and the new recruits quickly grew impatient.

After about a week at Camp Upton, the new recruits undertook more physicals, this time from doctors from the 4th Division located down south. Joseph knew that he and the other new recruits could not have looked less martial with their long hair and dirty clothing. Yet, he was one of 5,000 who boarded a train for the trip to Fort Benning, Georgia.

As soon as the train arrived the new recruits were fed, classified, and assigned to different divisional organizations. Joseph found himself classified as an infantryman assigned to a company in the 2d Battalion, 22d Infantry. Once assigned the men received their clothing issue, which included blue denim work uniforms, khaki field uniforms, and olive drab dress uniforms, and were divided into training companies. With no replacement training camps yet organized, the task of molding these civilians into soldiers fell to the regulars in the regiment, with every company providing a small cadre to basically train the recruits before joining their companies.

Every soldier also received a small blue book titled *Soldier's Handbook* with a drawing of the 22d Coat of Arms on the cover, which explained many of the rudiments of being a soldier. Inside was a description of the Coat of Arms, the regimental motto, "Deeds Not Words", a short history of the regiment, and 32 chapters on subjects ranging from the Articles of War, drill, and map reading to personal hygiene and care of feet. NCOs cautioned the new soldiers to study the book well.

The training Joseph and his comrades received in the training unit followed that of the 1940 mobilization plan, except that unit training was accomplished within their assigned units (see pages 49 and 99 for detailed descriptions of individual training.) The sergeants were very demanding and after demonstrating each step insisted that every task be done correctly and by the manual – even if there might be a quicker or better method to do something. It appeared to Joseph that the sergeants knew every regulation by heart, although he noted that they never failed to refer to the regulations when there was a question.

Sergeants knew their names by the first day; most were hard taskmasters but many took the time to explain a procedure. Everyone quickly learned the quirks of the different NCOs. Joseph found to his chagrin that getting on the bad side of his barracks' sergeant meant additional hours cleaning the latrine when he could have been at the enlisted men's club.

The recruits were issued brand new M1 rifles, and Joseph learned early on how to load the clip-fed weapon. The sergeant described and demonstrated the proper procedures, then watched

The "kitchen police"; these draftees wear the 1940 pattern blue-denim work uniforms, while their RA mentors wear khakis.

Soldiers in first pattern Herringbone twill (HBT) uniforms check their equipment. The equipment has been laid out exactly in accordance with page 134 of the 22d Infantry *Soldier's Handbook*.

as Joseph and his comrades practiced loading and unloading their rifles, with the occasional expletive when thumbs were smashed between bolt and receiver, the dreaded "M1 thumb" and mark of a rookie. Holding his rifle in his left hand, Joseph hooked his right forefinger over the operating rod handle and pulled it to the rear until it caught on the operating rod catch. Then with his right hand he inserted a clip of eight cartridges into the magazine, carefully forcing the clip down onto the clip latch with his right thumb. The engagement of the latch automatically released the operating rod and bolt to slam forward into the receiver. Joseph learned to swing his thumb to the right as soon as the bolt began to move forward, while at the same time pushing forward with the heel of his right hand on the operating rod handle to assist the bolt in stripping and chambering the first round in the clip.

To fire the M1 he had to squeeze the trigger for each shot; the empty clip automatically ejected out of the receiver with a "ping", upward to the right, while the bolt remained open, ready to receive another clip. Joseph was amazed that with a little practice he could load and fire 20 to 30 rounds a minute, and had observed one of his instructors fire five clips at a target at 100 yards (91m) hitting it with nearly every round.

It was nearly May when Joseph and the other inductees finally joined the companies that they would be with for the next eight months, with maneuvers on the horizon. He found that many of the older regulars in his company were from Alabama and Georgia, the states in which the 22d had been stationed since the 1920s. He also noted though that many of those who had enlisted during 1940 were from the Midwest, and that with the first shipment of draftees from New York, Pennsylvania, and New Jersey, this was a dynamic mixture to refight the Civil War.

Nearly all NCOs were old-time regulars; many of the corporals had ten or more years of service and the sergeants more. Joseph noticed some didn't have much schooling, but they displayed absolute mastery when field-stripping a weapon, demonstrating how to roll their pack, laying out equipment for an inspection, or any of the other tasks required of an infantryman. There were also distinct cultural differences between the regulars and the civilians in their midst. It seemed tradition and procedure counted more

Soldiers in HBTs practice the position of "Port Arms" with M1903 Springfield rifles. The soldier on the left wears the stripes of a Technician 5th Class.

than anything else did. Joseph and his fellow draftees listened with some amazement at the use of the third person in addressing the officers, although they quickly learned that it was not a sign of subservience but of tradition. There seemed different spheres within the Army; the officers of whom they saw very little, noncommissioned officers who lived away from the barracks or in the rooms at the end of the halls, and all the others who shared the large barracks rooms. Even with the camaraderie of the barracks, at times Joseph didn't think the regulars treated him and the other draftees like real soldiers.

Training

There were initially no training plans for motorized forces, and Joseph's leaders improvised as they went along. There was no idea of fighting mounted; the motorization, even with halftracks, was meant to move troops rapidly from one point to another on the battlefield.

Most of the motorized road marches along Fort Benning's rudimentary roads were in dust so thick that the drivers could not see the vehicles in front of them, and there was more than one accident. All Joseph and his comrades in the back did was eat dust and bump along from one point on the map to another, really having no idea where they were going. Many of the draftees with mechanical aptitude became mechanics and learned through intense training from experts how to maintain their vehicles. However nice it sounded never to have to walk, Joseph detested the motor pool and vowed never to drive.

There was a shortage of equipment even for Joseph's RA unit because most of what they initially had went overseas to support Britain. With mortars, antitank guns, and machine guns in short supply there was a lot of make-do: the soldiers trained and maneuvered with simulated equipment. His regiment was motorized during the Louisiana maneuvers only through borrowing vehicles from other divisions, and his squad rode in a 1932 Ford weapons carrier. Over time new equipment, such as the M2A1 halftrack and other vehicles, as well as machine guns, mortars, and radios, arrived bringing the unit to authorized equipment strength.

During the Carolina maneuvers, Joseph's division teamed with the 1st and 2d Armored Divisions in the Red IV Motorized Corps against the Blue First Army and fought what they called the Battle of Monroe.

In a civilian city in North Carolina, the streets were filled with halftracks, and white smoke from grenades and smoke pots, while soldiers fought hand-to-hand for street intersections; the only ammunition they carried was blanks. Umpires raised red flags during the night, halting the battle and leaving the town half red and half blue.

After the maneuvers, there was little inclination to hurry or correct their deficiencies, as there was still time in 1942 before they were discharged. There were few restrictions after hours, and with a pass in hand soldiers changed into civilian clothes to

M2 Halftrack personnel car used in armored and some motorized infantry formations.

go downtown. It wasn't until 1942 that haircut regulations changed to a more cropped military look and soldiers were required to wear uniforms at all times. In early 1941, everyone not on duty received Wednesday afternoons off. Asking one of the regulars why, Joseph was told that it came from 1933 when President Roosevelt had enacted the Austerity Plan, which cut the soldiers' salary by ten percent. The Wednesday afternoon, or ten percent of the week, was given off to make up for the pay cut. Once Congress restored pay to the 1932 levels, they began working the full week. The raise to $50 in September 1942 was quite a boon for privates; unfortunately, the day after they received their pay rise, Joseph and his comrades noticed a jump in prices in the businesses just outside the post gate.

On pass and while on post, Joseph and some of the others from up north were struck by the separate but equal policy regarding the races. Some restaurants served only whites, while others had rooms for "Colored's Only". The trains and buses were the same. Joseph was once on an Army bus that had all the rear seats filled with African American soldiers, however; the bus driver refused to pick up any more even though many of the seats up front were empty. It didn't seem right to Joseph that these soldiers, wearing the same uniform, were treated differently. Others in his company didn't see the problem.

Joseph, like many of the other draftees, made little effort to get promoted, preferring to remain a private for the months remaining in service. He had no decisions to make because sergeants made them for him, and had few obligations outside his own personal sphere. On August 18, 1941, draftees younger than 28 had their year-long tour extended an additional six months, while those older than 27 were released from active duty.

Along with many of the others, Joseph was planning his first furlough to New York for the Christmas Season of 1941. On December 7, 1941, all plans changed. On notification of the attack on Pearl Harbor, arms rooms opened to issue ammunition and the different companies scattered across Georgia to guard strategic installations and bridges. The US was at war and they were in a RA outfit, expected to travel overseas at any moment. Instead, at the end of December, Joseph and his comrades packed up their gear and organizational equipment and moved to Camp Gordon, South Carolina, which had been built especially for the 4th Motorized Division, and which would be home for the next 16 months.

After Pearl Harbor, everyone knew they were in for the duration, and those not yet drafted understood they soon would be. Those recently released were recalled, and on December 20, 1941, the draft was extended to those aged 20 to 45; and on November 13, 1942, altered to those aged 18 to 38.

Beginning almost immediately in 1942, drafts of trained men began departing the regiment as cadre for other regiments, which meant promotions for those leaving and for those who assumed their positions in the regiment. Most of the regular officers and many of the NCOs went to other units. By mid to late 1942 there was perhaps one regular officer in a company, and many of the squad leaders and some of the platoon sergeants were draftees or those who had enlisted through 1940–41. Although most had been in service just over a year, they had learned well from the old regular NCOs who had led and taught them by example. In late 1942, officers from OCS began arriving to the regiment; some had been in the regiment earlier as enlisted men.

For the two years after Pearl Harbor Joseph and his fellow "regulars" trained for combat, with proficiency and tactical tests from platoon through battalion level seemingly every month – with the requirement to pass each phase before progression to the next. Included at platoon level were proficiency tests based on the directives for tactical training in FM 7–10 Rifle Company that evaluated security on the march, the approach march, security during halts, tactical march, security in defense, attack as support, continuation of attack, hasty occupation of defensive positions, defense, defense as support, relief of front line platoons, daylight withdrawal, night attack, night patrol, and attack in woods; all logically sequenced into a scenario.

Long road marches broke up the different series of exercises. Soldiers went without sleep, and men became proficient in weapons manipulation and maneuver. With each stay in the field, Joseph and his comrades learned more about basic survival in the field, such as shaving with hot breakfast coffee when there was no water or how to pitch a tent so that one slept reasonably dry during a hard rain, as well as the tactics they were practicing.

On one two-day proficiency test, Joseph's company – a weary, mud-caked, unsmiling bunch – marched 35 miles (56km) mostly in rain, and spent the night in water to their ankles in a swamp.

US Army accessions and enlistment into the Army by age, 1940–42

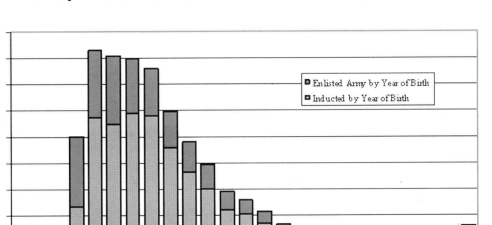

He vaguely remembered putting his haversack against a tree and trying to sleep while mosquitoes attacked like swarms of dive-bombers. At 0300 hrs, the sergeant woke those asleep and they moved out on a compass direction, wading a wide creek with mud coming to the knees, until they reached the company attack position. Artillery fire "crumped" in the distance.

Joseph's platoon objective was a hill 600 yards (548m) away. As the warming sun rose, they watched as artillery and the heavy and light machine guns fired indirectly, impacting on the hill. The platoon leader whistled and the squads moved out in tactical formation, each trailed by an umpire who at times would give information that demanded a decision or action from the group or individual leader.

As Joseph's squad crossed a large open area the umpire called out "for the last minute the squad has been subjected to heavy machine gun fire from the hill to the front right" and designated one man as a casualty. Joseph and his comrades went to ground dragging the wounded man under cover. The umpire announced "the machine gun's silent" when every man was under cover. The squad then slipped right and continued the move forward. As the squad maneuvered near the objective, the umpire announced, "a shell strikes 300 yards (274m) in front of you," a minute later, "a shell impacts 100 yards (91m) behind you," which suggested to the squad that they had been bracketed, and that the next round would land near them. The squad leader pumped his arm up and down to signify double time and pointed to the front right. Once the squad had run out of the impact area, Joseph and his comrades re-formed and continued onward.

Once in the last covered and concealed location near the objective, Joseph's platoon leader designated one squad to provide support while the other two maneuvered. Then the umpire announced there was an oily liquid on the grass and an unfamiliar odor. Now, instead of launching the attack, the men donned their gas masks and demonstrated how they would use their chemical paper to determine the type of chemical agent. The umpire announced the substance was not a chemical agent. The platoon unmasked and the attack began.

With the support squad firing at the targets on the hill, the two assault squads maneuvered onto the objective and consolidated, reorganized, and set into a hasty defense. Umpires counted the number of holes in the target and announced the percentage of hits by counting the hits against the number of rounds fired. Afterward the senior umpire briefed the platoon on its successes and failures. A failure meant that the platoon would perform another permutation of the attack, while success allowed the platoon to progress to other tasks. After a trip back to the barracks to clean self and equipment and to get a warm meal, it was back to the field.

The road marches were equally as hard. Although motorized, gas rationing hit Joseph and his fellow soldiers hard: instead of riding vehicles to the different ranges, they now marched and soldiers experienced countless tactical road marches each from six to 35 miles (9.6 to 56km), with most being between 12 and 20 miles (19 and 32km). Joseph remembered one that was especially grueling: the 25-miler with a full field pack weighing over 85lbs (38.5kg). The hot South Carolina sun, with the admonitions not to drink water caused hundreds to fall along the side of the road and was considered by many the worst road march ever. After a few such marches, it became a matter of pride that no one fell out and all canteens remained full. Many times, as an additional incentive, Joseph's company officers had kegs of beer waiting for the parched soldiers at the march completion.

On June 8, 1942, the 4th Division reviewed with all its vehicles for General Marshall and Lord Mountbatten. Joseph and many of the junior enlisted men took a perverse pleasure in being called the sloppiest of the 4th Division's three infantry regiments when on parade, but the best when out on maneuvers. Immediately thereafter, the men set out for the Carolina Maneuvers, for which everyone's haversacks, cartridge belts, and leggings were dyed green to blend with the terrain and all wore red armbands showing which side they were on.

Fully combat ready, and by now fully motorized, Joseph and his comrades participated in the Carolina Maneuvers in June and July

1942, only to be pulled out to pack their gear for overseas shipment. The alert was a false alarm, as was the order in December 1942, and to many of the soldiers it appeared that all they did was train and provide cadres to other units. The main reason Joseph and his comrades did not deploy overseas early in the war was that the 4th Division contained more than 3,000 vehicles which used almost as much shipping space as an armor division, although lacking the combat power.

The years passed rapidly, Joseph moved from post to post with the 22d, and he and the other draftees felt the ties to organization that long service makes. Many of Joseph's comrades married their hometown sweethearts or girls in the towns surrounding the camps. With the average age within the regiment at 28 in 1943, most thought they'd never go overseas as a regiment because they were too old, and that they would continue to provide cadres for other units.

In July 1943, after more than two years' service, Joseph was a corporal and assistant squad leader, but with every bit of knowledge of a squad leader, since they had all undergone the training together. The most enjoyable assignment for him and many others was Fort Dix, New Jersey, where they were near home; most of the training was on the small unit level, and there were ample passes to New York City and Philadelphia. Platoons went through Ranger training which included live demolitions training, more long road marches, rappelling, breaching wire obstacles, combat in cities, and training assault teams to eliminate fortifications.

On the lighter side, Campbell's Soup factory had large tomato fields in the areas, but no one to pick the fruit. With War Department approval, Joseph and his comrades received permission to assist Campbell's in harvesting the fruit to supplement their wages. Soldiers being soldiers, Joseph and his comrades soon engaged in unit-level tomato fights and began calling themselves "tomaterized".

It was at Fort Dix that the 4th Division lost its halftracks and its motorized designation. To Joseph and his comrades it meant more walking, but now the drivers and many of the mechanics were walking with them although still in technicians' grades.

From Fort Dix, they moved to Camp Gordon Johnston, Florida, where they practiced amphibious landings. Joseph and his comrades stayed in the water so much that they wanted to turn their boots in for fins. Once they were assigned a beach in heavy weather where they debarked 700 yards (640m) from shore and walked in through surf sometimes up to shoulder height. That exercise merited a commendation from the division commander, and comments from the soldiers of "please, never again". This training also signaled to many that they were being trained for something big. More officers from OCS and trained soldiers from the 83d Division joined as replacements for those who could not keep up with the intensified pace.

In November, although still with no official notice of movement overseas, the division shipped to Fort Jackson, South Carolina,

Soldiers attack into a mock German village during training in 1943.

where they began boxing equipment for overseas shipment and spending what they believed to be their last days with the families that had followed them from post to post. In December, they made the move to the overseas staging area at Camp Kilmer where they underwent a final overseas processing and medical examination. In this last session, some of the soldiers that Joseph had known since 1941 were determined unfit for overseas service and were replaced on the spot by soldiers waiting as replacements at Camp Kilmer.

In January 1944, when Joseph's regiment boarded HMS *Capetown Castle* to sail to England, he like many of the others was nearing the three-year mark within the same company. Although many of the original draftees had departed for new units, more than 70 soldiers in Joseph's company had been together since 1941. At no other time in the past had an army, regular or otherwise, trained so hard and so well over such an extended period before being committed to combat.

England

HMS *Capetown Castle* was a converted British luxury liner sailing under Royal Navy rules. In January 1944, it transported almost 5,000 soldiers of the 4th Division to Britain. Joseph had learned from others about the living conditions aboard ship. Officers lived quite well in prewar staterooms, while it seemed the enlisted existed where they might. Joseph's company and another were located on B-deck amidships: 361 men in a small compartment which also served as a mess. It was hard to find a place to sit and many men stayed in their hammocks strung from the ceilings over the tables. They ate their mediocre meals from mess kits twice a day, and there was a canteen which served Cokes and chocolate – until it ran out. The biggest problem for so many soldiers was the small latrine, especially with seasickness, and below decks reeked of men living too closely together. With the cramped conditions and wretched weather, about the only chance for fresh air was the daily abandon-ship drills, where Joseph and his comrades stood breathing in the cold clean air, watching the ocean heave and the convoy stretching as far as the eye could see.

Although Joseph and the other enlisted men had not been told where they were going, many quickly figured it out, noting the ship was heading east into the sunrise. Another sure indicator was the book on British customs the officers distributed to them.

On January 29, Joseph peered out at bomb-damaged Liverpool. The next day they boarded trains for the 12-hour ride to their new camps in southern England. Unlike the US where the regiment was together on one post, here the different battalions were scattered about at small camps. Joseph's battalion and regimental headquarters were at Denbury, the 1st Battalion at Newton Abbott, and the 3d Battalion and the separate companies at South Brent. The first road marches up and down through the rolling hills brought painful memories to unused muscles. The weather wasn't very cold, but the sky was a constant gray with rain and drizzle, keeping everything damp. Each hut received 4lbs (1.8kg) of coal per person per night to heat the little stove; the same ration the British lived under, and just enough to take the bite out of the air.

After being issued mattress covers filled with hay, the soldiers filed into closely grouped one-story buildings (they found out later it was an emergency hospital) which were to be their homes while in England. Chow was three times a day from their mess kits, but thankfully was essentially the same rations they had eaten in the US rather than the British Army ration. They carried their rifles in the camp at all times, including the latrine, which had the sign "Ablutions and Water Closets" above the door. They also learned of wartime rationing: they received coupons for seven packs of cigarettes, 21 cigars or three packs of pipe tobacco per week.

If they were not on duty, Joseph and his comrades were allowed to go on pass to the surrounding villages. To leave camp, they had to give the day's password, show their pass and dog tags and carry no weapons. When Joseph asked a local the size of Denbury, he received the reply "34 pubs". In the town they could all see the effects of rationing on the British. There was little to eat in the restaurants and the dances put on at the camp were well attended by the women in the area because there were always refreshments of meat sandwiches and beer. Joseph asked one how much meat she got and was told only a shilling's worth per week. Unfortunately, the soldiers weren't always allowed into town, especially after fights between "colored" and white troops erupted, so the commanders designated different nights for each race to go into town.

It seemed as if those in England didn't know that Joseph and his comrades had been training for three years in the States, and had just finished amphibious training. Nevertheless, they continued with more. There were more squad problems, more weapons training, more camouflage classes, use of artillery and mortars, assault tactics against bunkers using pole charges, the bazooka and the new beehive-shaped charges. More often on maneuvers, they

Training in the sand at Braunton, England. A soldier hunkers low as a dynamite charge explodes only yards away.

were hit with surprise situations that required them to improvise: what to do if the leader went down and then the next, or how to take out a masked machine gun located behind barbed wire and mines. Even though combat was nearing, however, Joseph and his comrades only participated part way, with the aside that "we know how to do this, and will do it correctly when the fighting begins."

In late April, Joseph and his comrades participated in a pre-invasion invasion at Slapton Sands on the coast of Devon, southwest of Dartmouth, although they still had no idea of the location they were heading for in France. His platoon was caught bunched-up and rout stepping down a road by one of the umpires who proceeded to write their unit down on his pad and reprimand them for not taking the maneuvers seriously.

Reorganization continued apace, and those leaders, officers and NCOs, who did not measure up were either transferred out, in the officers' case, or demoted in the case of the NCOs. Now with three years in service, Joseph found himself sergeant and assistant squad leader. New replacements from the US continued to arrive to take the place of those injured during training and his company received an additional 50 men who were to serve as the unit's initial replacements in France. In mid-May the company divided into what would land on D-Day and a residual force, with about 20 percent of the company strength designated to stay behind in England, and those who either were to arrive after D-Day or to serve as a cadre if the company were destroyed.

Some of the rifle companies reorganized for the initial assault and reduction of the fortifications into three assault platoons of 60 men each with two assault sections containing two rifle teams, a BAR team, bazooka team, demolitions team, flamethrower team and mortar squad. Two platoons organized with BARs and 60mm (2.36in.) mortars in the assault sections and the other with heavy machine guns and 81mm (3.16in.) mortars. After breaching the fortified area they were to reorganize into three rifle and one weapons platoon. Joseph's company was one of those that did not reorganize.

Everyone knew the big day was near when they had to lock their personal effects in footlockers and barracks bags and send them to the personal effects quartermaster in Liverpool. All identification outside dog-tags and ID cards was locked away. On May 18, they foot marched to the heavily guarded marshaling area near the coast – called "sausages" because of its appearance on a map. There Joseph and his comrades waterproofed their gas masks and other equipment, and toward the end of the month they began to enter guarded tents that had sandtables, which were an exact representation of the beach they were to assault. Now they became familiar with the terrain so that they could recognize physical features either by silhouette or by sight. No one other than the officers at battalion and the leading company commanders knew the exact location of the beach, but even they did not know the day or hour of the assault.

While in the marshaling area, Joseph and his comrades received their ammunition, with riflemen receiving 160 rounds to fill their cartridge belts plus an additional bandoleer of ammunition and other equipment required for the landing, as well as the incidentals for themselves: one K and one D ration for use after landing, one safety razor, seven packs of cigarettes, one half-ounce pipe tobacco, 200 safety matches, seven sticks chewing gum, one

Soldiers debark an LCVP during pre-invasion training at Slapton Sands, England.

two-ounce can of insecticide, four one-and-a-half-ounce heating tablets, for water purification one bottle of halazone tablets, and for the voyage across the Channel, ten motion sickness prevention pills – and if those didn't work, two vomit bags. Their lieutenant was the company censor who had the duty of reading all the soldiers' outbound mail for anything of military value, and who used a razor blade to cut out anything he deemed sensitive. Supposedly, he was to disregard anything else – to include derogatory comments about himself. Toward the end, outbound mail was impounded until they had landed in France.

Divine services were held daily for the different faiths, and Joseph and his comrades, who had expressed little interest in religious matters, now felt more of a need. He attended the services the division's Jewish chaplain conducted, while Catholics and Protestants filled the tents of their own chaplains.

Finally, the word came to move from the marshaling area, and Joseph and his comrades loaded closed trucks for the embarkation port. At about 0200 hrs the trucks halted: everyone sat and shivered waiting to move again. Smoking was allowed only in the trucks and any other lights were forbidden. Soldiers from a transportation company passed out sack breakfasts consisting of thick dry slices of English wholewheat bread with cold bologna and a cold, hard, fried egg; accompanied by cups of coffee that was cold and bitter, and so wound up on the ground.

They began loading the LST on May 30, and it was well past midday when Joseph and his squad went aboard and moved into their cramped quarters below deck. Unlike the *Capetown Castle*, officers and men alike crawled into web-laced horizontal bunks barely far enough apart for both the man and his equipment. No men were allowed on deck after they hoisted anchor, so they spent their time going over their assigned roles, as well as impregnating their clothing with a mixture designed to repel the poison gas that everyone expected to be covering the invasion beaches. Each man received a silk escape map of France, a small compass and 200 French Francs as invasion money (which many passed around for everyone to sign as a memento.) With all the necessary out of the way, many of the men settled down to throwing craps and playing blackjack until they had no money left.

There were no hot meals and the men ate the 10-in-1 ration, so named because it contained enough food for ten men. They thought it better than the K ration, with a greater variety, containing canned foods, soluble powdered drink, crackers instead of bread, jelly or jam, canned milk, and khaki-colored toilet paper, which received much derision.

On the night of June 4, the LST turned back toward England to ride out a hard storm. The men were keyed up, and Joseph hoped that none of those he had known for so long would be killed or wounded. He felt nervous about those whose lives now depended

22d Infantry soldiers preparing to sail for Utah Beach.

upon him and resolved to do the best that he could. The LST turned round again and during the night of June 5, with hundreds of aircraft flying overhead, the men loaded onto LCIs (Landing Craft, Infantry) that would take them to the beach at daybreak.

First blood, Normandy June–July 1944

On D-Day, Joseph's company contained one RA officer, two reserve officers, and six officers graduated from OCS. Of the 221 enlisted men, there were 16 pre-1940 RA soldiers – eight of whom were NCOs – and 86 pre-Pearl Harbor draftees. The remaining 119 entered service in 1942 and 1943, and joined the company Stateside and while in England.

As the LCI headed into shore, aircraft with three white stripes on each wing droned overhead, and Joseph spent his last moments of peace anxiously awaiting the unknown. Although well trained, he felt like a moth flying nearer and nearer a flame. Many times soldiers had been killed or wounded during maneuvers; however, they were always alive again for the next problem. He waved at a small landing craft traveling toward the beach, and watched in stunned surprise when it disappeared under a large plume of water, replaced by men thrashing in the water while other boats raced to rescue them. His LCI landed at H+210, and he walked down the ramp into waist deep water, passing his first dead soldier, who rocked softly in the waves against the beach.

There was some shelling, and at the rumbling sound of the first round someone yelled "incoming" and Joseph launched himself into the sand, only to have the round impact way down the beach, farther away than rounds normally landed during training. A twitter, a sheepish laugh, and the men continued to the beach wall. He and the others knelt in the sand and watched the officers gesturing

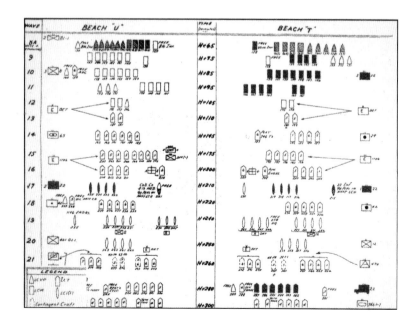

Formerly classified "Top Secret, Bigot" this is the landing order for Utah Beach. The shaded organizations are the 22d Infantry.

LCI similar to this carried the follow-on waves on D-Day. The landing was not bad, but worse lay inland.

toward landmarks and pointing to the map, trying to figure out where they were. Joseph had studied the terrain model and knew they were in the wrong area, but had no idea where they had landed.

Instead of moving inland on the heavily congested road, the officers led them over the dunes and into the marsh behind. Joseph's senses were working overtime as he noted the mined areas marked by white engineer tape, as well as baby German tanks filled with explosives sitting motionless in trenches. The water was first ankle, then knee and then crotch deep – soon everything in his HBT pockets was soaked again. During the long march that lasted until well after midnight, men exchanged heavy equipment so that everyone was equally tired. The bright moonlight made the night almost like day. From time to time, Joseph heard, and experienced more than once, the feeling of stepping into a bomb crater hidden under the water and completely submerging for the instant it took him to get to the other side. They halted along a bit of high ground, established a perimeter, and soldiers passed into sleep.

By the end of this long day, Joseph bordered on exhaustion – he had awakened early, landed, seen his first dead man, walked for seven hours across the marsh, watched German tracers fly overhead, and learned the difference between incoming and outgoing artillery. Joseph quickly learned the unmistakable sound of the German MG34 and MG42 machine guns – their rate of fire so fast they sounded like sewing machines – and the "whiz-bang" of the 88. Up before the dawn, gulping a quick breakfast from the rations remaining from the previous day, and ensuring his men rodded their weapons and changed their socks (since everyone was wet from the night before and the gun bores were fouled by the sand), at daybreak they were moving again.

Arriving near their original objective, Joseph's company mission was to clear the mutually supporting German fortifications along the narrow strip of land between the high water mark and the marsh they had waded through. They came upon the first bunker from the marsh side, and while Joseph's platoon provided support, another waded in water almost neck deep toward the rear entrance of the bunker. The Germans within waited until the Americans were near before they opened up with hidden machine guns, slaughtering those in the water. Joseph and the members of the support platoon immediately began firing but their shots were masked by those struggling in the water, so one of the officers drew fire from those trapped by running along the bank and firing at the bunker with his Thompson submachine gun, while another fired 57mm (2.22in.) antitank rounds at the position, and the mortars laid smoke so that the few men remaining in the water could retreat.

The next days were similar – with more losses and never a chance to rest and regroup. As an NCO Joseph awoke early, so that he could wake his men and ensure they ate, cleaned their weapons of the carbon buildup from the previous day's action, and changed their dirty wet socks for dirty dry socks. After the day's attack, they dug in for the night, resupplied and rotated on guard duty so that everyone got a little rest. Just about every day Joseph collected one dog tag from the dead (many of whom he had known for years) to give to his platoon sergeant, leaving the other on the body.

About three days into the battle, Joseph's battalion attacked the major fortifications at Azzeville. The four large pillboxes, each mounting a 150mm (5.9in.) gun and built of 6ft (1.8m) of reinforced concrete, were surrounded by smaller machine gun bunkers, barbed wire, and a minefield. Once the naval gunfire ended, the company moved forward with assault teams leading and Joseph's platoon in support. They picked their way through the minefield surrounding the pillbox, eliminating three small bunkers along the way. Joseph's platoon halted along a hedge about 100 yards (91m) further on, while the teams wormed closer. Two assault sections picked their way through the minefield surrounding the position without loss, reducing three small pillboxes along the way and then closed on near a hedgerow about 100 yards (91m) to the rear of the four large pillboxes. Joseph's platoon followed.

With the remaining machine gun positions masked by the nearest bunker's bulk, soldiers with bazookas, along with the one tank that had come up with the company, fired several rounds which penetrated only about 150 to 300mm (six to 12in.). Next, the assault teams ran to the back door, fired their flamethrowers and placed pole charges against it, all of which only dented the door. Then a soldier brought up a 40lbs (18kg) satchel charge, so powerful that he was knocked unconscious by the blast. The door remained intact. Joseph's company commander called for Joseph's flamethrower man, the last in the company with any fuel, to go forward. Joseph watched as he fiddled with the igniter while unlit liquid naphtha streamed onto the door; the soldier then bent over, struck a match, lit the stream and flamed the door until

Infantrymen jump off a wall to enter a fortified city. Their entrenching tools are attached to their web belts.

he too was out of fuel. It seemed to have no effect and a quiet desperation settled over the group of soldiers with Joseph: they had nothing left to attack the bunker with. A few moments later they heard small arms ammunition popping within the bunker that got louder as the minutes passed. The door opened and a white flag appeared, followed by an American parachute officer and a German officer who surrendered the fort and 169 men. The battle toll for the day, ten GIs.

The days passed, each as good or as bad as the last, but always with casualties. They'd expected casualties, but nothing like this. Losses mounted among officers and NCOs there were no replacements yet to take their place, and previously unknown leaders stepped forward. With no replacements for the first week, the company steadily grew smaller: sergeants led platoons and privates squads. Joseph felt almost detached from his fate, never knowing who among his group would be hit next; he was resigned to being killed or wounded like the others who had landed with him.

Every soldier could speak about a near miss. One soldier walked around showing off his helmet where a bullet had struck the inside of his helmet liner, cutting it like a band saw, yet not even scratching him. Another showed his Bible and a can of peanut butter that had stopped a killing bullet. Others were not so fortunate, especially those killed by friendly fire, be it artillery or a friend who fired into the night.

Quinéville finally fell on the 12th, the heights surrounding it in the days following. Joseph didn't remember much about the drive on Montebourg, or the pursuit up to the German main line of defense around Cherbourg, except that resupply arrived by tank at night, because roving bands of Germans, who had been cut off, were ambushing supply trucks driving alone. On June 26, Joseph and what remained of his regiment advanced against dug-in German anti-aircraft guns defending Maupertus airfield. They seized it then cleared Cap Lévy. The next day was their first true day of rest.

Soldiers resting in the sun sat by foxholes and listened as chaplains conducted non-denominational services. Joseph prayed more now than he had ever done in his life. He never thought about those friends who had been killed or wounded in days past; there was never any time and he was always bone-tired. But in the solitude of a rear area, he thought back on his last conversation with one of those killed, and remembered that they had talked about the good old days and what they was going to do when the war was over.

It was only when they pulled into reserve and looked around to see how many were not there that it struck them how fickle Fate was. Joseph felt it was initially only luck during the first days that had kept him from being wounded or killed. He still believed it was luck tempered with a hard-won experience. As one of the only NCOs left from pre-D-Day who had not been wounded, men followed him for his experience and his luck, hoping that he would keep them alive. Now he found his men depending on him where once they did not think twice about questioning his orders.

Between the 6th and 25th, Joseph's company had lost its company commander, six of its seven lieutenants, two first sergeants, five platoon sergeants, 12 staff sergeants, 16 sergeants, and 105 other ranks, and of the above all but 16 had landed on D-Day. Seventy-four replacements, some of them residuals, arrived to fill the empty files. What had taken three years to build was torn asunder in just weeks. His old squad now consisted of four old-timers and four replacements, and was four short of authorization. His squad leader had been wounded early on and Joseph had taken over. During the period, many of the 35 soldiers promoted, such as the recently promoted first sergeant, had already been wounded, and as one of the few surviving pre-invasion NCOs Joseph found himself promoted to staff sergeant on June 16, and now, just 15 days later, he was a platoon sergeant. However, he did not believe his good fortune would last.

He could not really remember how many men had cycled through his unit, but did remember their quality. The first who had been with the residual shipment were good, but with the heavy losses there was only one left, and the other draft of replacements that arrived late in the month were mostly non-infantrymen who had been assigned because there were no infantrymen left. They had to be quick learners or they weren't around long.

JOSEPH, SERGEANT, JUNE 6, 1944
(1) Here we see Joseph as on D-Day. He wears late-war HBTs of olive drab herringbone twill. Under his jacket, he wears a thick woolen brown army shirt. He also wears canvas leggings and standard issue boots. Joseph wears the M1 helmet with mesh netting. The rank insignia on his sleeve indicate that he is a Sergeant. On his left shoulder is the 4th Infantry Division shoulder patch (2). He wears an M1928 cartridge belt with a water canteen and first aid pouch attached.
He is armed with a .30 cal. M1 "Garand" rifle (3, also shown in top view, 4). The lettered parts of the M1 are as follows: (a) sling, (b) front sight, (c) front hand guard, (d) bolt, (e) rear sight, (f) safety, (g) stock, (h) plate butt, (i) barrel.
He bears two M1 sling bandoleers (9) of .30 cal. ammunition wrapped over each shoulder and slung across his chest, but these are obscured by the black invasion gas mask, which is carried across his chest and secured over his shoulders. The gas mask (5) is held in a black rubberized waterproof bag specially designed for amphibious landings.
He has two Mark II grenades (6) pinned onto his M1936 web suspenders at the chest.
On his back he bears the M1928 haversack without bedroll but with an entrenching tool attached. An inset detail (7) shows Joseph wearing his overseas cap with light blue infantry cord. The 22d Infantry Crest (8) appears on the front of this.

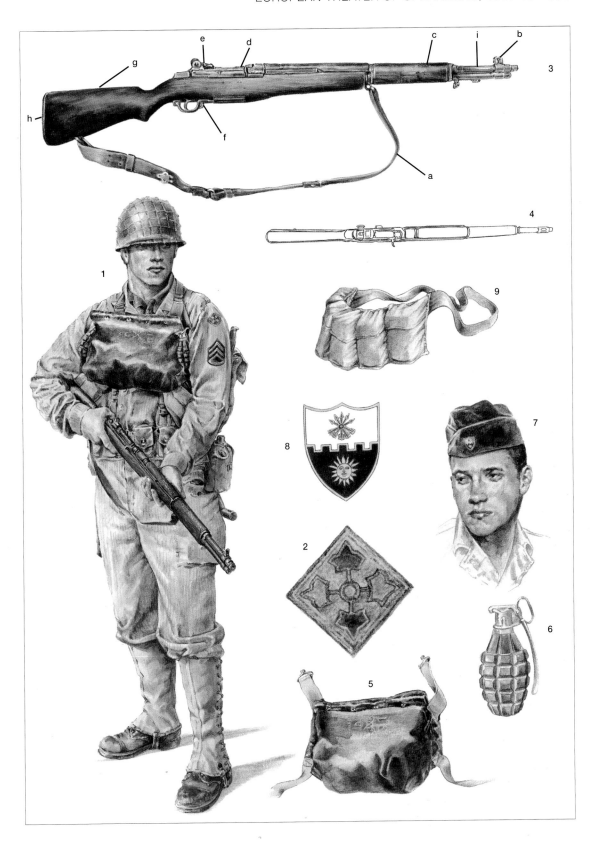

During his time out of the line, Joseph walked to the battalion aid station to visit one of his wounded friends. The aid station was located in a French farmhouse where he saw the family gathered by the fireplace, while dying Americans lay in one room and dying Germans in another. The medics told him his friend had been evacuated to England and, Joseph hoped, out of the war.

Between Cherbourg and Périers

On July 6, after only five days out of the line to rest, refit, and train replacements, Joseph and the 22d traveled east to the bocage country near Périers. Again the days merged one into another, and one field was similar to the next. They would seize one field only to be counterattacked, thrown back and then have to attack again to retake the field.

The Germans usually hid machine guns and mortars in each corner of a field to sweep the length of the

A church service in the field with foxholes nearby.

hedgerows as well as to cross and sweep the open field in front. Since there was no way to tell which hedgerow or which side of the hedgerow the "Krauts" were on, there was really no way to determine which approach was safest.

Joseph watched as his scouts crossed the field, and moved with his platoon in column along both sides of the embankment, which they found more effective than trying to cross in a skirmish line. He could see other platoons doing the same along other parallel hedgerows. The first platoon to reach the next lateral hedgerow would turn left or right to outflank the Germans in position along the embankment, which in turn allowed the other platoons to advance. Joseph thought it almost like playing chess, with each side devising one strategy, and the other working to overcome it.

Enemy tanks were another problem, especially when the Shermans could not get off the roads to support the infantry. With

Riflemen behind a hedgerow engage the Germans: two are reloading their M1s as one continues to fire. As became normal in the ETO, soldiers fought without haversacks and bedrolls, hoping that their equipment would arrive after they had gone into defensive positions.

only the 60mm (2.36in.) bazooka to use against Panthers, Mark IVs and SGIIIs, Joseph's men were leery of engaging in what they called "hand-to-hand" combat with a tank.

About the third day in the hedgerows, one tank-supported German counterattack sent Joseph's company scurrying back over the open ground to cover, with the Germans closely following. A 57mm (2.22in.) gun took out the first tank, while a second swung west into the nearby orchard with about a platoon of infantry, pushing back the platoon trying to defend there.

A third tank swung east into the orchard in front of Joseph's platoon. Joseph watched as Private Hix, an old regular, stood at a corner of a small house with his bazooka and waited for the tank to near. His first three rounds hit, but the tank continued forward. Hix then ran to the rear of the tank and fired another round and again hit the tank, this time blowing it up. The turret spiraled into the air as the tank tipped half over into a ditch. The second tank then pulled back, and Hix chased it almost 200 yards (182m) through a hail of small arms fire, before knocking it out. Joseph had never seen anything like it. The next day, Hix got another Panther; hitting it with three rounds at a range of 2 yards (1.8m) and suffering blast burns when the tank exploded. He was killed by a sniper on July 13.

With this feat of heroism, the men realized that German tanks were as helpless against infantry at close range as the American tanks were, and soon hunter-killer teams were chasing tanks out of the bocage. They learned through experience that the front end on the left side of the Panther was the most vulnerable, because the shell hitting there killed the driver. In two days Joseph's battalion knocked out ten German armored vehicles, three self-propelled

Exhausted infantrymen with equipment and rations scattered about. The soldiers sleep, read, and ponder the next day.

guns, and seven Mark Vs: six with bazookas, three with 57s, and the other stopped by a bazooka and killed by either a 57 or a bazooka. Joseph didn't care who killed it as long as it was dead.

Casualties continued to be heavy. His company commander was killed on one day, and the next the new company commander (who had been the XO) was killed by a mortar round hitting him on the shoulder. As there were no officers left in the company, the first sergeant assumed command until an XO from one of the sister companies arrived to take command; he was the only D-Day rifle company officer left in his battalion. Joseph remembered the lieutenant from the training days in the States when he was in the company as a platoon leader.

Joseph and his comrades could sense that the tide was turning in the hedgerows when they found that the Germans were leaving their wounded, and more and more prisoners were taken. If the well-trained company they had begun with had remained, Joseph felt they could have pushed right through.

This phase of the battle had cost Joseph's company 67 casualties: five officers, 12 NCOs and 50 other ranks, which reduced the numbers of the pre-D-Day soldiers remaining to just 80. With the continued flow of replacements, the company's on-the-ground strength stood at 149 or about 75 percent of authorized strength.

The St Lô breakout

Joseph's regiment received a short breather when they left the line after the attacks on Périers. They loaded trucks and moved into an assembly area with the 2d Armored Division's 66th Armored Regiment, and those who did not know quickly figured out their next mission would include fighting alongside armor. Battalions of the 22d married to battalions of the 66th for what many hoped would be the battle to break them out of the beachhead. Joseph remembered fighting alongside the 2d during the 1941 maneuvers and the many years of training as an armored infantry regiment. However, now instead of halftracks, they would be riding on tanks or in the backs of trucks. Over the next several days, Joseph and his comrades practiced combined arms tactics with the armor company they would fight with, and learned the combat techniques of this particular company.

Men loaded up with extra grenades, bandoleers and K rations; they had heard that they might be cut off for a while. Joseph knew that with the tanks sometimes spread 200–300 yards (182–274m) apart the squads following them were gong to be hard to control, so much was left to the squad leaders' discretion.

As long as there was no resistance, men rode on tanks. When contact was imminent or they were receiving fire, the soldiers hugged closely to the tank's rear, with the leader hanging onto the intercom phone that was mounted on the tank's rear hull so that he could maintain contact with the tank commander.

The attack began on July 26; initially with Joseph's platoon team leading. At first they moved across the hedgerow fields with two tanks leading as scouts and the remaining three following in overwatch positions. On entering the field, the lead Shermans would shell the corners with their 75mm (2.95in.) and rake the hedge in front with machine gun fire as they traversed the field. Once on the other side, the overwatching tanks moved forward while the infantry went past to secure the hedge against any Germans with Panzerfausts and to find the best place for the tanks to break the embankment. Finished, they ran back behind the tanks and repeated the procedure. There were casualties, but not many.

Darkness fell about 2230hrs and they received word to continue the attack. The long armored column wound through the burning village of Canisy with tanks silhouetted against the flames. After Canisy, Joseph's column turned off onto the road leading to Le Mesnil Herman. Just after midnight when they were outside the northern edge of town, Joseph heard Germans shouting just on the other side of a hedge about 15 yards (14m) away. He jumped off the tank and threw a grenade over the hedge, which exploded just as a Panzerfaust fired. His men dismounted and formed into a skirmish line to clear the hedge, while Germans fired other Panzerfausts. One hit a tank, and it blazed so brightly that it lit the night sky. The tanks began pulling back while Joseph's platoon provided security as they turned round. Joseph called up to the platoon leader asking if his men should ride back on the tanks but was told no, with the light they would all be shot off.

As the other tanks roared past the burning one, more Panzerfausts fired and missed. For the infantry it was a different matter. Germans were in front and behind them, and Joseph's platoon had to pull back or risk being captured or killed. Now with only 14 men, some wanted to make a break for it, but Joseph decided to

These soldiers, dressed in straw hats, are taking some hard-earned rest. Note that their bayonets are fixed.

A soldier on the march to Paris. He has a bazooka slung over his shoulder, and his M1 at the ready. He is in stripped marching order, carrying only his raincoat tucked into his web belt.

move back in staggered column so that he had some control. As they passed the burning tank he saw some Germans off to the right, threw a grenade, fired a clip of ammunition and yelled, "Come on, men, let's go," and ran up the road with the Germans returning fire into the dark. Two of Joseph's men went down wounded, but the others grabbed them under the armpits and dragged them out of the line of fire. About an hour later, they staggered into the tank laager, where Joseph found that, because of casualties, his platoon was to be split up between the two other rifle platoons.

Over the next days there were other memorable instances: German vehicles joining the moving columns at night, with neither side the wiser until they passed by a checkpoint; or German artillery firing red smoke, which was the American signal used to indicate enemy positions and which resulted in Joseph being shelled by his own artillery. However, this was not nearly as bad as being bombed by the two American P-47s, normally good at identification, that struck them while they marched through a village, killing seven and wounding six. There was a three-day fight at Tessy-sur-Vire, where the tank company Joseph was with made the final assault on the village with one tank, with all the others knocked out or disabled.

About four days later with the breakout well established, Joseph was riding on one of the tanks in the lead. There had been no contact for hours and the vehicle pulled ahead to reconnoiter a piece of open ground on the side of a gently sloping hill. As soon as

22d Infantrymen mounted aboard 66th Armored Regiment tanks during the St Lô breakout.

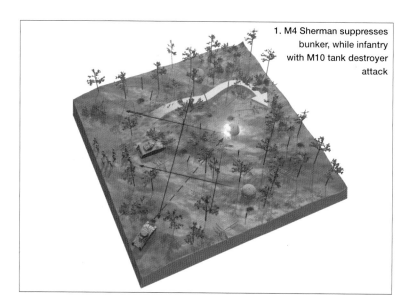

1. M4 Sherman suppresses bunker, while infantry with M10 tank destroyer attack

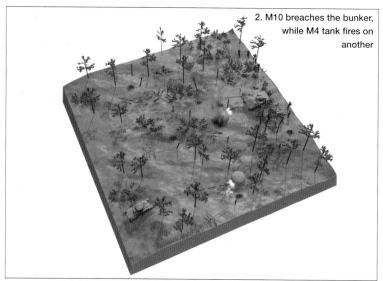

2. M10 breaches the bunker, while M4 tank fires on another

they crested the hill, Joseph saw a flash, felt a bang and then heat as an antitank round slammed into the turret, flinging him off the tank to land hard on the ground.

Siegfried Line and Hürtgen Forest

Joseph had been knocked unconscious by the antitank round and woke up in a collection station with a nasty gash on his head. A doctor sutured his wound, gave him an initial shot of penicillin, and sent him by ambulance to a convalescent hospital where he took his first real bath since leaving England, slept between sheets, and ate hot food. This was nothing like the front: no one was shooting around him or at him. Two weeks later he returned to duty with a scar on his scalp and a Purple Heart. He met up with the friend who

LEFT AND OPPOSITE
TAKING OUT BUNKERS ON THE SIEGFRIED LINE, SEPTEMBER 1944
This illustration shows the stages and principles of how to clear German bunkers and pillboxes on the Siegfried Line (West Wall), and is set on the borders of Germany in the fall of 1944. The Americans are attacking a section of large bunkers, and will remove the Germans from there. The four stages shown are as follows.
(1) The Americans suppress and smoke the bunkers using an M4 Sherman, while infantrymen accompanied by an M10 tank destroyer attack in a narrow column until they are behind the bunker.
(2) The M10 tank destroyer fires point blank at the rear door or aperture until a breach is made. There is now smoke/dust pouring from the front of the first bunker where the M4 tank shell has hit. The infantry have their rifles trained on the bunker, to cover exiting Germans. The Sherman M4 tank fires on another concrete bunker at the front.
(3) A soldier with a flamethrower advances, first firing unlit naphtha through the openings and then firing a burning blast, either smoking out or killing the Germans within. Other infantrymen from the first squad of men stay under cover.
(4) The M4 Sherman ceases firing against the second bunker, as US troops are now behind it. The M10 tank destroyer and the 1st rifle squad now move to the rear of the recently blasted 2nd bunker. Once again, they try to stay under cover. The second rifle squad maneuvers around the destroyed bunker to attack another one.

had been wounded earlier and returned to England for hospitalization. His friend told him that the doctors there did a wonderful job, but once he was convalescent they sent him to Fees' Farm for recuperation. There, he said, they overdid the rehabilitation program; day and night training with lectures, hikes, inspections, and details, and full field inspections every day – almost as if they intended to make it so miserable that infantrymen would want to go back to the front.

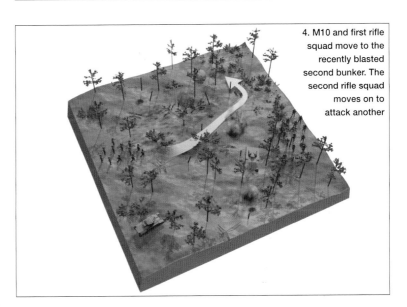

3. Soldier with a flamethrower fires unlit naphtha through openings and sets the bunker alight

4. M10 and first rifle squad move to the recently blasted second bunker. The second rifle squad moves on to attack another

Joseph returned to his squad in time to participate in the fight at Le Teilleul, and then the liberation of Paris. He stood in an awards ceremony where he received the Silver Star for his actions on the first night of the breakout and later in a mass ceremony where infantrymen who had been in combat 30 days received the Combat Infantryman Badge. What griped Joseph and his comrades was that those who weren't there because of wounds hadn't been submitted for a CIB. With the CIB came an increase in pay of $10; in addition, foreign service added another 20 percent of base pay.

After Paris, with the German forces in quick retreat back to the German border, Joseph's regiment mounted any vehicles they could find, and now motorized, drove toward Chauny, seized St Vith, and entered Germany at Bleialf. They all enjoyed motoring across France and Belgium, with American aircraft flying overhead, tanks, and tank destroyers close at hand if they made contact. Casualties were not nearly as high as they had been earlier, and many soldiers wounded earlier in the bloodletting of Normandy returned. The only problem with some returnees was that they were listed as limited duty, and there weren't any assignments in a rifle company for a soldier who was unfit. Joseph and his comrades

An awards ceremony: the division commander stands on the hood of a jeep, extolling the virtues of the men receiving the awards.

did what they could to see them assigned to headquarters and the Service Company.

With the slowdown in casualties, Joseph noted that marginal or burnt-out officers were being relieved of their assignments and sent to the rear for reclassification. They were replaced by officers wounded earlier during the campaign and now rested, new officers from the US, or battlefield commissionees. The same situation applied to NCOs; however, they were normally demoted to private and kept in the line instead of being sent to the rear. Others made it back to the Service Company as privates. It didn't seem fair, especially for those who had been through it all and bordered on combat exhaustion.

By mid-September, Joseph's regiment had reached the crest of the Schnee Eifel ridge and his battalion was overlooking Hontheim with orders to take Brandscheid. They began their attack to bust the Siegfried Line using the technique that worked best in the bocage: attack in column along a narrow front and then roll up the positions from the sides and rear. As Joseph's platoon worked their way into the rear of the pillbox line, German machine gun fire was initially heavy, but it tapered off once they got behind the pillboxes. Joseph's main worry now was to defend against the small German elements either trying to retake lost bunkers or trying to escape from bypassed ones.

While the men in his platoon forced the Germans in the trenches and foxholes surrounding the bunker to pull back, Joseph motioned for the tank and supporting machine guns to fire into the embrasures, forcing the Germans to close them, which permitted his platoon to get close to the bunker without being

fired on. One of the squad leaders maneuvered a tank destroyer about 15 or 20 yards (14 or 18m) from the rear door and then signaled it to begin firing. The solid armor-piercing rounds of the 76mm (3in.) gun soon tore gashes in the steel door, at which time a man with a flamethrower squirted unignited naphtha through the hole, followed by a burning blast. In some positions, Germans surrendered before being roasted by flamethrowers, in others they did not, and their screams echoed through the woods. Joseph just wished he had more of the old men left who had trained with demolitions and flamethrowers.

The bunker destroyed, they went to the next in line. Joseph's platoon leader had a map overlaid with all the known German bunkers that really helped, however, there were others well camouflaged, so they were careful in searching the area.

In instances where they couldn't get the tank destroyer in close, they had the tank and tank destroyer suppress the bunkers while infantry teams, some with rifles and BARs, and others equipped with satchel charges, Panzerfausts (which they found much more effective than their 60mm (2.36in.) bazookas), and flamethrowers got in close. With Joseph's support team of riflemen giving covering fire, he watched as one of the assault team soldiers ran to the right

Soldiers pass through the West Wall and into Germany.

A German machine gun bunker on the West Wall.

side of an embrasure, pulled the fuze of a 30lb (13.6kg) satchel charge, let it burn down until there were only a few seconds left, and then threw the charge into the bunker. A "Whoom!" and the rear door and closed embrasures popped open from the concussion. Then the flamethrower operator went to work.

They kept what they had captured that day; however, German counterattacks prevented them from taking the town. After a few more days they settled into what the leadership called

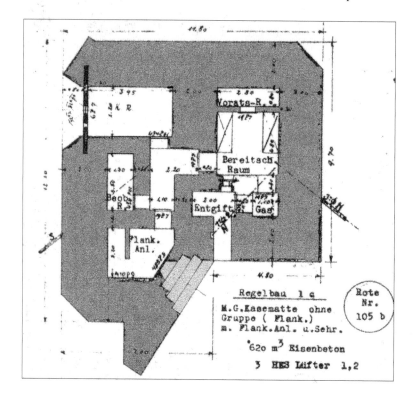

A bunker schematic. As with most permanent bunkers, the walls were 6½ft (2m) thick.

"aggressive patrolling" and those in the line called "letting sleeping dogs lie". Here they spent a month recuperating and they received what infantrymen usually went without: showers, movies, Red Cross donuts and coffee, and USO shows, not to mention mail and hot food.

Promotion

In September, Joseph's battalion commander had recommended he be commissioned, and in October Joseph left the line. During a five-day period he bathed, slept on clean sheets, received new clothes, was discharged as an enlisted man, and appointed as an officer in the AUS, receiving a seven-digit serial number beginning with 199. Regular officers had numbers ranging from 01 (General Pershing) up to 99,999: Reserve and National Guard officers six-digit numbers, and AUS OCS and battlefield commissioned officers seven-digit numbers.

When he returned to the 22d, the now Lieutenant Stein met with Colonel Lanham, his regimental commander. Joseph remembered the colonel's admonition, "If you ever fail to do your duty it is the penitentiary for you." Next, he met the regimental executive officer, who assigned him to a company in the 1st Battalion, away from the company he had been with since February 1941.

The Combat Infantryman in the Hürtgen Forest.

Hürtgen Forest

In early November, they moved into the town of Rötgen. Before they moved, however, division instructed everyone to remove their shoulder patches and to muddy the bumper numbers so that the Germans would not know who was facing them. When Joseph cut the light khaki square from the Parson's jacket he had worn since 1942, he found the original olive drab coloration of his jacket underneath and thought of the years that he had worn it.

They spent their first days in the forest preparing for the coming attack, supposedly including a bombing attack as big as the one that had sprung them from Normandy. Some of the new sleeping bags arrived for the front line infantry, as well as the officers' liquor ration, which Joseph and the other officers shared with their NCOs. Rain fell constantly and temperatures stayed in the thirties. As the junior officer in the company, Joseph passed the

Riflemen in raincoats on alert in their newly dug foxhole.

absentee ballots for the presidential election around, but there didn't seem to be much interest.

The attack began on November 16, with everyone expecting to be through the forest in a day and at the Ruhr River the next. A series of ridges running north and south crossed the region, thickly wooded ridges with great hardwood and fir trees standing 75 to 100ft (23 to 30m) tall. The bodies of the firs hugged close to the ground and interlocked with their neighbors, making it appear as if the forest were a sea of green, which the midday sun seldom broke through, leaving an eerie twilight effect.

However, try as they might, they couldn't break the shell of the German defenses. Walking up the steep slope on the first day, most of the company machine gun section was wiped out by artillery, and the next morning was even worse, with barrage after barrage catching the company forming for the day's assault. As the days passed it seemed almost routine to take 20 percent casualties and be replenished that night with replacements. By the fourth day there were only a few originals left.

The battle seemed never to end. Joseph didn't think it possible, but this current battle in the forest with the constant artillery, rain, and cold was worse than what they had experienced in Normandy. In the half-light of the forest, soldiers on both sides traded small arms fire in the frozen slush, while artillery cracked overhead and men swore softly and died, or cried and collapsed – hoping to be evacuated. With the heavy rains and night frosts the men huddled together in mud- and water-filled foxholes, one in three pulling guard, and shivered until the sun came up. Here there was no rear area and companies almost never pulled out of the line unless there was nothing left of them and replacements did not keep up with losses. Joseph had heard that his battalion commander had been killed early on and that many of the remaining old men had been wounded, and he had a premonition that he would not make it either.

It was damned cold. Joseph knew like the other old men to bundle up with as much clothing as he could because the chance of getting his bedroll brought forward at night was nil. He wore everything he could get his hands on in an effort to keep warm. The enlisted overcoats were really warm; however, when they got wet and muddy they seemed to weigh a ton; with everything else they were carrying, many opted to wear their Parson's jackets and raincoats if they had them. As outerwear, Joseph wore his enlisted man's raincoat. Under that he wore a Parson's jacket and a pair of fatigues; beneath the fatigues, a pair of ODs; beneath the ODs, long underwear and long socks; and on his head his knit cap underneath his helmet. He began with gloves, but quickly lost them, so put socks on his hands to ward off the cold.

They had been issued the M1943 combat boot in September, but once wet, they bred cold feet, trenchfoot, and frostbite: soldiers quickly learned not to lace the boots too tightly because it

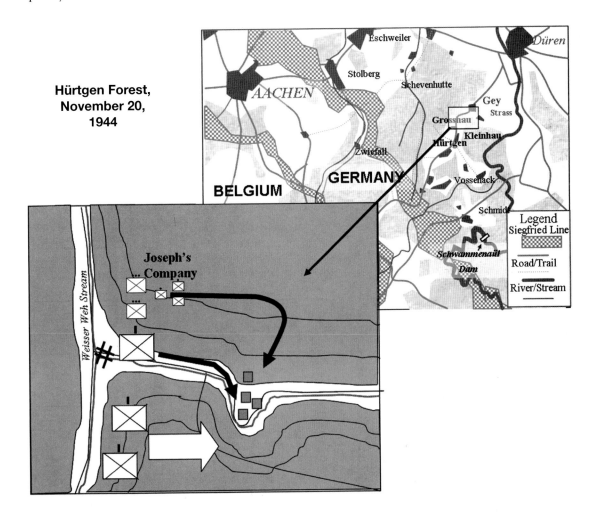

Hürtgen Forest, November 20, 1944

constricted the blood flow. Many of those who had galoshes threw them away because they were too exhausted to clean them. As trenchfoot cases went up, exhaustion cases went down.

About six days into the attack, with only about 90 men left in the company, they attacked again, this time toward a hill that overlooked the east–west road. Joseph's platoon led, with the other platoons following. Joseph's platoon attacked in a "V" with two squads nearest the enemy and one back.

Joseph's scouts were about 100 yards (91m) out and moving up the hill when one stopped, signaled that he saw enemy on his right and motioned Joseph forward. Joseph spotted six or seven small bunkers and radioed the information to his company commander, who then put everyone into a long skirmish line that flanked the pillboxes. Joseph's platoon moved forward in a skirmish line of riflemen and light machine guns supported by a pair of heavy machine guns and BARs on each flank, taking one bunker out at a time with few casualties of their own. The Germans did not offer much resistance because the bunkers' firing ports all faced south and southwest and Joseph's company had attacked from the north.

Overseas shipment of replacements to the ETO

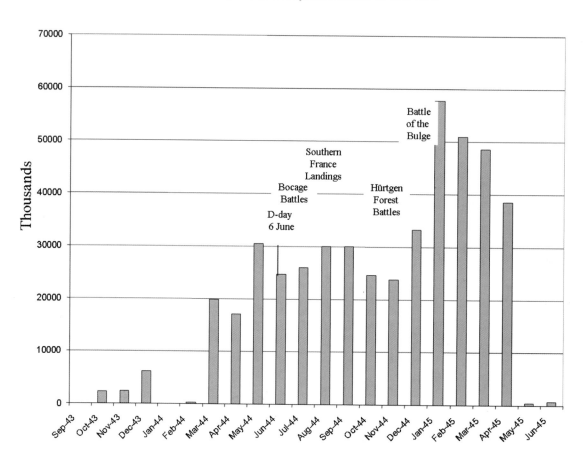

After eliminating the bunkers, Joseph's platoon continued its march northeast to the crest of Hill 136. A German machine gun fired on his lead squad as it crossed an east–west firebreak, splitting Joseph's platoon. One of the machine gunners attached to his platoon picked up his M1917A1 water-cooled heavy machine gun and moved forward firing it from the hip, walking his rounds onto the target, and allowing time for soldiers in the platoon to flank the position to knock it out. As Joseph walked up the trail,

ETO replacement camp. A smoky haze hangs over as men gather by the fire.

he stopped and knelt for a moment beside the seriously wounded gunner, grasped his hand, and thanked him.

As soon as they reached the top of the hill, everyone began digging in. Not more than 20 minutes later, they heard tanks off to the north and soon saw German infantrymen working their way through the trees. While Joseph's platoon engaged with rifles and machine guns, the forward observer for the 44th Field Artillery called in repeated fire missions and the Germans fell back.

Resupply and replacements

Joseph's company commander was wounded the day before Thanksgiving and the executive officer took his place, with Joseph becoming the XO. Now he was concerned more with resupply and replacements than he was with fighting. Joseph used the weapons platoon and German prisoners to carry the wounded back, then with the newly arrived replacements the weapons platoon men brought forward water cans, ammunition, and rations over 1,500 yards (1,372m) of rough terrain. His company's daily requirement amounted to about a ton and a half of ammunition, about 40 cases of rations, 20 five-gallon (23l) cans of water, and all the dry socks they could find. It was a never-ending struggle to keep the company supplied. It would have been nice to bring up the bedrolls, but there was only so much the men could carry.

Outside the heavy attritional combat of Normandy and the Hürtgen, there was seldom a time when Joseph's platoon had not been near full strength. Replacements usually arrived to occupy the positions left by soldiers killed or those who had been evacuated wounded. When a soldier was killed or wounded, the company clerk entered his name on the daily company Morning Report, which was the company's daily history: assignment, departure, promotion, demotion, casualty, return to duty of individuals, and location, current status, and strength of the company. Once the clerk completed the report the regimental adjutant compiled all of the company reports and from them submitted requisitions for soldiers. The clerk dropped soldiers from the company roster after he had received notice they had processed through the division clearing station. Those non-battle casualties leaving because of sickness remained on the rolls until they had been gone five days.

As he looked over his newest batch of replacements, Joseph thought with some wryness that the longer the war lasted, the more competent leaders became, while the quality of the individual soldier declined. These were good kids, but they just did not have the training that he and his earlier comrades had experienced before being committed to combat. Even better was getting back those soldiers who had been previously wounded. No matter what corps they were in, soldiers returned to their original companies. Upon recovery, these so-called "casuals" were reassigned to the same company with the priority going to those soldiers who had been with the unit longest. Joseph knew they were seasoned veterans but from his own experience, he also realized they were usually skittish in their initial action. Now they all understood they were mortal.

Joseph was wounded on Thanksgiving Day, 1944, after only one day as XO, when units were reconstituting and preparing for the next attack. The attack through the woods continued until the 22d was withdrawn on December 3. Soldiers in rifle companies on November 16 had a 92 percent chance of being wounded or killed during the next 18 days, and counting replacements, losses reached an average of 138 percent in rifle companies. Total regimental casualties numbered 2,805, with the three battalion commanders being killed or wounded during the first three days, and commanders for the nine rifle companies numbering more than 30. On December 3, they moved 90 miles (145km) to the quiet sector near Luxembourg City, where on December 16 elements of the German Seventh Army struck the regiment during the initial stages of the Battle of the Bulge.

Soldiers beginning the climb into the Hürtgenwald. The rear soldier appears to be carrying an M1936 musette bag.

US Doughboy meets German Landser.

Casualties

One of Joseph's men, wounded earlier at Brandscheid in September, arrived midway through the Hürtgen Forest battle, and in days had transitioned from a clean, warm environment to one of utmost barbarity. He had spent the first days back as an observer for the mortar section and had been caught in an artillery barrage that had killed the radioman next to him. Unable to dig in, he stayed motionless throughout the shelling until the next morning.

When Joseph found him the soldier's eyes were mindlessly staring straight ahead, and his arms were wrapped tightly around the radio. Joseph instantly knew that he was "out of change" and sent him back to the aid station. The soldier didn't recognize Joseph as he picked up the radio and started back. Joseph watched him as he hit the ground when shells came near, then got up and continued walking as soon as his concussion had passed. When he arrived at the aid station, he simply sat down and waited until a medic asked his problem: he didn't answer, only stared straight ahead. The medic snapped his fingers a couple of times in front of the vacant eyes, and then wrote on the tag "exhaustion". When ordered to, the soldier climbed into an ambulance with other exhaustion cases for the ride to 622d Exhaustion Center.

The ETO based its standard treatment for combat exhaustion on experience from the Mediterranean, a process known as narcotherapy. This consisted of putting the man to sleep for three days using sodium amytal, hooking an intravenous tube of saline solution to keep him hydrated, and waking him only long enough to help him to the latrine. While he slept the soldier lived the nightmares of his days in combat, and was hollow-eyed and frail upon awakening. Next came showers, hot food, and more sleep.

Then there was rehabilitation with a psychiatrist so that hopefully he could rejoin his unit of the front line, but this seldom worked, because once he found that a medical tag reading "Combat Fatigue" removed him from the horrors of combat, a neuro-psychiatric casualty sometimes made an almost continual circuit between the exhaustion center and the front lines until he was killed or the war was over.

In 1945, studies in the ETO reflected the same findings as the MTO, that as the war progressed, more veteran officers and noncommissioned officers with extended time on the front lines fell victim to neurosis, and like the MTO infantrymen had an aggregate of 200–240 days on the line until they had "no change left" and cracked-up.

When Joseph was wounded on Thanksgiving Day, he was shepherding the hot marmites of turkey sandwiches forward. An artillery shell hit a tree alongside the white tape he was following, showering everyone below with tree splinters and shell fragments. Joseph felt a burning in his leg and a sharp blow to his left foot. A medic hastily bandaged his leg and sent him hobbling back to the battalion aid station, supported by two other more mobile wounded. They followed a group of four litter bearers carrying a soldier up and down the muddy hills and across the streams, sometimes slipping and dropping the litter.

At the aid station, Joseph was triaged with the others, with each quickly examined and sorted into different categories of need. They told him that they could do nothing for him there but give him morphine, as they started a plasma drip into his arm and placed him into a corner until an evacuation ambulance arrived. He looked around and found the station looked like a slaughterhouse; a pile of bloody bandages in one corner, and shoes and clothing crumpled in a heap in another. The blankets on the stretchers were more red than olive drab. Finally, he climbed into an ambulance along with other wounded, two litter cases slung in racks with him, and the others sitting on the seat and floor. The ambulance started down the trail pock-marked by artillery, bomb, and mortar craters, and the vehicle sharply jolted left and right. The driver called out that they were nearing the bridge and to hold on because the Germans were intermittently shelling. The vehicle picked up speed and at every bump Joseph felt the jars traverse his leg and spine, worse than any medieval torture he could imagine. At least he was out of the forest.

They arrived at the regimental collection station, where wounded soldiers from throughout the regiment were collected. Again they were triaged with the walking wounded being sent to wait in one room, while the more seriously wounded, Joseph among them, lay on litters in another.

JOSEPH, LIEUTENANT, FEBRUARY 1945
Joseph is now 27 years old. He is a lieutenant and proud of his accomplishments, but has been beaten down by wounds and war.
(1) He wears the Parson's jacket, with the blue Combat Infantryman Badge above his left breast pocket. The CIB was only awarded to infantrymen at regiment level or lower who had served at least 30 days in the line or had been wounded previously. The 4th Infantry Division shoulder patch is on the left shoulder of his jacket, and Second Lieutenant bars on his shoulders. Under his jacket, he wears a thick woolen brown army shirt, and he wears HBT trousers, tucked into his 1943 buckle top combat boots. Under his HBTs he wears his woolen army trousers to keep warm. He wears the M1 helmet, without netting, and under this a wool knit cap. He is armed with the M1 .30 cal. carbine instead of his favored M1 rifle, and the ammunition for this is stored in the pouches attached to his M1936 belt. The M1 carbine was authorized to platoon leaders. Lieutenants sometimes also carried the M1 Thompson submachine gun. He is carrying the M1936 musette bag strapped over his shoulders, worn like a small rucksack. A pair of binoculars hangs around his neck. (2) The lensatic compass was used by infantry combat leaders. (3) An M1938 dispatch bag, more commonly called a map case. (4) The SCR 300 radio was used at company level, whereas the SCR 536 radio (5) was used at platoon level.

An aid man looked at Joseph's foot and began cutting through his layers of clothing from the knee down. With the shoe exposed, Joseph saw that his foot lay oddly twisted. The more the medic cut, the more sharp jabs of pain cut through his drug-induced haze. Cutting through the shoelaces was excruciating, and Joseph fainted when the medic began cutting through the boot leather. Joseph remained unconscious while they lifted him into another ambulance for shipment to the Division Clearing Station. Those who had died were placed outside the building with a blanket over their bodies.

At the clearing station, ward boys moved down the line of wounded with pans of hot water, the first hot water most had seen since early November, so that they might clean the grime, shave, brush their teeth, and comb their hair. Once processed, the wounded were separated into categories and sent to field hospitals in Eupen, Verviers, and at Malmady. This was where Joseph and the other officers, were separated from the enlisted men and put into their own wards.

Joseph not only had a lacerated and broken foot, he also had the onset of trench-foot, one of the reasons he was able to walk from the company back to the battalion aid station. He had not been able to feel the pain. He'd been wearing overshoes over his combat boots; however, once his boots got wet they never dried. Overshoes were so unsatisfactory when worn over combat boots that 60 percent of the cold-injury victims in the division were found to have become disabled while wearing them.

A medic dresses a wounded man while another soldier in the background continues fighting.

A battalion aid station in the Hürtgen Forest.

From the evacuation or general hospital within the army boundaries, soldiers normally rode a hospital train to one of the hospitals near Paris. From there, trains might further evacuate them to the coast for a ship to England or for a longer recovery to the US. Alternatively, if circumstances were favorable, a soldier might be loaded aboard an aircraft for the trip to England.

The convalescent hospital was a place where postoperative soldiers who had not yet recovered could rest and recuperate. Those whose expected recovery was longer than the theater's evacuation policy (between 1944 and 1945, evacuation policy to the US varied between 90 and 120 days) transferred to a hospital in the US.

Joseph remained in hospital through the month of December, while his regiment was fighting in Luxembourg on the southern flank of the Bulge, and through much of January when the regiment was moving into position to continue its attack on the West Wall. During the latter part of his stay at the rehabilitation hospital for officers at Bromsgrove in Worcestershire, when he wasn't going through reconditioning, making him fit for duty, he was able to do the sightseeing he had been unable to do as an enlisted man. In marked contrast to the multitude of medals the flyboys were wearing, Joseph wore only his Combat Infantryman Badge, knowing that only infantrymen could earn it.

After a short furlough in Paris, Joseph rejoined his company in early February, just after his regiment had finally taken Brandscheid, an objective that had eluded them in September 1944. There were already seven officers in his company; however, they assigned him back to his platoon as a "spare" in the likely event there were further officer casualties.

Walking wounded in the Hürtgen Forest leave the line as other soldiers move up.

Prüm, R&R, and crossing the Rhine

Joseph was happy to be back; however, after being wounded twice he didn't harbor any illusions as to whether he would survive the war. He found that he had missed the opportunity to return to the States for a furlough granted to those twice wounded. Although he qualified, they had already filled the allocations through March.

Arriving just as his platoon had taken Brandscheid, Joseph had orders to continue the attack the next day. His heart was in his throat as he motioned his men forward. He wished that he were a private so that he could hide, instead of being one of the few combat veterans remaining from D-Day – and as an officer commissioned from the ranks, he couldn't let his men down.

They swept through one small village and were at the top of a crest when a German attack boiled out of the town below. It was not serious, but it stopped the attack for the day. Joseph looked out over the long rolling hills surrounding Prüm and could observe anything that moved for miles. He called his artillery observer up and they adjusted fire on the different groups of German soldiers they observed.

There were more days of fighting through the hills, the most memorable of which was when Joseph's company and another were cut off on the opposite side of a stream by machine gun fire. Friendly tanks were unable to cross and they had to fight up the ridge unassisted. A German tank-infantry attack hit them while they were re-forming, and they were just able to hold on using bazookas against the tanks and calling in artillery against the infantry.

To Joseph, it seemed that they settled into a routine of attack, take casualties, seize the day's objective, and prepare for the next day's attack. It was debilitating work in terms of human endurance, but at least the men could see measurable progress. In nine days Joseph's regiment captured 12,373 Germans and knocked out more than 150 Siegfried Line bunkers.

On the last day of February, they crossed the Prüm River in a night attack, moving into real tank country as they drove toward the Rhine. Joseph's company teamed with a company of the 11th Armored to take some towns, until finally they were outside Hillesheim, expecting to have to fight their way through to the river. However well the town was fortified, it was undefended and Joseph and his comrades were again able to sleep under roofs.

In mid-March they found out that they were moving out of the line for rest and refit in southern France – the only time they'd been away from artillery fire in 199 days. For two glorious weeks, soldiers sunbathed, drank, slept, chased women, and saw the sights; as well as

Taking cover behind a tank: two soldiers in raincoats and galoshes smoke cigarettes until the artillery fire lets up.

pulled motor maintenance and conducted some weapons training. Joseph slept the first two days and then went sight-seeing. He purchased a camera and took pictures of all the men in his platoon, as well as the sights in Paris when he visited. Those going to rest camps around Paris received a bag full of cigarettes, chocolates, and nylons for barter purposes with the natives. They all agreed that Patton might be an ass when it came to uniform rules, but when it came to taking care of soldiers out of the line there was no equal.

Alerted to move on the 28th, the 22d crossed the Rhine River on a pontoon bridge in a long convoy of trucks on March 30. Joseph looked out from the truck cab at a huge steel girder bridge with its center collapsed into the river. Once across they entered the largest highway he had ever seen and then turned off onto one of the secondary roads heading east. They could tell they were nearing the front lines again because here and there they saw untended dead Germans. They were back at war.

In comparison to previous fights, early April was a quick motor across southern Germany; casualties were light and movements

A safe and dry company command post inside a captured German bunker.

were 20, 35 and even 50 miles (32, 56 and 80km) a day across hilly terrain on secondary roads. German towns hung white sheets from the windows signifying surrender and no Wehrmacht forces within the confines. The entire regiment suffered only 54 casualties during the new drive, and Joseph's company only lost nine in a vehicular ambush. On the night of April 2, they were inside the town of Hofstetten.

On April 3, the sun was shining and the sky was a dark teal blue as Joseph walked from the door of the company command post. He felt that, with the rapid advances, the war had to end soon. He heard a shell screeching in, felt an explosion, and the blue faded to black. Of the 22 battlefield commissionees in the 22d, of which Joseph was one, six were killed, ten were wounded and two became non-battle casualties.

Once evacuated by grave registration, Joseph was buried in the Third Army cemetery at Bensheim, Germany, and his personal effects including his medals sent home. His parents found six: the Silver Star, a Bronze Star that Joseph had never mentioned, his Purple Heart, a Good Conduct Medal, American Defense Medal, and a European-African-Middle Eastern Theater Campaign medal with arrowhead and five campaign stars.

At war's end there were 61 United States Military Cemeteries in Europe. Outside these established military cemeteries there were an estimated 12,000 US soldiers buried in graves by the German

A surrendered German town, displaying white sheets.

To the everlasting glory of the infantry.

Army. Another 6,000 were buried by civilians, and a further 3,000 were isolated battlefield burials. In June 1945, Congress approved ten permanent cemeteries in Europe where soldiers were re-interred. Beginning in 1947, those soldiers whose families requested it were returned to their homes in the US. Today, military cemeteries overseas are cared for by the American Battlefield Monuments Commission.

In the days remaining in the war in Europe, the 22d continued its sweep to the southeast and cleared Bad Mergentheim, Röttingen and its surrounding hills, Crailsheim, Adelmannsfelden, and crossed the Lech at Schwabstadl; on April 30, they crossed the River Isar at Unter Schäflarn and drove southeast to Miesbach-Gusteig. The war for the 22d was practically over on May 4, when it left for the Neumarkt area for occupation duty.

On the day of the German surrender, the regiment's soldiers received a mimeographed page describing the feelings of the old-time members of the 22d.

"This evening Admiral Doenitz has announced to the German people the unconditional surrender of all German fighting forces.
Had this surrender occurred the 1st of September on

OPPOSITE April 1945: an overloaded halftrack passes marching soldiers who wear the M1943 field jacket.

22d Infantry battle casualties	KIA Officers	KIA Enlisted men	MIA Officers	MIA Enlisted men	WIA Officers	WIA Enlisted men	Total Battle Casualties
D-Day and Carentan Jun 1944	25	401	1	228	121	2,164	2,940
Périers Jul 1944	16	249	1	56	39	897	4,198
St Lô Breakout, Paris Aug 1944	8	56	0	30	19	273	4,584
Siegfried Line Sep 1944	11	92		10	17	333	5,047
Schnee Eifel Oct 1944	1	14		1	7	71	5,141
Hürtgen Forest Nov 1944	27	233		12	70	1,472	6,955
Hürtgen Forest, Luxembourg Dec 1944	2	197		41	22	345	7,562
River Our Jan 1945	1	16		7	2	59	7,647
Prüm Feb 1945	10	145	1	47	29	446	8,325
Prüm Mar 1945	2	100		4	8	188	8,627
Pursuit Apr 1945	7	86		4	10	244	8,978
End of War 1945		1			1	1	8,981

our wave of optimism when we hit the Siegfried Line, or immediately after the defeat of Von Rundstedt and the successful crossing of the Rhine, we would have been wild with joy. The news of Germany's surrender was received by all of us with a calmness very nearly approaching indifference about the feeling deep within our hearts.

There was no revelry last night, no drunkenness, no shouting, no flag waving, no horns blowing; there was a sober realization that it was all over … and that we, by the strength of our arms and by our own courage, had, with the help of God, completely and finally defeated everything that the warped and twisted soul of a perverted nation could hurl at us …

There is not one single fighting day of which we must be ashamed or for which we must make excuses. No regiment in the ETO has more right to hold its head high and to march with shoulders back, colors streaming, than this one. Its record, its casualties, its achievements, and the respect it instilled and the terror it struck in the heart of the German Army speak for themselves."

And Taps played over the many cemeteries in Europe.

Day is done, Gone the sun,
From the lake, from the hill, from the sky
All is well, Safely rest, God is nigh
Thanks and praise, for our days,
'Neath the sun, 'neath the stars, 'neath the sky
Rest in peace, Soldier brave, God is nigh

Going home
The 22d deployed overseas in January 1944, had entered combat on June 6, 1944, and had suffered casualties much higher than most deployed to the European Theater. The average infantry regiment in the ETO lost 41 officers and 668 enlisted men killed and 133 officers and 2,413 enlisted wounded. In approximately 11 months of combat, the 22d Infantry Regiment suffered 111 officers and 1,594 enlisted men killed, three officers and 209 enlisted missing or captured, and 419 officers and 7,287 enlisted wounded, most of whom were lost during the Normandy Campaign and in the Hürtgen Forest. This does not include the thousands of non-battle casualties due to trench-foot, frostbite, combat fatigue or other illnesses. Combined battle and non-battle casualties for the 22d Infantry reached 351 percent and 560 percent for the rifle companies.

The 22d departed France aboard the USAT *General James Parker* on July 3, and arrived in New York Harbor on July 11. There were still many soldiers remaining who had sailed overseas with the 22d just 18 months previously, most of whom had served in the different headquarters and in the regiment's separate companies. The great majority of soldiers who had landed in rifle companies with Joseph on D-day were long gone, either wounded, shipped home as high pointers on furlough, discharged in May and hipped-home as high pointers on furlough, discharged in May and June 1945, or buried in cemeteries throughout France, Belgium, Luxembourg, and Germany. By the end of the war, of the 229 soldiers assigned to his company prior to D-Day 54 had been killed, 22 captured or missing, and 192 wounded – 60 percent of those seriously – amounting to 268 battle casualties for the initial cohort of this one rifle company.

On arrival in the US soldiers received a 30-day furlough. Those not discharged earlier were scheduled for redeployment to the Pacific after reassembling at Camp Butner, North Carolina. With Japan's surrender, the remaining high point officers and men received their discharges and went home.

The 22d Infantry in its 11 months of combat lived up to its motto "Deeds not words", garnering two Distinguished Unit Citations (the equivalent of the Distinguished Service Cross being awarded to every man in the unit), for the St Lô breakout and the Hürtgen Forest, and its 3d Battalion another for the Normandy landing. Its soldiers were also honored with the Belgian Fourrageré for the operations in Belgium and the Ardennes. The 22d remained at Camp Butner, until it inactivated on March 1, 1946, and remained inactive until July 15, 1947, when it was activated at Fort Ord, California.

CHAPTER 7

SOUTHWEST PACIFIC THEATER OF OPERATIONS, 1944–45

"His name and fame are the birthright of every American citizen. In his youth and strength, his love and loyalty, he gave all that mortality can give. He needs no eulogy from me or from any other man. He has written his own history and written it in red on his enemy's breast."
General Douglas MacArthur

The Southwest Pacific Area (SWPA) encompassed large island land masses that were jungle-covered, and infested with malaria, where the high temperatures and humidity along

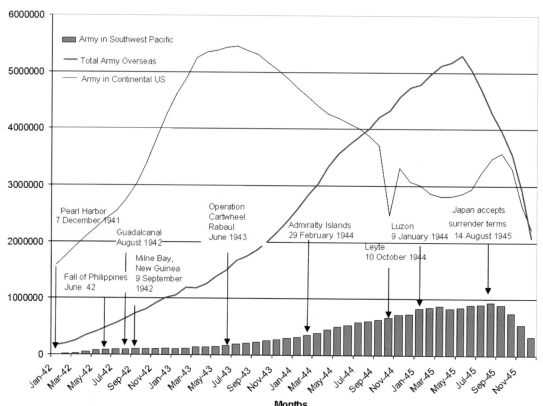

US Army strength in the Southwest Pacific, 1942–45

Campaigns in the Pacific

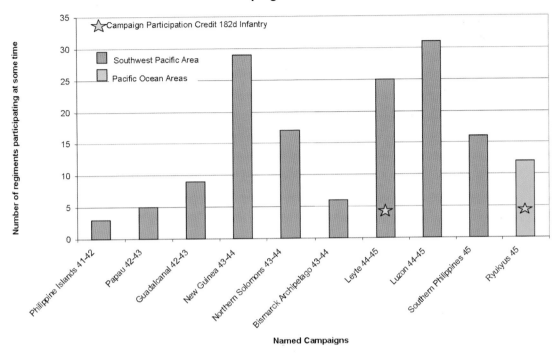

US Infantry Regiments in Combat, Southwest Pacific

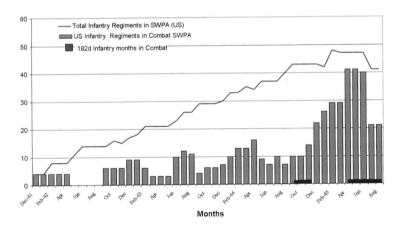

with the muck, filth, and debilitating diseases combined to send a great many more soldiers to hospital as non-battle casualties than did battle wounds. In 1942 and 1943, soldiers in the SWPA fought through the jungles of New Guinea, New Britain, and the Solomon Islands in vicious hand-to-hand fighting, with little support from armor, artillery or air power. The large numbers of non-battle and battle casualties, primitive infrastructure, as well as the slow arrival of replacements ensured that once committed to combat, units never again reached authorized strength.

Daily Average non-effective rate (per 1,000 strength), Southwest Pacific			
	Disease	Non-battle injury	Battle injury or wound	Total daily admissions per 1,000
Southwest Pacific	46.25	7.23	10.39	63.87
Continental US	27.06	4.24	.01	31.31

Like the Pacific Ocean Area, every move from one island to another required shipping. It was only in late 1944 that there was sufficient shipping to allow major campaigns in both the Pacific Ocean Area and the Southwest Pacific, culminating in the invasion of the Philippines and Okinawa.

The US Army entered combat in the Southwest Pacific on December 8, 1941, with its four prewar regiments stationed in the Philippines. Between that date and September 1945, there were nine campaigns that the US Army infantry fought in the SWPA, from the fall of the Philippine Islands through the recapture of the Southern Philippines in 1945. There were 513 regimental months of combat in the SWPA of the 1,271 total regimental months in theater on Guadalcanal, New Guinea, New Georgia, New Britain, and in the Philippines and other islands. Although regiments entering combat in 1942 were untrained in jungle warfare, they learned to combat the Japanese the hard way – by fighting them. However, by October 1944, divisions and regiments invading the Philippine Islands had the measure of their Japanese opponent, having either learned through combat or, if new to theater, through extensive pre-combat training in Hawaii, Guadalcanal, and New Guinea, utilizing lessons learned from other units.

The incidence of disease in the SWPA was highest of all theaters. For every soldier felled through combat, more than five others were stricken with disease or non-battle injuries, compared to the average daily casualty rate for the worldwide US Army of one battle casualty for every four and one half rendered ineffective through disease or non-battle injury.[1]

THE 382D INFANTRY

The 382d US Infantry is the regiment into which our composite soldier was assigned in August 1944. Constituted in 1918 in the NA and later in the OR as a prewar component of the 96th Division, its headquarters was in Medford, Oregon. In 1942, the 382d received orders calling it to active military service and reorganized at Camp Adair, Oregon. The regiment trained for a year and then participated in maneuvers in the Oregon maneuver area in 1943 and participated in the IV Corps Oregon Maneuvers later in the year. In 1944, the 382d underwent amphibious training at Camp Luis Obispo and went from there to Camp Stoneman and the San Francisco Port of Embarkation.

It sailed on July 22 to the Hawaiian Islands, arrived on Oahu on July 28 and continued training there until September 13, 1944 when, along with the other regiments of the 96th, it departed the

Hawaiian Islands for its first combat, which came when it landed in the initial waves onto Leyte Island in the Philippines. The 382d earned two campaign streamers for its work on Leyte and for Okinawa. At war's end, the regiment was on Palawan Island rehabilitating and preparing for the invasion of Japan. In February 1946, the 382d returned to the US where it inactivated on February 3, 44 months after activation and 17 months after shipping overseas.[2]

GORDON'S STORY

Gordon Cockrell was born in December 1920 in Los Angeles, California. He was an only child and had graduated high school in 1939. He had enrolled in university after high school and was in his sophomore year when the Japanese struck Pearl Harbor. When Gordon was drafted in late July 1942 he became one of 421,462 soldiers drafted from California, which during World War II supplied 24 percent of its total male population to the different services.[3]

Induction, reception, and service in the 89th Division, 1942–44

Gordon was preparing to go home on Christmas break when he learned of the Japanese attack on Pearl Harbor. He had not yet registered for the draft since he was below the age of 21, and was called to register during the third registration call in February 1942, which enrolled all males aged 20 to 44 for selective service who had not previously done so. In June he received his draft notification that read "Greeting: Having submitted yourself to a local board composed of your neighbors for the purpose of determining your availability for training and service in the land or naval forces of the US, you are hereby notified that you have now been selected for training and service therein." In July 1942, Gordon was one of 270,391 men drafted that month.[4]

After processing through the reception station, Gordon and other new recruits found themselves assigned to the newly activated 89th Infantry Division forming at Camp Carson, Colorado. On the road to the camp they drove through barren desert, meadows of hay, softly rolling grass-covered hills, and as they got off the train, he noticed the Cheyenne Mountains towering high over the camp. For the first few days until their permanent barracks were completed they lived in tents and practiced learning to be a soldier while waiting for other train loads of recruits to arrive and the individual phase of their training to begin. Over time, Gordon found that the division cadre came from the RA 6th Infantry Division.

The first 13 weeks of Gordon's training were devoted to basic and small-unit training up to battalion. During this training, Gordon put on weight and muscle like the others who arrived thin, while those who had arrived fat and flabby grew lean until everyone

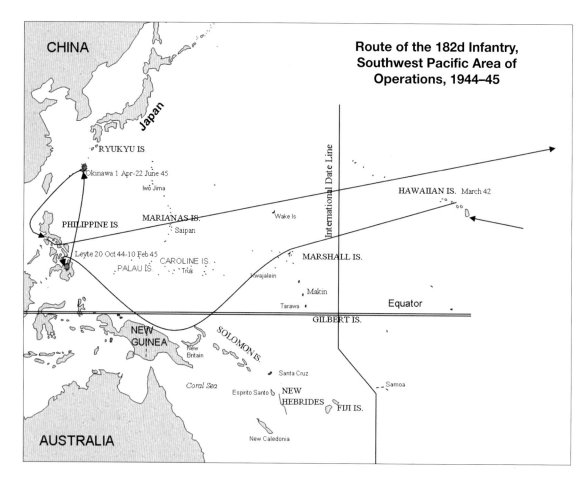

looked pretty much the same. The hard training broke some while it conditioned others, and a steady stream of soldiers returned to civilian life because they could not keep up.

Gordon and the others learned military courtesy, discipline, sanitation, first aid, map reading, individual tactics of the soldier, and drill – much of it by listening to lectures, watching films, and observing practical demonstrations. With their two weeks of basic recruit training completed, they proceeded to the tactical phase designed to teach soldiers to act as part of squads, squads as part of platoons and platoons as part of companies. The young recruits learned basic soldiering skills and then proceeded to practice weapons firing at the end of August. They wore new uniforms but besides their new M1 helmets, carried practically the same field equipment that Gordon's father had had during the earlier Great War. All fired the M1 Garand, although each only had a few rounds to fire. By the end of their training in 1943 though, every infantryman would have fired thousands of rounds.[5]

Weather did not stop the training and the soldiers slogged over the countryside in endless marches day and night. They learned by the John Dewey principle of "learn by doing" and once they had been shown how to do something they practiced it until they got it right:

long days on the rifle range learning how to shoot; how to negotiate obstacle and the dreaded infiltration courses; the technique of pin-pulling and tossing hand grenades; from their squad leaders how to disassemble and assemble their weapons and how to parry and thrust with the bayonet into straw-packed effigies of Hitler and Tojo.[6] Gordon noticed that with the constant repetition even the slow soldiers were learning what it took to be a soldier.

As training progressed men once privates began wearing noncommissioned officers' chevrons, especially with the formation of a cadre from the 89th to be sent to activate the 66th Infantry Division, and Gordon found himself a corporal with less than a year in service. Soldiers within his platoon were always coming and going although most remained. Some including Gordon had volunteered for Officers' Candidate School, and were waiting their class dates while others attended technical schools.

During the last month of the basic period, Gordon's rifle platoon began spending more time in the field training on tactical subjects. They completed their qualification firing on the known distance range, familiarized themselves with other weapons and then began training on the squad problems in attack and defense, and then progressed to squad combat firing. Although Gordon fired well on the known distance qualification range, he like many of the others had problems moving from static firing to firing while maneuvering on the combat courses. In 1943, when they fired again for qualification, they completed a transition course consisting of firing at pop-up silhouettes at varying distances, before going through the squad combat course.

During the combat course, Gordon noticed they were not allowed to maneuver as they had been trained. Instead, umpires and safety officers with their red flags kept the units generally on line instead of allowing them to maneuver as they would on the battlefield, with units advancing in uneven lines. Artillery and mortar fire from the flanks impacted on the objective while they moved forward and they had a seemingly endless supply of ammunition to fire.[7]

Gordon remembered the weather at Camp Carson as pleasant in the fall with warm days and chilly nights to deeper cold as the months progressed, especially in the rugged training areas of Deadman and Rock Creek Canyons. Snow arrived on Christmas Day, his first but not last Christmas season in service. He remembered pulling guard duty during the night of January 20, 1943, when a 75-mile-an-hour (120km) wind storm swept down from the Rockies, smashing some wooden buildings, wearing paint off others as if they'd been sandblasted, uprooting trees, knocking out electricity and starting fires in the prisoner of war compound. The wind and blowing snow seemed to cut right through his layers of uniform and he chilled to the bone. Areas of bare skin appeared sunburned and sensitive to the touch.

At the end of their individual training they took the Mobilization Training Program tests administered by the corps

"GI Party" Soldiers cleaning barracks – rear soldiers sweeping the floor in front of the soldiers working their way back with scrub brushes. The double bunked bed, footlocker and a set of pegs on the wall comprised the GIs domain in these WWII brracks.

headquarters. These tests covered all subjects included in the 13-week program of individual training. Not every platoon tested on all subjects but each tested on several. Gordon's platoon took the physical fitness test, the squad tactical proficiency test and the individual skills hands-on test.[8]

Unit training

The next phase involved unit training that progressed from squad to regiment. Much was the same to Gordon as he and the others had already been operating at squad level. To him and others in squads it appeared to be the same thing: march, obey their sergeants when moving tactically, and fire their weapons. Until he was a leader, he really was not so concerned about how platoons maneuvered together.

Now they seemed to be always in the field under tactical conditions. They spent a minimum of 16 hours night training each week, which included night marches, scouting and patrolling, and establishing night defensive positions. It was not only the night they contended with, but also the snow and mud of winter and spring. Gordon had been cold before, but never for such extended periods of time.

To acclimatize them to the sights, sounds, and sensation of battle and to train them to react appropriately regardless of noise, confusion, and surprise the men went through more advanced training with live ammunition. They first attempted the day infiltration course that began in a trench with everyone watching a demonstration of some of the officers crawling out of a trench and low crawling over the muddy field under barbed wire and through entanglements while dynamite charges exploded, sending geysers of dirt and mud onto them and fixed M1917A1 water-cooled machine guns fired streams of bullets 30in. (760mm) above their heads. When it was Gordon's group's turn, the muddy captain told

Soldier stands at attention while a lieutenant in Class A uniform "pinks and greens" examines his equipment layout.

them with a grin that it was not hard, all they had to do to get to the other side was keep low, not freeze, and keep crawling forward. Then they got to do it at night under tracer fire.

Next was the close-combat firing course, conducted over a large area with rough terrain interspersed with wire obstacles. This time Gordon and the others got to shoot back at the silhouette targets that would pop up unexpectedly at ranges from five to 50 yards (4½m). Since every target was timed they had to be fast and accurate in engaging it. And again, there were soldiers throwing dynamite to keep those on the course on their toes. Neither Gordon nor the other soldiers minded this type of exciting training and yearned to do more of it.

Lastly, they fought their way through Beauclair, a replica of a French village of six square blocks, that contained hotels, stores, banks, shops, residences, outbuildings, trees and shrubs. The map even showed a cemetery, which when they crossed through it Gordon noticed had names of late residents inscribed on the tombstones as well as the name Hitler, Hirohito, and Mussolini. Again there were pulley-controlled dummies, appearing in windows, on stairways or jumping from closets. For the first time Gordon experienced the zip of rifle rounds passing nearby whenever he spent too much time in the open. They had been told that specially trained snipers would be firing ball ammunition over them if they got too careless.

Some of the soldiers who were older than 38 who had job offers in critical wartime industry went home in February 1943 – their places taken by soldiers of 19 and 20 who had just graduated from RTCs. Others left to go back to university under the Army Specialized Training Program (ASTP) where soldiers with high intelligence went through accelerated engineering, medical or foreign language training. Gordon was tempted to do the same, however he was still waiting for confirmation of his class date to Officers' Candidate School.

Mock village – soldiers practice Combat in Cities.

In April, they went through chemical training, learning the smell of tear gas and traversing an area filled with live mustard gas. Gordon also had the "opportunity" of digging a foxhole, being handed two dummy grenades and then having a light tank run over his position while he cowered deep inside waiting for it to pass. Once the tank had crossed, he stood up and threw the grenades on its back deck.

The next month, Gordon's platoon completed the Platoon Combat Firing Proficiency Tests which were much like the squad tests except now the platoon leader had to maneuver the three squads. Next up were the infantry battalion field exercises and combat tests, after which they moved to the field for regimental force-on-force maneuvers.[9]

Combined training

Twelve weeks of combined-arms training followed that included regimental and division maneuvers. Gordon found that now they had a field artillery battalion, engineer company and a medical company supporting them, making his regiment a combat team. The exercises comprised both night and day operations and included an assault on a fortified position that included replicas of pillboxes. Gordon found it interesting to watch the little L-3 "Grasshopper" observation aircraft direct artillery fire onto targets, and occasionally air corps conducted bombing runs with bags of flour while everyone engaged them with blank small arms fire.

They moved to the field in June for three weeks to finish the combined training phase. Gordon and the others welcomed the change from the barren terrain of Camp Carson – an area where they knew every nook and cranny. The grassy ridges they were now training on with trout-filled streams nearby were something

Massed weapons fire power demonstration. BARs and M1917A1 water cooled machine guns in the first rank and M1 firing riflemen in the second and third.

to behold. The days grew warmer but there was still a chill in the air at night. They began learning to cope with water rationing by living on one quart (0.95l) of water per day during training, so that by the hot summer they would not have problems on the long road marches.

During the first three exercises one infantry battalion represented the Red force. Corps umpires used flags to indicate the presence and firepower of hostile troops, artillery fire impacting, bombed-out bridges, and other activities. The flags and simulated enemy troops were not very realistic to Gordon or the other soldiers at squad level, and the soldiers were pretty lackadaisical in performing the different missions, but they saw the umpires and controllers frequently taking notes. As a result, instead of resting after the exercise ended they went back over the ground and corrected the faults reported by the umpires. When not training, they were maintaining their equipment or retraining and correcting those tasks incorrectly executed.

It was different when they went regiment against regiment during what was termed the "D" Series, a series of six problems that pitted the three regiments against one another in small-scale maneuvers. Here it was a matter of pride as to which unit was best. Their combined-arms training ended with infantry field exercise tests and infantry battalion combat firing tests. A cadre of officers and noncommissioned officers from the corps evaluated both tests. When Gordon's battalion went through the Infantry Battalion Combat Firing Test, they attacked a defensive position that had been prepared by another battalion, and when they finished they prepared the position for the next battalion.

Gordon learned, in mid-July 1943, that his division was reorganizing into a light division. At the time he had no idea what this meant, except that they were going to be "Truck", and after the countless 25-mile (40km) marches with full field equipment in eight hours it seemed they would finally be riding.[10]

In August once they had certified as a combat ready division, the 89th Infantry Division reorganized as one of three light divisions. With the change, Gordon's regiment contracted from 19 to 13 companies, with each battalion now consisting of a headquarters and three rifle companies. Each battalion now had 250 fewer soldiers due to the elimination of the heavy weapons company and some soldiers from each rifle company; although Gordon's rifle squad and platoon did not lose any strength. Gordon watched those soldiers now surplus, pack their duffle bags to join either the 71st Light (Pack) Division forming at Camp Carson, or the 10th Light (Mountain) Division, stationed at Camp Hale, Colorado.

Gordon's dreams of riding quickly disappeared. Although the division carried the title "Truck" in its designation, Gordon saw it drop from 1,400 trucks, weapons carriers, and jeeps to 267 jeeps and 207 quarter-ton trailers. Battalions lost all of their motorized vehicles; replaced by the soon-to-be-hated handcart – not easy to pull loaded over gently rolling terrain, and a nightmare when traversing rough terrain or mud.

There were many lessons learned coming in from the combat theaters, with many being incorporated into their training. They practiced mine removal, and concentrated on tasks that emphasized small unit leadership such as scouting and patrolling, night fighting, infiltration, and physical conditioning. Some soldiers who had served overseas in combat were now also serving as instructors.

For what they termed postgraduate training, each squad negotiated a combat course that offered the nearest thing to realistic battle conditions and, as when they fought through the village of Beauclair, there were snipers firing live ammunition when they failed to take advantage of cover and concealment. The medics also ran the course carrying litters with simulated casualties. With the rounds zinging nearby, everyone's adrenaline was pumping fast as they crossed the open areas going to the next covered position. There were many near misses. Gordon learned of a medic who, while carrying a litter patient on the open ground between cover, had a bullet rip through his sleeve, lightly wound his arm and rip off his chevron.[11]

With so few vehicles most movement was on foot with full field pack and the men taking turns pulling the handcarts. Even though many soldiers had survived a year as infantrymen, many of those either injured in training or who were physically broken had to leave the unit, and almost 20 percent of the division, not counting those earlier departed for the other light units, were reclassified as limited service and assigned within Service Command units by November 1943.

In November 1943, Gordon's division departed Colorado for maneuvers in the sunny south. They arrived at their bivouac site near Alexandria, Louisiana, just before Thanksgiving and the company messes served turkey with all the trimmings. After that

Soldiers pulling the "damned" handcarts in Colorado.

day, soldiers quickly learned not to leave food in their pup tents or even at ground level. The wild boar living in the area marauded through the camps in large herds, rooting through the garbage and tents. Gordon ruefully thought that this was the perfect opportunity for some rifle firing practice if he had had the ammunition.

The first exercises were again of the flag variety but at the division level, and as before there were some problems. Gordon heard soldiers from other units commenting on the "pushcart outfit" with some awe. However, others thought that the light division was a "light duty division" and many soldiers arrived from hospital without adequate clothing or equipment and their records showed they were in the wrong assignment. When asked they told the story, "The docs said we had to go on light duty for six months, so they assigned us to a light division."

In mid December they began the two-sided phase of the maneuvers with the 89th Light and 9th Armored Division on one side and the 86th and 97th Divisions on the other. As the problem progressed, the weather grew steadily worse and Gordon and the other infantrymen found that they could not walk fast enough or far enough to keep up and when they did, with their handcarts mired in the mud, their supplies did not.

By the time they broke for Christmas, Gordon was dirty and tired, his face smudged from the pitch-pine campfires they lit whenever they could. However, no sooner had they pitched their pup tents than the rain began, froze over night and turned to ice. The unsurfaced roads turned to Louisiana gumbo and any type of vehicular movement was difficult. The companies resorted to sending carrying parties back to pick up the Christmas meal and they drank the rainwater. Worse of all, the mail did not arrive.

Soldiers in full field equipment including M1928 haversack and shovel boarding a train for maneuvers.

After their ordeal in the mud, the soldiers wearily stood formation in a downpour to hear their commander read a commendation from the division commander that said in part, "Vehicles were pulled out, and pulled out again. I cannot commend you too highly for the spirit that you all showed. We should have a feeling of pride and confidence in the future based on this experience. We know now that we can take anything which either God or man can send against us."

The next problems were just as bad, with snow and sleet covering the trees and turning the ground into a morass. Gordon was so tired of picking up and putting down his galoshes in the mud that his mind seemed to go numb. It was only later that he learned they had marched 20 miles (32km) through the mud in one day; taking far longer than normal. For their sixth and last exercise they conducted an assault across the Sabine River which all of the umpires said was the most effective in the history of the maneuver area. Everyone was happy when the series of exercises ended and when they began convoying to Camp Polk for rest and refitting.

Gordon was promoted sergeant during the maneuvers in Louisiana. In January, he received his orders for Officers' Candidate School at Fort Benning, Georgia, and a two-week furlough home, while his unit packed up for more force-on-force maneuvers at Hunter Liggett Military Reservation in California.[12]

Officers' Candidate School

Gordon arrived at the officer candidate reception station at Fort Benning, Georgia, in late January, 1944. There he received another physical and the Basic Education Test that covered reading, grammar, spelling, geography, and mathematics. Although it was a mental requirement to score a minimum of 110 on the AGCT, a specific level of education was not required, and many soldiers although intelligent were academically deficient. No one left for failing the test; it was just an indicator of the problems they might have during the course. With preliminaries completed the commandant briefed them on the coming 17 weeks. Everything they would learn focused on making them into successful infantry platoon leaders, with most of the time devoted to basic infantry weapons and the tactics of the rifle platoon and company. He left them with the principal question they would ask themselves and each other, "Would I be willing to follow this man in battle?"

Gordon and the others were evaluated not only by their grades in class, but were continually monitored by their tactical officers for leadership in class and while performing in different leadership positions in garrison and in the field. The candidates rotated weekly through the duties of company commander, executive, platoon leader, and so on, down to assistant squad leader. He felt fortunate that as an NCO he had had to conduct drill and physical training for his soldiers because how he presented himself in front of his peers and his cadre was also evaluated. Lastly were the peer reviews that he had to make on his classmates and they had to make on him. Of the three principal ratings made on each man, the academic, the tactical officer's, and fellow candidate's rating, Gordon found the last two were the most important because they reflected his leadership ability. A man with high leadership ability would probably be commissioned, while one whose grades were high but who lacked leadership probably would not.

Besides the academic and leadership positions, the tactical officers assessed penalties for even minute errors; much more rigorous than anyone would impose upon their soldiers. Gordon was called aside by his tactical officer during the second week after he had failed to ensure there was a 1in. (25mm) spacing between his uniforms in his wall locker. Braced against the wall, standing as straight as possible, chest out, shoulders back, chin in while he listened to his tactical officer tell him: "Mr Cockrell, you are intelligent. That is why you are here. You are inattentive to duty and that must cease. Use your intelligence. Any questions? That's all, dismissed." NCOs had yelled at Gordon before; however, no one had ever reduced him as had this officer.

Gordon and the others had to sweat through three screenings of their capabilities and capacity to be an officer. The first occurred during their sixth week of training and eliminated those candidates who were failing academically or lacked aptitude for the work at hand. The second was during the 12th week when all those put on probation the first time were reevaluated and those failing academically eliminated, as well as those who lacked leadership aptitude. The last board was during their last week. Those on the cusp of success or failure received their decision and qualified candidates their recommendation for commission. Gordon had problems sleeping the nights before the postings of results; although more than once he had resigned himself to being an enlisted man again, and in fact early on with the intense scrutiny he was under had thought about being a sergeant again. His doubts and fears were needless and on completion of Officers' Candidate School, Gordon received the gold bars of a second lieutenant and swore the following oath:

> *I Gordon Cockrell, having been appointed a second lieutenant in the Army of the United States, do solemnly swear (or affirm) that I will support and defend the Constitution of the United States against all enemies, foreign and domestic; that I will bear true faith and allegiance to the same; that I take this obligation freely, without any mental reservation or purpose of evasion, and that I will well and faithfully discharge the duties of the office upon which I am about to enter. So help me God.*

With his new gold bars, Gordon saw his pay increase from $78.00 as a sergeant to $150.00 base pay and $21.00 subsistence allowance as a second lieutenant. He received a one-time sum of $250 to purchase his officer uniforms and accoutrements. Thankfully, the supply room of the company he would be assigned to provided most of his field equipment.[13]

Joining the 96th Infantry Division

Upon his graduation from OCS, Lieutenant Cockrell received orders assigning him to the 96th Infantry Division, and after a two-week furlough joined the 382d Regiment, 96th Division along with three other officers. He arrived in his regiment while it was undergoing the final phases of advanced amphibious training at San Luis Obispo, California. During in-processing, he found that the division's sobriquet was "Deadeye" and later learned the story behind it. In earlier years the assistant division commander had served on the US Army rifle team and while the division was in training he spent hours on the rifle ranges training and insisting that soldiers be satisfied with nothing less than bull's eyes.

His new regiment and the 96th Division had been activated just one month after his old division the 89th. It had gone through the same training and exercises as the 89th except its maneuvers had been in Oregon and, instead of becoming a light division, it was designated an amphibious division. Moreover, like in the 89th, soldiers unable to keep up had been weeded out, their place taken by high quality soldiers from the now defunct Army Specialized Training Program (ASTP) college program. All they needed was rebluing as infantry soldiers.

Officer candidate observed by tactical officers, displays perfect form during bayonet practice.

The battalion adjutant assigned Gordon as a rifle platoon leader after interviewing with the 2d Battalion Commander. He now had the responsibility for a platoon of 41 infantrymen, a responsibility that weighed above that of his own safety or well-being, and one that he took very seriously. He did not want to let his men down, and worked hard to gain their trust.

When amphibious training ended in mid-July, Gordon's division made the move to Camp Beale, California, where they prepared for overseas movement. Events moved rapidly, and instead of the normal three weeks to pack out it only took nine days. Packing completed, Gordon Cockrell found that practically everyone was going on furlough, and having just finished one, found himself staying behind. Although not announced, every man knew this would be his last time home before shipping overseas.

On July 18, they moved to Camp Stoneman for the final five days before they shipped overseas. From that point passes were cancelled, officers began censoring mail, and the long-distance calls from the telephone building were monitored. The company commander assigned Gordon, as the company's junior officer, those details no other officer wanted; one of them was to censor the enlisted soldiers' mail home. Whenever the enlisted man made any comments pertaining to military activities he underlined it and sent it back to him for correction. If the soldier did not make the correction, Gordon blotted the words out. Sometimes it seemed his men took a perverse pride in writing to embarrass him; at other times, they were upset that he was reading their mail.

In mid-September, the regimental headquarters passed out an officers roster listing every officer in the regiment. Gordon found that of the line officers there were eight RA officers including the regimental commander and two of the lieutenant colonels; 29 officers commissioned through the officers' reserve corps with most in the rank of captain but with two as lieutenant-colonel battalion commanders. The remaining officers were OCS graduates (AUS) like him, comprising the vast majority of lieutenants within the regiment; although there was one AUS major and 13 captains, with three commanding rifle companies. Gordon's company commander was OR as was the other second lieutenant. The three first lieutenants were AUS, as was he.[14]

On July 21, they boarded the old river steamer *Delta Queen* that ferried soldiers between Camp Stoneman and San Francisco harbor. A band played on the pier as they climbed aboard the steamer and it slipped out into the harbor. Every boat they passed blew a farewell salute to the soldiers massed on the deck. They were not in San Francisco for long. Gordon listened to the roar of traffic on the bridge that spanned the bay directly above him as they debarked from the steamer and walked down the pier towards their transport ship. Red Cross workers passed out coffee and donuts while everyone formed for the final muster. As the first sergeant called each soldier's name, he shouldered his weapon, picked up his barracks bag and climbed the gangplank onto the USAT *Sea Sturgeon*. Early the next day the ship raised anchor and headed west into the Pacific. It was only at sea that they learned they were heading for the Hawaiian Islands.

On the voyage to Hawaii, the junior officers were bunked six to a room. His billet was above decks, but as one of the battalion's most junior officers his commander assigned him to conduct daily inspections of the soldiers' living conditions in the troop compartments below decks. Cramped as they were, with no opportunity for the men to shower and with little fresh air, the living area smelled worse than any locker room he had ever used. Like many of the other officers he felt uneasy eating in the officers' mess on plates, while his men stood in what seemed a continual line with their mess kits for the two meals they received each day.

After six days at sea, they reached Honolulu and once debarked, loaded onto flatcars of the Oahu Railroad, and took the slow train past Pearl Harbor, through pineapple and sugar fields to the massive brick quadrangles of Schofield Barracks. Gordon quickly gathered that the wooden huts on the edge of a large pineapple field were to be their homes while they trained in Hawaii.[15]

In Hawaii for just over a month, division, regiment, and battalion headquarters engaged in planning the coming invasion while the platoons refined their small unit tactics, using the most up-to-date information they had from the combat zone. They learned Japanese camouflage techniques and practiced throwing live hand grenades into bunkers. Everyone fired their weapons on the different ranges, including a new one that had them walking a combat course engaging Japanese cardboard-silhouette targets that popped up from spider holes, from behind trees, and from trenches. Gordon really enjoyed the weapons courses, until one day his commander pulled him aside and said, "Lieutenant, I really like your enthusiasm; however, remember if you are shooting, then you are not commanding."

They also went through the Green Valley Jungle Training Course where as individuals they learned jungle survival, which meant learning to eat off the land and how to build a lean-to from palm fronds. At squad level, the soldiers learned to cross tropical streams with their equipment wrapped in field expedient rafts made from their shelter halves, and to conduct day and night patrols through the thick jungle. Gordon heard more than once sarcastic comments from his men on how they had trained hard in the Oregon desert to wind up fighting in jungles. On another day, the soldiers received paint with which to camouflage their helmets.

Although security was tight, by the end of August the latrine scuttlebutt had them assaulting the island of Yap, however no one confirmed it. Everyone knew that they would fight alongside the 7th Infantry Division, veterans of Attu and Kwajalein and the division that had cadred the 96th Infantry Division, as part of the newly formed XXIV Corps. On August 21, the soldiers began combat loading the ships with the equipment and ammunition for the lead waves going on top. The assault elements of Gordon's battalion climbed aboard the USS *Warhawk* at the end of August for final invasion rehearsals. Afterwards, during the battalion commander's exercise review, Gordon found that the exercise did not go as well as it should have, with troops being landed at different beaches away from their equipment, several landing craft sunk, and communications gear breaking down. He was glad that as a platoon leader he was only responsible for the functioning of his platoon and did not have to be overly worried about the grand scheme of things.

The rehearsal complete, the ships sailed back into harbor and the soldiers finished the final details before departure into the combat zone. Gordon conducted inspections of his soldiers' clothing and equipment: what they would carry aboard; combat gear and a barracks bag; and what would be stowed in the hold, their duffle bags with the clothing and equipment they did not need, and would not see for months. On September 15, with the 2d Battalion aboard, the *Warhawk* sailed in convoy from Hawaii en route to Eniwetok. Once under way the commanders gathered the officers to brief them on the upcoming invasion of the island of Yap, and then instructed them to brief their men. Days later at Eniwetok, Gordon learned the Yap operation was cancelled and that they were going to be one of the assault battalions in the invasion of Leyte Island in the Philippines.[16]

First blood, Leyte, October 1944
Japanese aircraft greeted the convoy as they entered Leyte Gulf, but they were driven off by the ships' anti-aircraft fire and escorting fighters. Before they reached anchor, the assault waves transferred

Officer occupation specialties within an Infantry Regiment

Officer MOS	Description	Location
200	Communications Officer	HQ
600	Motor Transport officer	Svc Co
1189	Artillery Observer, Forward	CN Co
1192	Cannon Commander, Infantry	CN Co
1424	Antitank Unit Commander	AT Co
1542	Infantry Unit Commander	Co, Bn and Rgt
1930	Combat Liaison Officer	HQ
2162	S3 Ops and Tng Officer	HQ
2260	S1 Personnel Staff Officer	HQ
2622	Unit Officer Training Center	HQ
2900	HQ Co Commander	RHHC
2901	HQ Commandant	RHQ
2910	Service Co Commander	Svc Co
4010	S4 Sup and Evac Officer	Svc Co
5310	Chaplain	RHQ
9301	S2 Intelligence Staff Officer	HQ
9312	Reconnaissance Officer	HQ

to a Landing Ship Tank (LST) that contained "Alligators" of the 728th Amphibious Tractor Battalion (AMTRAC), and as H-hour approached Gordon led his platoon into the back of one of the AMTRACs. The clamshell bows of the mother ship opened and the vehicle lumbered into the water. They did not know what to expect. Just four months ago the Marines landing on Saipan were hard hit at the water's edge by fierce Japanese resistance. At least the AMTRACs would get them over any reef and drop them on the beach while offering protection from small arms.

The assault wave beached at 0958hrs on October 20, and although the 3d Battalion on their right made heavy contact on Hill 120, all Gordon's battalion had to contend with was harassing fire as the Japanese withdrew. There was little fire as they rolled up and over the beach, everyone exiting the vehicle to the left and right. After a few minutes reorganizing they began the push to the company's first objective. Gordon placed his platoon in a V formation with two squads forward and one back. He had the rear squad examine what appeared to be empty Japanese positions some distance off the beach. A grenade in, an explosion and while one soldier covered, another would jump into the hole with a cocked automatic pistol. The enemy foxholes were 7 to 8ft (2 to 2½m) deep and about 2½ft (0.75m) in diameter with a firing step. Below the firing step was a cavern that held four or five men.

They continued pushing forward and had made about 2,500 yards (2,286m) before settling in for the night. The roads that appeared on the map were really only muddy trails impassable to wheeled vehicles. M29 Weasels and AMTRACs brought supplies part of the way forward but could not cross the numerous streams and waist-deep swamps that hopelessly mired every type of vehicle imaginable. That left resupply up to soldiers and native bearers carrying ammunition forward on their shoulders or on caribou and evacuating wounded by the same method. With supply limited to what they needed most, Gordon and his men lived on the little food and two canteens of water they came ashore with on D-Day, supplemented by whatever else they could find.

They carried ashore an assault ration of candy along with a day's worth of K rations. The candy stuck together in the heat and took too much energy to eat, and the soldiers much preferred the D ration, a 4-ounce (113g) bar of concentrated chocolate. The soldiers liked the ten-in-one ration for its menu, but they usually only got it when they were in reserve, and that was days away. The K-rations were also liked, and they existed on them for days at a time. However, Gordon and the others steadily lost weight because they only ate two of the three meals.

Soldiers practicing climbing down cargo nets during amphibious training.

It rained incessantly, and with the movement through the swamps, the soldiers never dried out. Although there was water everywhere, the high heat and humidity caused heat exhaustion among those not drinking enough water. To supplement what they had in their canteens, Gordon had his men dig seepage pits in the wet ground from which they filled their canteens. He told his NCOs to ensure the men purified the water with halazone tablets regardless of whether the water was clear or cloudy.

With the wetness, Gordon's feet looked like he had just spent days in a bathtub, and his skin sloughed off in his wet socks, leaving ugly patches of raw and dead skin. The only way he could forestall this was by changing his socks frequently, but both of his pairs were soon worn through. His soldiers suffered the same, some to the extent that they had to be evacuated as a non-battle casualty. Many soldiers quit wearing their canvas leggings because of the chafing and wore their fatigue trousers unbloused and rolled up over their combat shoes. As an officer, Gordon felt obliged to wear his leggings, at least until he saw Brigadier-General Easley wearing his trousers rolled over his boots while he rode a caribou.

Outside some short engagements, the Japanese did not seem to want to fight, and did not live up to their reputation of being tenacious defenders as Gordon had been taught about them. There would be short firefights during the daytime, with the Japanese pulling back at night. Gordon was surprised at the elaborate gun positions, foxholes, and pillboxes they abandoned without a fight as they continued their withdrawal towards the foothills west of the town of Dagami.

Gordon quickly learned not to allow his BAR men and attached machine guns to fire tracer ammunition as it gave away their positions, which were then harassed the remainder of the night. He insisted that his men respond to probes with rifles and grenades, and to save the automatic weapons for serious thrusts, and then to fire the final protective fire.[17]

Tabontabon

The Japanese decided to fight at Tabontabon, a town lying astride the Tanauan–Dagami Road and the linchpin to the Japanese defense of the central valley. Gordon's company was last in his battalion's order of movement. They had fought not so much the Japanese as the swamp terrain in their struggle to get there. In position on the opposite side of a small river separating them from the town at about 1200hrs, Gordon heard the first rounds of artillery going in to soften the target. At 1600hrs he watched as the two lead companies forded the shoulder-deep river under a heavy crossfire and entered the town's outskirts. His company soon followed and once across they wheeled right to establish the battalion's right flank. It appeared to Gordon that there were Japanese dug in under every one of the raised houses. With casualties heavy on both sides and night approaching, the Americans pulled back across the river and dug in.

They attacked again the next morning. Gordon heard heavy firing over to his left where the 1st and 3d battalions were fighting their way west along the road leading out of the town, but the big show was in his area. Gordon's company again followed the other two companies as they recrossed the river, and he watched as each of the lead companies began slowly working their way down the streets, while his company again secured the battalion's right flank. However not for long.

Gordon received the call to take his platoon to assist George Company and was told that the remainder of the company would soon follow. As he had suspected, there were Japanese snipers and machine guns in and under every house and the streets were honeycombed with trenches that connected one strong point to another. With them went a platoon of Cannon Company with their self-propelled M7 Priests to act as assault guns in rooting out the Japanese with direct fire from their 105mm (4.1in.) howitzers. However, on this day they were ineffective as the Americans and Japanese were so intermingled that they could not get good shots at the Japanese positions. Gordon's company could not break free

The 382d Infantry's fight at Tabontabon

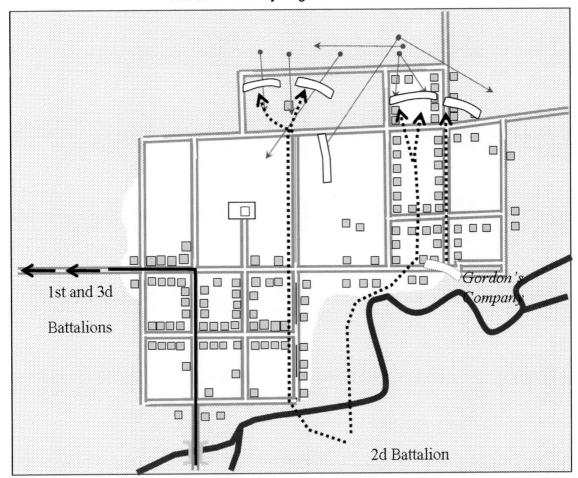

of the town as every exit was covered. The Japanese had machine gun-fire directed down each of the north-south streets, with others placed in mutually supporting positions so they could not be outflanked.

Unable to clear the town by nightfall, the battalion fell back into the middle of the town and set up a night defensive perimeter. Bugles sounded during the night and small groups of Japanese attacked the perimeter by Gordon's platoon, as well as in other locations. The fight was short and one-sided, with many of the Japanese dying under the flash of machine guns and rifles. When it was dark again, Gordon heard the foe dragging the dead and wounded away from the battlefield.

After that short night, his company led the attack into the northwest quadrant of Tabontabon, with his platoon leading the company. Three tanks, one a flamethrower tank, accompanied them. They had gone about four blocks when a Japanese soldier ran from one of the buildings carrying an antitank mine. Although everyone was firing at him, he managed to place the mine between

the first tank's road wheels and tread before dying. The resulting explosion tore off the tread and disabled the tank in the middle of the street. Gordon found his platoon pinned down by enemy machine guns at the same time and, although he tried, he could not get his men back. He saw one of his squad leaders go down and then the two men who had raced to pull him back under cover were also hit. Gordon hoped that the squads he could not see were faring better.

The entire company was being hit hard and Gordon watched in amazement as his company commander ran to one of the still running tanks and while standing in the open had them maneuver so as to engage the enemy machine gun position. Then there appeared an American running toward them from the direction the tank guns were pointed and beckoning for them not to fire, but it was too late. After a few rounds, the company commander was beating on the turret and the tanks stopped firing. Gordon saw his battalion commander emerge from cover near where they had been concentrating their fire. His group had come in through another direction and had inadvertently gotten in front of Gordon's company.

During the mid-afternoon soldiers arrived from their sister company and joined with the tanks. As the armored vehicles slowly advanced, the riflemen of both companies walked alongside them

Debarking from an Amphibious Tractor (AMTRAC) during the assault on Leyte Island.

keeping the Japanese suiciders away from the tanks, while the tanks blasted each machine gun position in turn. Even as they moved forward, infantrymen fell killed and wounded. The many casualties were brought back to the battalion aid station about two blocks behind the fighting. Gordon's company supply sergeant kept running his jeep up and down the road to the front lines, bringing ammunition forward and the wounded back.

One of Gordon's messengers motioned to him and pointed to a group of GIs making their way up the street that had caused them so much consternation. Unlike the morning there was no fire and the group got as far as the disabled tank before being fired upon. This group began driving the Japanese out of the positions that had held up Gordon's platoon. He could sense the Japanese were losing heart, and becoming more desperate as the flame tank flushed each group into the open where the riflemen picked them off.

By 1700hrs it was over and Gordon's company and another one set up a defensive perimeter along the outskirts of the town, with the weapons and headquarters company in the town itself. The next day, when they resumed the attack, there was very little opposition. The Japanese had departed, leaving more than 360 dead outside the town. During the three days of combat the 2d Battalion lost 34 killed and 80 wounded, however, the last heavily defended Japanese strongpoint within the Corps beachhead zone was eliminated. Gordon's unit proceeded north up the road to Kiling where they made contact with the 3d Battalion, 381st Infantry. They captured Kiling the day after Tabontabon and were

Comrades pull a heavily laden soldier from the muck during the crossing of the swamp just off the Red Beach.

Soldiers cautiously move forward. One soldier scans for snipers while the other creeps forward.

amazed at the size of the supply dumps that included all classes of supplies, including rice, sugar, gasoline, sewing machines, phonographs, radios, tires, and dynamite, not counting the small arms and ammunition.[18]

Gordon found out that the Corps beachhead line for the 382d was secured on October 30; but he had no way of knowing when that was, as each day seemed to merge into the last, and he had a hard time remembering incidents occurring much more than 12 hours previous. There was no rest for the weary and Gordon with his and other platoons from other companies had to go back into the swamp to recover the vehicles mired during the first days of the operation.

In 31 days of continuous combat Gordon's 382d Infantry Regiment had fought elements of the 16th Japanese Infantry Division and its 9th, 20th, and 33d Infantry Regiments, and killed 4,353 Japanese while sustaining 785 battle casualties, of which

236 were killed or missing. This equated to about 75 battle casualties of all types in each rifle company, assuming they sustained 85 percent of the regiment's casualties; however, this does not list those evacuated for non-battle injuries or sickness, such as battle fatigue, malaria, dysentery, etc. Gordon's platoon, like most others, numbered in the high teens. He only hoped that those lightly wounded and injured would return soon.

Almost a month later Gordon's company was patrolling west of Mount Cauncajunag searching for Japanese stragglers hiding in the bush. During this mop-up phase, he found that many of the Japanese they killed were in poor condition, having existed on coconuts and sweet potatoes and whatever else they could steal. Many had no weapons, but would not allow themselves to be captured unless too feeble to resist. From all appearances it seemed to Gordon that the Japanese had broken their units into small groups fending for themselves from the very outset of the campaign in the hills. However, once broken they were unable to reestablish themselves into cohesive platoon size or larger units. As casualties mounted the men were left to shift for themselves with many of the wounded dying for lack of care.

Infantrymen recently returned from combat in the Philippines stand formation under the palm trees with their pup tents in the background.

Soldiers engage Japanese in a Leyte village.

Gordon's regiment moved to Buri on December 9 to defend against the Japanese airborne assault against the near Burauen and on December 19, they again moved into the mountainous area near Cabang to hunt for the remaining Japanese in the area. On Christmas Day 1944, General MacArthur declared Leyte secure.

Gordon and many of the others did not believe the vaunted Japanese 16th Infantry Division lived up to its reputation and they thought the Japanese on Leyte Island were second class fighters. The enemy's tactics in the hills and dense jungles were far below the standard that other Japanese units had set in past campaigns. During nighttime, the enemy did not attempt to maintain contact with the US front lines and usually he pulled out of his prepared positions during the night, leaving fully operational artillery pieces and ammunition to be captured by the Americans.

Even with the uneven resistance, there were lessons to be learned. Once, Japanese machine gun fire pinned the company down for several hours, and it was only by the maneuver of another company that they were able to withdraw without too many casualties. From this experience they learned as they had in training that they needed to send scouts forward to reconnoiter so the larger element did not walk into an ambush. A bit different from what they learned during their training in the States was that, at least in the Philippines, a long skirmish line was the best technique when advancing against unknown opposition. Whenever a Japanese position began firing, it was relatively easy to assault it since the line

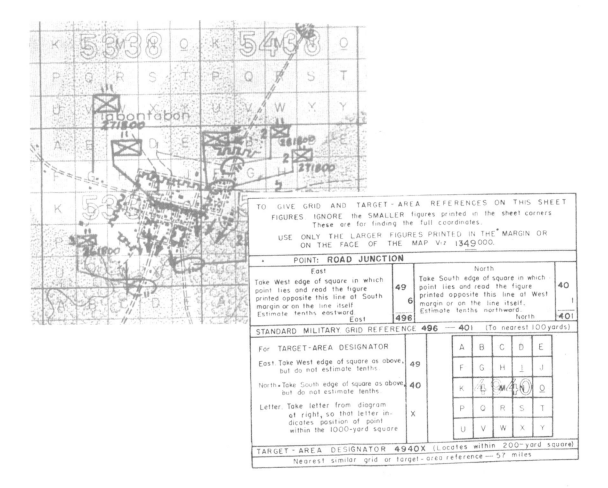

1944 Tactical Map of Tabontabon and an explanation of the grid system located thereon.

usually overlapped the position on both flanks. Most of the Japanese machine guns fired fixed lanes of fire between 4in. and 1ft off the ground, and it was a simple matter to take the position from the flank. The American soldiers had to be especially careful when trying to rescue wounded or recover dead because the Japanese were good at converging their fires to cut down the would-be rescuers.

They also better understood the capabilities and limitations of their weapons systems. Everyone thought the M1 Rifle far superior to anything the Japanese had, and believed the BAR was best suited for the type of combat they experienced: lots of firepower, and only one man to operate it. The only problem Gordon's BAR men saw with it was that the bipod kept catching on the jungle vines and there never seemed enough spare parts. The M1 Carbine was weak in knock-down power and when rusted its magazines failed to function properly, and the men hated the Thompson Submachine gun for its jamming at the most inopportune moments, failure to feed and its habit of rusting quickly. The light and heavy machine guns were also thought highly of as long as spare parts were available and they were used for what they were designed. Everyone liked the flamethrower, although few wanted to carry it.

Infantrymen following an M4 Sherman tank during clearing operations on Leyte Island.

This weapon was very effective against Japanese pillboxes, which usually had only one aperture, and was also effective against Japanese hiding in the thick Kunai grass. The naphtha flames set the grass on fire and forced the enemy into the open where they were easy targets for the rifle and BAR men.

Gordon heard of a helicopter evacuation of two seriously wounded soldiers from the mountains. What would have taken 20 to 30 men two or three days of heavy exertion getting them through the rough terrain only took a few hours. He thought this was the wave of the future; however, he had never seen a helicopter or even knew how it operated.

The 2d Battalion was stationed on Samar Island guarding airfields for six weeks beginning in January. It was a nice break: good and plentiful food, a roof over their heads, and sleep without worry. What more could an infantryman ask for? In February, they began training for their next operation. Gordon found the best way to train the few replacements he received was through sending them on patrol with the old hands. Although there was little chance of contact with the enemy, just the sense that they were around did much to heighten their learning curve.[19]

Okinawa

Rumors ran rampant about the upcoming operation, and it was not until March 6 that Gordon learned his unit's next objective was the island of Okinawa. Between that time and March 13, when they boarded transports, training was hectic with strong emphasis on further developing small unit leaders. Everyone considered that courageous leadership by officers and noncommissioned officers along with the individual soldiers' resourcefulness and initiative were the key to success on the battlefield.

Every company had received about 50 replacements, thankfully including some of those previously wounded on Leyte. However, there were not enough to make up for combat and non-battle casualties suffered during their first combat, so each rifle company had about 155 assigned soldiers, which also included those in hospital and expecting to return. Gordon had heard in passing of the high casualties suffered by the Army fighting in Europe during the Battle of the Bulge but that was in another world far away. With his squads averaging between nine and ten instead of the authorized 12, his major concern was that his platoon was going into combat understrength.[20]

The 382d Infantry landed behind the assault regiments on April 1 and remained in reserve until April 3 when they passed through the 383d Regiment for their first attack. From that day forward Gordon and his soldiers experienced nothing like what they had encountered on Leyte. Here the Japanese were fighting a battle of attrition from well-designed defenses. Riflemen and machine gunners occupied the forward slopes, pulling back to prepared positions on the reverse slope during bombardments and then reoccupying when they were over. When forced from the forward slope they fought from the crest of the ridges, and when forced from the ridge tops, fought a tenacious reverse slope defense. In this campaign, Gordon did not see much of the Japanese on the surface. Instead they were in cleverly camouflaged caves interlocked with pillboxes and communications trenches.[21]

The advance through the series of ridges took a toll on all. Casualties were heavy, especially among the leadership. His company commander and several of the company officers were killed or wounded as were many of the noncommissioned officers, with Japanese artillery causing many of the casualties. The attacks themselves resembled a chess match. The scouts moved forward to draw fire. Once the Japanese had disclosed their position, Gordon would then maneuver his platoon to eliminate it. Usually though, the route to the objective was covered by machine gun and 47mm (1.85in.) fire located on another hill, so to take out the first meant coordinating for someone else to take out the flanking fire. At night, there was no rest and the next day they began again.

On the 12th day of the campaign, while waiting for the artillery to soften up Tombstone Ridge, Gordon's company commander told him to destroy one of the caves they had bypassed earlier. The cave was dug into the solid coral wall of a 100ft (30m) escarpment, with two of its entrances, each protected by a coral parapet, at the base of the cliff about 50ft (15m) apart. Two other smaller holes were above the bottom entrances and two more holes dug into the sheer wall of the cliff; much smaller and about the size of a firing port, they were offset a bit from the others. A pair of pillboxes at the top of the escarpment overlooked the valley. The front of the cave was covered with large coral knobs and the left edge of the cave concealed by brush.

Gordon's platoon numbered 17, with many of the casualties among his NCOs. Now, instead of three squads of 12, he had reorganized his men into one squad of seven and one of eight, with

81mm mortar squad firing in close support of infantrymen fighting on Okinawa. The high trajectory of the mortar's round's enabled it to engage Japanese on the reverse slope of the ridges where field artillery with its lower trajectory could not.

him and his messenger with whichever squad he designated as the lead squad. The seven-man squad consisted of a two-man BAR team, a two-man bazooka team carrying nine rounds, one man carrying the flamethrower and two men carrying satchel charges. The eight-man squad was organized into two two-man BAR teams, with the remaining four men each carrying a satchel charge. Each man also carried four fragmentation and one white phosphorous grenade and two bandoleers of ammunition. The squad leader carried a rifle grenade launcher.

Gordon planned to assault the cave from below and from its right side. One of the artillery rounds in the preparatory concentration hit one of the cave openings high up on the cliff, but after the dust had settled Japanese riflemen continued to fire from it. As his men moved forward, they encountered rifle fire and grenades being thrown out of the upper entrances and from the top of the cliff. Pausing behind coral, Gordon talked by radio with his company commander, who told him they could see Japanese soldiers running out of one of the exits by the pillboxes. Gordon directed his riflemen to put covering fire on the escarpment to keep those on top from observing where their grenades were landing and ordered his BAR men to neutralize the two high ports. He then popped smoke in front of the cave mouths to screen those within the cave's vision while he and others got close enough to use the bazooka and grenades against the bottom entrances.

The bazooka man fired nine rockets at 20 yards (18m) distance into parapets protecting the cave entrance. Gordon's squad leader then fired fragmentation grenades into the cave mouths. The rifle grenades went deep into the caves before exploding. Next, using white phosphorous grenades they checked for other entrances. The smoke rose within the tunnels and along with the smoke coming out the openings in the top came several coughing Japanese, rapidly dispatched by those infantrymen offering covering fire.

Gordon popped smoke again so that one of his men could get in close enough to throw a satchel charge into the bottom entrance. Its explosion raised a cloud of dust but did little else. Next came the flamethrower. The soldier carrying the torch stood at the mouth of each entrance and fired a two- to three-second burst into them. Next he hosed the holes just above the entrances. The heat and flame forced many of the Japanese out of the cave and a heavy machine gun section on another hill had a field day shooting them as they exited the top. Gordon knew that although neutralized, there were still Japanese within and that they would have to wait until the escarpment was taken. As long as soldiers maintained a watch on the cave, they could wait for the engineers.[22]

Nineteen days into the campaign – and he only knew the exact number of days because one of his soldiers had been notching his rifle – Gordon crossed the line of departure with his platoon at 0640hrs to occupy one of the small, hopefully undefended hills to his front and to the right of Tombstone Hill. Sniper and mortar fire greeted them, but not with the intensity of earlier days. The tanks with them were negotiating the steep turns of the trail going up the hill when a Japanese soldier jumped out of a small cave adjacent to the trail and hit the lead

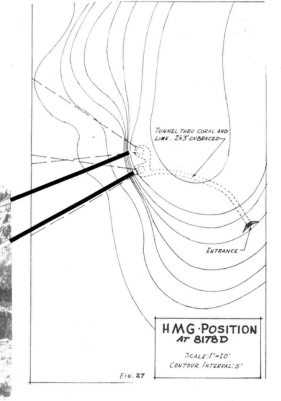

**Japanese Heavy Machine Gun
Position, Kakazu Ridge, Okinawa**

tank with a satchel charge. The resulting explosion tipped the tank onto the cave and worse, blocked the other tanks' passage. Now without tank support, Gordon's men continued forward to the crest of the hill when a salvo of grenades thrown by Japanese on the other side landed amongst them.[23]

Wounded and return home

Gordon saw out of the corner of his eye a Japanese grenade come from out of nowhere. With no time to dive to cover he turned away, curled into a defensive ball and instinctively threw his hand up to protect himself. An explosion, dirt flying, and Gordon felt a sudden feeling of numbness in his left hand and arm. Dazed, he looked at the two fingers that were different from the others, shook his hand and then began walking down the hill. One of his soldiers caught him, wrapped a bandage around his hand and then guided him down to the battalion aid station located about 300 yards (274m) behind the lines. After initial treatment, they put him in a jeep ambulance for the bumpy ride back to the collecting station, where doctors from the attached portable surgical hospital tried to save his fingers. From there he went to a field hospital and then onto a hospital ship bound for the Marianas. Ten days later, he was on another hospital ship bound for San Francisco, and a convalescent hospital in the US.

His first stop was Letterman Army Hospital at Presidio, San Francisco where his wounds were re-evaluated and arrangements were made for his transfer to a hospital nearer to home. Letterman was the nation's busiest hospital during World War II, and its sheer size astounded Gordon. With 100 buildings and 3,500 beds, it was the largest military hospital in the nation and admitted 73,000 patients in 1945 alone. Hospital trains departed daily transporting wounded to hospitals closer to their homes.

Gordon spent his remaining months in the army convalescing and rehabilitating at Hoff Army Hospital in Santa Barbara, near his home of Los Angeles; one that specialized in general and orthopedic surgery. Not only were there medical facilities but bowling alleys, swimming pools, and tennis courts to assist in the

Okinawa, infantrymen attend Mass before re-entering battle.

patients' recreational therapy.[24] During his convalescence he lived in a ward with other officers who had been wounded during fighting in the Pacific and he was transferred to a smaller dormitory while he was rehabilitating. Like many of the other veterans of infantry combat he wore his Combat Infantryman's badge on his hospital gown. In late 1945, Gordon had recovered from the amputation of his two fingers to the greatest extent possible and received his discharge papers.

Now at age 23, Gordon was a disabled war veteran who received a disability pension and who had to decide what to do with the rest of his life. He made up his mind to continue his university education, which had been interrupted by the war. He enrolled in the University of California under the auspices of the Servicemen's Readjustment Act or GI Bill that President Roosevelt had signed in June 1944. "The GI Bill" offered a wide array of benefits to veterans ranging from home loans to educational stipends, in the hope that the veterans would be spared the economic hardships that accompanied the return of those who fought in World War I.

The 382d Infantry Regiment deployed overseas in September 1944, entered combat on October 20 1944, and suffered casualties higher than most other regiments deployed to the Pacific. The average infantry regiment in the Pacific Theater of Operations lost 25 officers and 365 enlisted men killed and 57 officers and 1,091 enlisted wounded. In approximately six months of combat, the 183d Infantry Regiment lost 44 officers and 712 enlisted men killed, one officer and one enlisted man missing or captured, and 115 officers and 2,538 enlisted men wounded on the islands of Leyte and Okinawa. This did not include the many non-battle casualties due to malaria, combat fatigue or other illnesses.

96th Infantry Division casualty being administered plasma on the front line on Okinawa.

The 382d Infantry in its six months of combat lived up to its motto "We Lead", garnering one Distinguished Unit Citation, (the equivalent of the Distinguished Service Cross being awarded to every man in the unit) for is participation as part of the 96th Infantry Division during the Battle of Okinawa. In January 1946 the 382d departed Palawan, Philippine Islands, arriving Los Angeles Harbor on February 2, 1946, and inactivating the next day at Camp Anza, California. Many of the soldiers who sailed to Hawaii in September 1944 were still with the organization when it landed. On arrival in the US soldiers spent a few days processing for discharge and then received their tickets home. The 382d remained inactive until January 10, 1947 when it was reactivated in the OR with Headquarters at Boise, Idaho.[25]

CHAPTER 8

CONCLUSION

The United States entered combat woefully unprepared in December 1941. Units sent overseas during the early days, although relatively well trained, lacked combat experience. Those divisions organized in 1940 and 1941, filled with the first draft class of single men aged 21 and over, carried the war for the United States. Many of the divisions landing on hostile shores in 1944 had been in training for three years. Individual training also improved markedly, and by 1943–44 the individual soldier was far better trained than his counterparts in any other country. Whether training units or soldiers, the Army was profligate with using live ammunition, something other countries could not afford. What became apparent, though, was the longer the war lasted, the better the quality of combat leadership while the poorer the quality of soldier. However, no number of exercises can replicate combat and that was what was needed to produce competent battalion and higher commanders.

THE NATURE OF COMBAT

In every theater infantrymen combated the enemy and their primal environment: the constant rain and mud, and never drying out; the unforgiving hard ground; the heat or the cold; almost indigestible rations; everyone bearded and gray; the dirty, almost rotting feet and unwashed bodies; the unceasing movement forward, and never catching up on the missed sleep of night movement or guard and patrolling. Men passed the point of being tired, and went on only because there was nothing else they could do. Days merged into other days, until dates and days did not matter.

On the front line, there was a reduced military formality, with little difference between officers and men. The social divide was between veterans and replacements; in the rear areas it was different – it became again officer and enlisted men. The veterans were hard and wise in keeping themselves alive and knew they had survived initial combat only because they were lucky. And replacements after a time became just as wizened as the original cadres. Everyone wanted to go home, but they knew that they would not until it was either over or they had been wounded too seriously to continue.

Casualties

The American Infantryman suffered 661,259 of the 936, 259 battle casualties of the US Army in World War II, with the great majority occurring in the European Theater of Operations. The price of success in Northern Europe amounted to 377,858 battle casualties in the 45 Army infantry divisions deployed there. In the 957 months of infantry regiment combat, 74,718 (19.8 percent of total battle casualties) lost their lives. In the Pacific Theaters of Operations in the 20 US Army infantry divisions (including the 1st Cavalry Division but not including Marine divisions) there were 96,034 battle casualties in 660 months of infantry regiment combat with 22,660 killed. The 12 Army infantry divisions deployed in the Mediterranean Theater of Operations suffered 106,131 battle casualties in 446 months of infantry regiment combat with 19,719 men killed.

Replacements

Once entered into heavy combat, organizations remained viable either through receiving replacements to bolster units on the line (European Theater and to some extent the Mediterranean) or by consolidating units as they grew ever smaller (both Pacific Theaters), with such replacements as available arriving normally after the battle was over.

Within the US Army there were different types of replacement systems in the different theaters. In the PTO, units committed to combat were seldom at full strength and only occasionally received replacements while in combat, ensuring that the company steadily fell in strength during combat. Soldiers remained on the company books as long as they were scheduled to return to duty within 60 days, the normal occurrence for those injured or sick. The above was exacerbated by the slow influx of replacements entering theater. The procedure in the MTO was essentially the same,

Soldiers exhausted from combat catching sleep when and where they can.

except that the policy changed to immediate replacement beginning in October 1944. This was not possible in the ETO, where once committed to combat there was little relief for the "dogfaced" soldier. Here a soldier wounded or injured was dropped from the company rolls once he passed beyond the division rear boundary, with a replacement normally assigned within 48 hours, and in November perhaps even before the casualty occurred. Those soldiers healed of their wounds, injury or illness and remaining physically qualified to perform their duties returned to their organization.

Thus, this was the story of the American infantryman in World War II; neither the hero nor the goat, but one who did his duty.

Weary combat infantryman offering C-rations to an Okinawan child.

CHAPTER 9

FORMATIONS AND POSITION SCHEMATICS

PLATOON FORMATIONS
The four basic movement formations for infantry platoons were: Platoon column, which was easy to control and best for movement in woods, through smoke, at night, and through defiles and along trails; Platoon on line, which allowed greatest firepower forward and was usually used during the assault phase of an attack; Platoon "V" with the bulk of the firepower to the front and flanks and balanced movement and control; and the Platoon wedge, which was used when the enemy situation was uncertain and provided a high degree of flexibility and control.

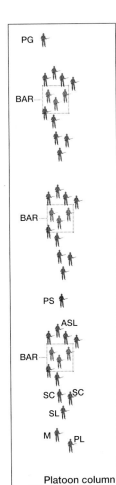

Platoon column

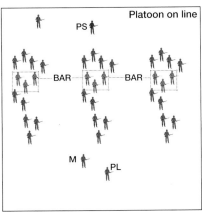

Platoon on line

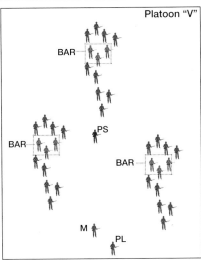

Platoon "V"

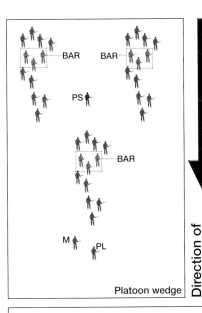

Platoon wedge

Direction of movement

Key

ASL	Assistant Squad Leader
BAR	Browning Automatic Rifle Team (three men)
M	Messenger
PG	Platoon Guide
PL	Platoon Leader
PS	Platoon Sergeant
SC	Scout
SL	Squad Leader

Browning Automatic Rifle
defensive fire

Squad
defensive
perimeter

R	Rifleman	AB	Ammunition Bearer for BAR
BAR	Browning Automatic Rifleman	SL	Squad Leader
ABAR	Assistant Browning Automatic Rifleman		

Browning
Automatic
Rifle
defensive
fire

Squad
defensive
perimeter

SQUAD DEFENSIVE POSITIONS 1942 (left top) AND 1944 (left bottom)
The top half shows the rifle squad defensive positions in 1942: a squad of men would lay themselves out as shown and dig their foxholes to defend against enemy attack. The bottom half shows the rifle squad defensive positions in 1944: note the different layout. Early doctrine recommended individual foxholes because they were harder targets to hit and did not collapse as easily as larger two-man foxholes when shelled or driven over by tanks. Later leaders found that although this was true, the isolation of a soldier in a foxhole negated all advantages, so opted for larger two- and three-man positions, in which one soldier could sleep while the other pulled guard.

RIFLE COMPANY WEAPONS POSITIONS (page 256)
(1) shows the dug-in position for an M1919A4 light machine gun from a side view, and (2) shows the position from above. This "horseshoe" emplacement was protected by a raised parapet about 3ft (0.9m) wide all the way round. The internal trench was about 2ft (0.6m) wide: the gun platform was roughly at chest height, and was $3^1/_2$ft (1.06m) square. The man firing the gun is the gunner, and the man next to him feeding the ammunition is the assistant gunner.
(3) shows the dug-in position for 60mm (2.36in.) bazooka from the side, and (4) shows it in cutaway view and without figures. (5) shows the bazooka position from overhead and with the spoil removed. The overall depth of the position is $5^1/_2$ft (1.67m), including the foot hole at the bottom which is 2ft deep and 2ft in diameter. The gunner fires the weapon, while the assistant gunner feeds the ammunition into the rear of the bazooka.
(6) shows an open emplacement for a 60mm (2.36 in.) mortar, from the side; (7) shows it from the rear and facing the enemy; and (8) shows it from above. The assistant gunner loads the shell into the mortar, the gunner aims it and adjusts firing. The position is dug to a depth of $3^1/_2$ft (1.06m), and is about 5ft (1.5m) long by 4ft (1.2m) wide. Spoil is piled all around the position to provide protection and camouflage. (9) shows the maximum elevation for the 60mm (2.36in.) mortar and (10) the maximum traverse. These mortars did not have 360-degree traverse as current mortars do, allowing the positions to be much smaller than those of today.

DIGGING A TWO-MAN FOXHOLE (below)
This plate shows the dimensions and function of a two-man foxhole as per period regulations. The soldiers could crouch in the bottom of their hole when shells were bursting nearby. Although the rifle company infantry manual recommended one-man foxholes because two-man positions were easily collapsed by tanks, the war in the Pacific and the constant Japanese infiltration necessitated two- and three-man positions.

WEAPONS COMPANY HEAVY WEAPONS POSITIONS (opposite)
Top illustration: this shows the dug-in position for an M1917A1 water-cooled heavy machine gun, from several different views. The gunner fires the weapon, and the assistant gunner next to him feeds the ammunition (note that the assistant gunner has been removed from the illustration so as to show the gunner's position more clearly).
Bottom illustration: this shows the dug-in position for an 81mm (3.18in.) mortar, from several different views. The World War II mortars did not have the 360-degree traverse of current mortars, that allows the positions to be much smaller. A vignette shows the angle of maximum traverse of the mortar. The assistant gunner loads the shell into the mortar, and the gunner aims it and adjusts firing.

Irregularly piled soil and spoil

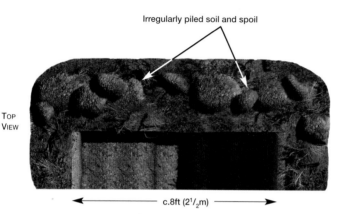

TOP VIEW

← c.8ft (2½m) →

SIDE VIEW

← 2 ft (0.6m) →

Branches and bush placed in 'growing' position

FRONT VIEW (ENEMY)

4–5ft (1.2-1.5m)

cut-out for foot room

← c.8ft (2½m) →

REAR VIEW

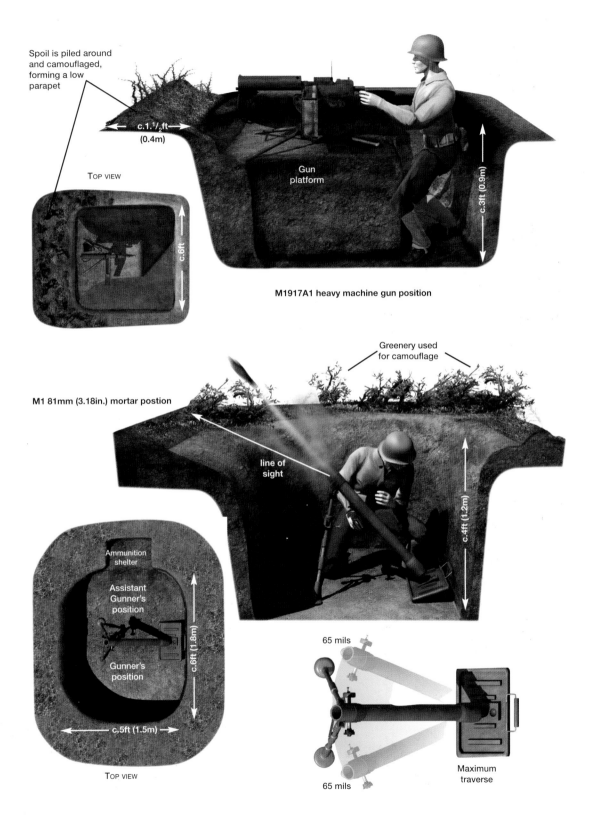

Spoil is piled around and camouflaged, forming a low parapet

c.1.¹/₂ft (0.4m)

TOP VIEW

c.6ft

Gun platform

c.3ft (0.9m)

M1917A1 heavy machine gun position

Greenery used for camouflage

M1 81mm (3.18in.) mortar postion

line of sight

c.4ft (1.2m)

Ammunition shelter

Assistant Gunner's position

Gunner's position

c.6ft (1.8m)

c.5ft (1.5m)

TOP VIEW

65 mils

65 mils

Maximum traverse

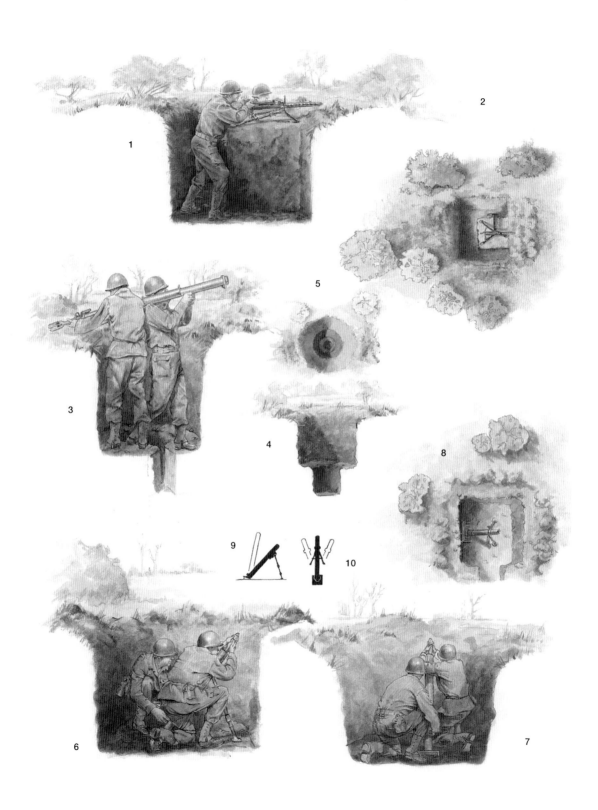

NOTES TO CHAPTER 7

1   Lada, John, *Medical Statistics in World War II* (Washington DC: Office of the Surgeon General, 1975), 70–71.

2   Historical Report 1943, 382d Infantry. (National Archives and Records Center, NARA) Record Group 407.396-INF (382) 0.1), 2; Shelby L Stanton, *Order of Battle U. S. Army, World War II* (Novato, CA: Presidio Press, 1984), 255.

3   *Selective Service and Victory: Fourth Report of the Director of Selective Service*, 1944–47 (Washington DC: Government Printing Office, 1947), 610; 588.

4   Ibid., 60; *Selective Service in Wartime: Second Report of the Director of Selective Service*, 1941–42 (Washington DC: Government Printing Office, 1943), 159; 173.

5   R R, Palmer, B I Wiley, and W R Keast, *The Procurement and Training of Ground Combat Troops:* The Army Ground Forces, US Army in World War II (Washington DC: Government Printing Office, 1948), 445; The Eighty-Ninth Division, 35–6.

6   Davidson, *The Deadeyes*, 4; Palmer, *Procurement and Training*, 445.

7   Ibid., 451.

8   Palmer, *Procurement and Training*, 446.

9   Palmer, *Procurement and Training*, 446; 447; The Eighty-Ninth Division, 43;

10 The Eighty-Ninth Division, 38; 44.

11 The Eighty-Ninth Division, 49.

12 Ibid., 57.

13 *Officers Guide* 1944, 332; 365; PAM 21–13 *Army Life* (Washington D.C.: War Department, August 1944), 19.

14 Headquarters, 382d Infantry, "Roster of Officers as of 15 September, 1944" (NARA RG 407 396-INF (382).01, 1–4. The sample company was Company E 2d Battalion 382d Infantry.

15 Davidson, *The Deadeyes*, 11; Dencker, *Love Company*, 45.

16 Ibid., 13.

17 Headquarters, 382d Infantry, "Summary of Lessons Learned, Leyte," 5.

18 Ibid., 39; Headquarters 382d RCT, "Unit Report Number 11," 1–2

19 Headquarters, 382d Infantry, "Ryukyus Campaign, 1st April–30th June, 1945: Training Phase and Rehearsals" (NARA, RG 407.396-INF(382)0.3), 1.

20 Dencker, Love Company, 152; Headquarters, 382d Infantry, "Training Phase and Rehearsals", 2.

21 Headquarters, 382d Infantry, "Ryukyus Campaign, 1st April–30th June, 1945: Chapter VIII Infantry Combat (NARA, RG 407.396-INF(382)0.3)", 1. "Infantry Combat", 1.

22 Headquarters 96th Infantry Division, "Action Report Ryukyu Campaign, 96th Infantry Division "Operation Features during the Assault" (NARA RG407.396.03) 13-14 Although this cave reduction occurred in June 1945 and was carried out by soldiers of the 381st Infantry, it is used as an example of the ferocity involved in clearing caves throughout the campaign.

23 382d Infantry, "Ryukyus Campaign, 1st April–30th June, 1945: Chapter 5 Narrative" (NARA, RG 407.396-INF(382)0.3), 5; Okinawa, Last Battle, 97

24 Okinawa, Last Battle, 412; Clarence M. Smith, The Medical Department Hospitalization and Evacuation, Zone of the Interior, U.S. Army in World War II (Washington, DC: Government Printing Office, 1956), 345.

25 "An act to provide Federal Government aid for the readjustment in civilian life of returning World War II veterans, June 22,1944" Enrolled Acts and Resolutions of Congress, 1789-1996; General Records of the United States Government; Record Group 11; National Archives; Lineage and Honors 382d Regiment, U.S. Army Center of Military History.

ABBREVIATIONS

1SG – first sergeant
AGCT – Army General Classification Test
AGF – Army Ground Forces
A & P – ammunition and pioneer
AUS – Army of the United States
BAR – Browning Automatic Rifle
CO – Commanding Officer
EMT – emergency medical tag
ETO – European Theater of Operations
HBT – herringbone twill
LCI – Landing Craft, Infantry
LCV – Landing Craft, Vehicle
LCVP – Landing Craft, Vehicle, Personnel
LST – Landing Ship Tank
LVT – Landing Vehicle, Tracked
MOS – Military Occupational Specialist

MTO – Mediterranean Theater of Operations
NA – National Army
NCO – noncommissioned Officer
NG – National Guard
OCS – Officer's Candidate School
OR – Organized Reserve
ORC – Organized Reserve Corps
POA - Pacific Ocean Area
PX – post exchange
RA - Regular Army
ROTC – Reserve Officers' Training Corps
RTC – Replacement Training Center
SWPA – Southwest Pacific Area
T&E – traversing and elevating
USAT – United States Army Transport
XO – executive officer

BIBLIOGRAPHY

PRIMARY SOURCES

"Company A 165th Infantry Diary October 1940–December 1945." np. National Archives and Records Administration (NARA) RG 407.327-INF(165)-0.1

Double Deucer, 1942–43. Issues 1–17, 25–36, 40, 45–49. The weekly newspaper of the 22d Infantry

22d US Infantry *Soldier's Handbook*, Infantry Journal Inc., Washington, DC: 1940.

Appel, J. W., MD, *Prevention of Manpower Loss from Psychiatric Disorders*, March 22, 1945 (unpublished study)

FM 100-5 *Operations, 22 May 1941*, Government Printing Office, Washington, DC,1941.

FM 21-100 *The Soldier's Handbook, 11 December 1940*, Government Printing Office, Washington, DC,1941.

FM 21-5 *Military Training July 16, 1941*, Government Printing Office, Washington, DC, 1941

FM 22-5 *Infantry Drill Regulations, 1 July 1939 and 4 August 1941*, Government Printing Office, Washington, DC

FM 7-10 *Rifle Company, Infantry Regiment, 2 June 1942*, Government Printing Office, Washington, DC, 1942

FM 7-10 *Rifle Company, Infantry Regiment, March 18, 1944.*: Government Printing Office, Washington, DC, 1944

FM 7-15 *Heavy Weapons Company, Rifle Regiment, May 19, 1942*, Government Printing Office, Washington, DC, 1942

FM 7-20 *Infantry Battalion, October 1, 1944*, Government Printing Office, Washington, DC, 1944

FM 7-25 *Headquarters Company, Intelligence and Signal Communication, Rifle Regiment, October 1942*, Government Printing Office, Washington, DC, 1942

FM 7-30 *Service Company and Medical Detachment, Rifle Regiment, July 18, 1941.* Washington, DC: Government Printing Office, 1941.

FM 7-35 *Antitank Company, Infantry Regiment, March 15, 1944,*: Government Printing Office, Washington, DC, 1944

FM 7-37 *Cannon Company, Infantry Regiment, March 28, 1944*, Government Printing Office, Washington, DC,1944.

FM 7-40 *Rifle Regiment, February 9, 1942*, Government Printing Office, Washington, DC 1942

FM 7-5 *Organization and Tactics of Infantry; the Rifle Battalion, 1940*, Government Printing Office, Washington, DC, 1940

General Order #80, First Army, Nov 14, 1944. Posthumous D.S.C. Private Eugene Hix, 22d Infantry.

Headquarters First United States Army, *Report of Operations, 1 August 1944–22 February 1945.* n.p., n.d.

Headquarters First United States Army, *Report of Operations, G1 Section, After Action Report of the G1 Section, 1 August 1944–22 February 1945*, n.d.

Headquarters, 133d Infantry Regiment, *133d Regiment History*, n.p. NARA RG 407.334-INF(133)-0.1

Headquarters, 133d Infantry Regiment, *S3 Operation Report*, np. NARA RG 407.334-INF(133)-0.3

Headquarters, 165th Infantry Regiment,*165th Regiment History*, n.p. NARA RG 407.327-INF(165)-0.1

Headquarters, 165th Infantry Regiment, *S3 Operation Report*, n.p. NARA RG 407. 327-INF(165)-0.3

Headquarters, 22d Infantry Regiment, *22d Regiment History*, n.p. NARA RG 407.304-INF(22)-0.1

Headquarters, 22d Infantry Regiment, *S3 Operation Report*, n.p. NARA RG 407. 304-INF(22)-0.3

Headquarters, 382d Infantry Regiment, *382d Historical Report*, n.p. NARA RG 407. 396-INF(382)-0.1

Headquarters, 382d Infantry Regiment, *S3 Operation Report*, n.p. NARA RG 407. 396-INF(382)-0.3

Headquarters, 4th Infantry Division, *Action Against Enemy, Reports After/After Action Reports, Jun 1944–May 1945*, NARA RG 407.304.

Headquarters, 27th Infantry Division, *Action Report, Forager Campaign 1944*, NARA RG 407.327.

Headquarters, 34th Infantry Division, *Action Against Enemy, Reports After/After Action Reports, February 1943–May 1945*, NARA RG 407.334.

Headquarters, 96th Infantry Division, *Action Report, Ryukyu Campaign 1945*, NARA RG 407.396.

Roster of killed and died, 22d Infantry Regiment. NARA

Roster of killed and died, 165th Infantry Regiment. NARA

Roster of killed and died, 133d Infantry Regiment, NARA

Roster of killed and died, 382d Infantry Regiment, NARA

Selective Service in Wartime, *Second Report of the Director of Selective Service, 1941–42*. The 2nd Report of the Director of Selective Service 1941–1942, Government Printing Office, Washington, DC 1943.

US Selective Service System, *Selective Service as the Tide of War Turns: The 3rd Report of the Director of Selective Service 1943–1944*. Government Printing Office, Washington, DC, 1945.

US Selective Service System. *Selective Service and Victory: The 4th Report of the Director of Selective Service 1944–1947*, Government Printing Office, Washington, DC, 1948

US Army Military History Institute, *WWII History, 133d Infantry, 34th Infantry Division*, file #603–133, 1945

US Department of Army. Adjutant General's Office, *Army Battle Casualties and Nonbattle Deaths in World War II: Final Report, December 7, 1941–December 31, 1946*. Government Printing Office, Washington, DC, June 1, 1953.

US War Department. Adjutant General's Office, Historical Documents World War II: 4th Inf. Div: 22d Inf. Regt. interviews. Microfilm Reel 2178.

SECONDARY SOURCES

A World War II and "Cold War" Mediterranean Retrospective http://www.milhist.net/index.html#mto

Ankrum, H. R., *Dog/aces Who Smiled Through Tears: The 34th Red Bull Infantry Division*, Graphic Publishing Company, Lake Mills, Iowa, 1987

Appleman, R., et al., *Okinawa, the Last Battle. Pacific Theater of Operations, US Array in World War II*, Government Printing Office, Washington, DC, reprint 1998.

Babcock, R., *War Stories: Utah Beach to Pleiku, the 4th Infantry Division in World War II. the Cold War and Vietnam*, Saint John's Press, Baton Rouge, Louisiana, 2001

Bergerud, E., *Touched with Fire: the Land War in the South Pacific*, Viking Penguin, New York 1996.

Blumenson, M., *Breakout and Pursuit. European Theater of Operations, US Army in World War II*, Government Printing Office, Washington, DC, 1989

Blumenson, M., *Salerno to Cassino*, Government Printing Office, Washington, DC, 1969–88

Boice, W. S., *History of the 22d United States Infantry in World War II*, Published by author, Phoenix, AZ, 1959

Cannon, M. Hamlin, *Leyte: The Return to the Philippines. The War in the Pacific*, Government Printing Office, Washington, DC, reprint 1996

Cole, H. M., *The Ardennes: Battle of the Bulge. European Theater of Operations, US Army in World War II*, Government Printing Office, Washington, DC,1965

Condon-Rall, M., et al., *The Medical Department: Medical Service in the War Against Japan*, Government Printing Office, Washington, DC, 1999

Conn, S., et al., *Guarding the United States and its Outposts. The Western Hemisphere, US Army in World War II,*: Government Printing Office, Washington, DC, reprint, 1989

Conn, S., et al, *Guarding the United States and its Outposts. The Western Hemisphere, US Army in World War I.*, Government Printing Office, Washington, DC, reprint 1989.

Crowl, P. A., and Love, E G., *Campaign in the Marianas. The War in the Pacific, US. Army in World War II*, Government Printing Office, Washington, DC, reprint 1995

Crowl, P A., and Love, E .G., *Seizure of the Gilberts and Marshalls. The War in the Pacific, US. Army in World War II*, Government Printing Office, Washington, DC, reprint 1995

Davidson, O., et al, *The Deadeyes, the Story of the 96th Infantry Division*, Infantry Journal Press, Washington, DC, 1947

Diamond, M. et al,. *The Eighty-Ninth Division 1942–1945*, Infantry Journal Press, Washington, DC,1947

Dencker, Donald O., *Love Company: Infantry Combat Against the Japanese World War II: Leyte and Okinawa*, Sunflower University Press, Manhattan, KS, 2002

Fisher, E. F., *Cassino to the Alps*, Government Printing Office, Washington, DC, 1977–89

Harrison, G. A., *Cross Channel Attack. European Theater of Operations, US Army in World War II*, Government Printing Office, Washington, DC, 1989

Historical Division, War Department, *5th Army at the Winter Line, November 15, 1943– January 15, 1944*, Government Printing Office, Washington, DC, 1945, 1990

Historical Division, War Department, *Anzio Beachhead January 22–May 25, 1944*, Government Printing Office, Washington, DC, 1948, 1990

Historical Division, War Department, *From the Volturno to the Winter Line October 6–November 15, 1943*, Government Printing Office, Washington, DC, 1945, 1990

Historical Division, War Department, *Salerno, American operations from the beaches to the Volturno, September 9 October 6, 1943*, Government Printing Office, Washington, DC, 1944, 1990

Historical Division, War Department, *To Bizerte with the II Corps, April 23, 1943 May 13, 1943*, Government Printing Office, Washington, DC, 1944, 1990

Historical Division, War Department, *Small Unit Actions. American Forces in Action*, Government Printing Office, Washington, DC, 1948

Historical Division, War Department, *The Capture of Makin, American Forces in Action*, Government Printing Office, Washington, DC, 1946

History of the 34th ("Red Bull" Infantry Division http://www.dma.state.mn.us/redbull/HISTORY/History.htm

Howe, G. F., *Northwest Africa: seizing the initiative in the West*, Government Printing Office, Washington, DC, 1957–91

Linderman, G. F., *The World Within War: America's Combat Experience in World War I*, The Free Press, New York ,1997

Love, E. G., *The 27th Infantry Division in World War II*, Battery Press, Nashville, reprint 1973

MacDonald, C. B. , *The Last Offensive. European Theater of Operations, US Army in World War II*, Government Printing Office, Washington, DC, 1972

MacDonald, C. B., *The Siegfried Line Campaign, European Theater of Operations*, US Army in World War II, Government Printing Office, Washington, DC, 1963

McCarthy, J., "Iron-Man Battalion," *Yank Magazine, European Edition*, Vol 1:38, pp. 2–5, December 22, 1944, Great Britain

Palmer, R. R., Wiley, B. I., and Keast W. R., *The Procurement and Training of Ground Combat Troops. The Army Ground Forces, US Army in World War II*. Government Printing Office, Washington, DC, 1948

Public Relations Office, *96th Infantry Division, 1942–1944*, Shannon and Firth, San Francisco, 1944

Pyle, E., *Brave Men*, Henry Holt and Company, Inc. New York, 1944

Rothbart, D., *World War II Army Journal*, Pittsburgh, PA, Published by the author, 5864 Phillips Avenue, 1977

Rush, R. S., *Hell in Hürtgen Forest: Ordeal and Triumph of an American Infantry Regiment*, University Press of Kansas, Lawrence, KS, 2001

Trindal, W., "And Then There Were None," Marietta, GA ed. 22d Infantry Society, 1997

Wilson, John B., Armies, Corps, Divisions, and Separate Brigades, Army Lineage Series Government Printing Office, Washington, DC, 1987

Wiltse, C. M., *The Medical Department: Medical Service in the Mediterranean and Minor Theaters*, Government Printing Office, Washington, DC, 1987, 1965

INDEX

Page numbers in **bold** refer to illustrations.

Adjusted Service Rating 92-93, **92**, 152-153, 154, **152**, 213

Admiralty Islands 39

aid stations 81-82, 202-203, **205**

Alam Halfa, battle of 38

Alife, Italy 130

allegiance, oaths of 101, 162, 228

American Battlefield Monuments Commission 210

ammunition 63, 88, 108, 125, 136, 150, 175

see also weapons

amphibious landings 61-63, **62**, **63**, 232

amphibious tractors (AMTRAC) 232, **236**

Anzio 39, 40, 135-142, 154

Arcadia Conference 38

Army Air Corps **56**

Army General Classification Test (AGCT) 18

see also tests

Army Ground Forces (AGF) 11, 18

Army Serial Numbers 49, 100-101, 161, 195

Army Specialized Training Program (ASTP) 221

Atlantic Charter 38

atomic bombs 41

Army of the United States (AUS) **11**

accessions and enlistment by age **169**

composition 9

military strength

European Theater of Operations (ETO) **156**, 158

Mediterranean Theater of Operations (MTO) **96**, 123

Pacific Ocean Area (POA) of Operations 42-44, **43**

Pacific Theater of Operations (PTO) **43**, 44

Southwest Pacific Area (SWPA) of Operations **43**, **214**

see also infantry; National Guard (NG); Regular Army (RA)

atrabrine 121-122

Attu 39

Austerity Plan 167

Austria 37, 41

Axis powers 38, 39

Azzeville, France 180

Balkans 38

Bataan, siege of 38

"Battle of the Hedgerows", Normandy 40, 184-190

battlefields commissions 17, 19, 192

Belgium 37, 40, 41

Berlin 41

Bismarck Sea, naval battle 39

Borneo 38

Bradley, Omar, General 156

Brandscheid, Germany 206, 207

Britain 37, 38

battle of 37

"Blitz" 37

US Army support 166

see also England

bunkers, German **190-191**, 192-194, 198, 207, **208**

Calvert, USS 46, 61
Camp Butner 213
Camp Carson 217-220
Camp Gordon 168
Camp Gordon Johnston 171
Camp Kilmer 116, 172
Camp Smith 48, 49
Camp Stoneman 228
Camp Wheeler 102-114, **106-107**
Cape St. George, battle of 39
Capetown Castle, HMS 172-173
Casablanca Conference 39
Cassino, battle of 39, 131-135, **131**, **132**, **133**, 154
   house clearing 131, 132-133, **134**, **135**
casualties 44, **44**, **93**, 93-94, **94**, **249**
   European Theater of Operations (ETO) 158, **160**, **211**, 212-213, 243, 249
   France 178, 180, 181, 182, 184, 186, 189, 191-192
   Germany 197, 199, 200, 201-205, **204**, **206**, 208-212, **210**, **211**
   Italy 124, 126-128, 130, **130**, 131, 134, 135, 141, 142-144, **144**, 146-148, 151, 153, 154, **154**, 155
   Leyte 236, 237, 238-239, 247
   Makin 71, 94
   Mediterranean Theater of Operations (MTO) 97, **154**, 249
   non-battle 123, 130, 133, 140, 154, 158, 200, 204, 209, 215, 216, **216**, 233, 239
   North Africa 121, 122, **154**
   Okinawa 88, 90, 94, **247**
   Pacific Theater of Operations (PTO) 71, 75, 76, 77, 78, 79, 80-84, **82**, 88, 90, 94, 243, 247, **247**

   psychoneurotic/neuropsychiatric 83, 144, 201-202
   Saipan 75, 76, 77, 78, 79, 80-84, **82**, 94
   Southwest Pacific Area (SWPA) of Operations 216, **216**, 236, 237, 238-239, 247
   in training 123, 170
   transportation of 204, 205
   see also "friendly" fire
cemeteries, military **93**, 209-212
censorship, mail 176
chemical warfare 108, **110**, 129, 170, 177
China 37, 41
Churchill, Winston 38
Cockrell, Gordon (382d Regiment, 96th Infantry Division) 217
   Leyte 231-242, **240**
   Okinawa 242-246
   training 217-228, 230-231
combat fatigue 83, 144, 201-202
   see also casualties
Combat Infantryman Badge **85**, 85-86, 191, 247
Conroy, Gardiner, J., Colonel 71
Coral Sea, naval battle 38, 57
Crusader offensive 38
Czechoslovakia 37, 41

Delta Queen, steamship 230
Denmark 37, 41
Die Suedfront 129
discharges 49, 155, 213
discipline 48, 102, 105, 115, 149, 155
disease/illness
   European Theater of Operations (ETO) 158, 197-198, 204
   Mediterranean Theater of Operations (MTO) 97, 128-129, 130, 133
   Pacific Ocean Area (POA) of Operations 44, **44**, 71, 80

seasickness 172, 176
Southwest Pacific Area (SWPA) of
    Operations 216, **216**
treatment 71, 121-122
trenchfoot 197-198, 204
see also casualties
Distinguished Unit Citations 213, 247
draft extension 54
draftees 13, 14-15, 16, **16**, **17**, 50, 157, 159,
    160-166, 217

Eagle Day 37
Easley, Brigadier-General 233
Eastern Solomons, naval battle 38
Egypt 37, 38, 39
83d Division 171
86th Division 225
89th Division 12, 24, 225, 228
Eisenhower, Dwight D. 38, 39, 40, 118
El Alamein
    first battle of 38
    second battle of 39
England 172-178, **176**
Eniwetok 231
enlisted soldiers 14, 15-16, **16**, **17**, **18**, 38,
    47-48
    pay **53**, 113, 115
equipment 47-48, **51**, **54**, **59**, **60**, 71, **75**,
    95, 102-104, **103**, 114-115, 116, **118**,
    124, **127**, **147**, **181**, **183**, **200**, **203**
    canteens **65**, **86**, **118**
    compasses 60, **203**
    field **226**
    gas masks **103**, 108, **110**, **116**
    handcarts 224, 225, **225**
    haversacks **58**, **65**, **75**, **140**, **161**
    radios **203**
    shortages 166
    sleeping bags 150
    stoves 150

see also uniforms
Espiritu Santo 83, 84-85
Ethiopia 37
European Theater of Operations (ETO)
    12, 156-213
    campaigns 157, **157**
    US Army strength **156**, 158

Fifth Army 98, 151
Fifth Army Battle School 123
Finland 37
Fondouk 39, 98, 118-121, **120**
formations, platoon **251**
Fort Benning 159, 162-167
Fort Dix 171
Fort Jackson 171-172
Fort McClellan 49-50, 53
Fort Meade 114
4th Division 159, 172
    22d Regiment **158**, 159-160, 162-163,
        165-166, 171-172, **177**, **189**
    campaigns, European Theater of
        Operations (ETO) **157**
    England 172-178, **176**
    France 178-190, 191-192
    Germany 190-212
    route, European Theater of
        Operations (ETO) **160**
foxholes **184**, **196**, **252**
France 37, 39, 40, 174, 176, 177, 178-190,
    191-192, 207-208
    Cherbourg–Periers 184-186
    St Lo 186-190, **189**, 213
"friendly" fire 60, 63, 64, 65, 70, 140,
    181, 189
Friendship Treaty (Soviet–German) 37

General James Parker, USAT 212
German troops 118, 124-125, 184, **201**
Germany 37, 38, 39, 40, 41, 190-212, **209**

Siegfried Line **190-191**, 192-195
    Hürtgen Forest 195-199, **197**, **200**,
        206, 213
Gothic Line 40, 41, 99
Greece 38
Guadalcanal, naval battle 39
Guam 40
guard duty 113
    General Orders 113, **114**
Gustav Line 40
Gusukama 87, 88-90

handcarts 224, 225, **225**
Harakiri Gulch 79, **79**
Harris, USS 72, 73
Hawaii 42, 43, 46, 56-61, **56**, **58**, **59**, 71-72,
    230-231
Hawaiian Department Ranger School 60
Hill 120, Leyte 232
Hill 609, Tunisia 98, 121, 122, **122**
Himmler, Heinrich 41
Hiroshima 41
Hitler, Adolf 37, 38, 41
Hix, Private 185
hospitals 142-144, 204, 205, 246-247
Hungary 41
Hürtgen Forest 195-199, **200**

Iceland 38
illness *see* disease/illness
induction 13, 14-15, 16, **16**, **17**, 50, 160-163
infantry 20-36, **44**, **122**, **136**, **142**, **143**, **186**,
    195, **200**, **201**, **211**, **237**, **238**, **239**,
    249, **250**
    antitank companies 24, **24**
    barracks **104**
    battalion headquarters **25**, 25-26
    cannon companies 23, **23**
    campaigns, European Theater of
        Operations (ETO) **158**
heavy weapons companies 32-33
"kitchen police" **163**
medical detachments **22**, 22-23
Mediterranean Theater of Operation
    (MTO) 97, **97**
regimental headquarters 20-21, **20**, **21**
regimental organization **20**
rifle companies 26-32, **26**, **27**, **28**, **29**,
    31, **54**
service companies 22, **22**
Southwest Pacific Area (SWPA) of
    Operations **215**
specialties **109**, **232**
tradition 165-166
see also individual infantry divisions
infiltration methods 69, 129, 140
Italy 37, 38, 39, 40, 41, 98-99, 123-151

Japan 15-16, 37, 38, 39, 40, 41, 42, 160
Japanese Mandates 42
Japanese troops 64, 65, **66-67**, 238,
    240-241, 243
    subterfuges 69
    suicides 77, 237
    see also Leyte; Makin; Okinawa; Saipan
Java Sea, battle of 38
jungle warfare 214-215
    training 60, 72, 85, 216

Kakazu Ridge, Okinawa 243-246, **245**
Kauai 56, 60
Kef-el-Amar Pass 117
Kolombangara, battle of 39
Kula Gulf (Kolombangara), battle of 39
Kwajalein Atoll 42, 72, 80, 82

Landing Craft, Infantry (LCI) **179**
Landing Craft, Vehicles (LCV) **62**
Landing Vehicles, Tracked (LVT) 70
Lanham, Colonel 195

Lear, Ben, General 53
Lemnitzer, General 133-134
Lend-Lease Act 38
Leyte 231-242
    naval battle 40
Libya 38
losses *see* casualties
Low Countries 37

MacArthur, Douglas, General 38, 42,
    214, 240
Makin 39, 46, 61-71, **65**, **66-67**, **68**, **69**
    Red Beach 62-63, **63**, **64**
Malaya 38
Manchuria 41
manuals, training 14
Marines 42, 83, 91
Marshall, George C., General 37, 42, 170
massed formation **11**
Maui 60, 72
medals 72, 85-86, 91, 144, 152, 153, 190,
    191, 213
    award ceremony **192**
medical examinations 100, 116, 162
medics **73**, 80-83, **81**, **144**, **204**, 224
Mediterranean Theater of Operations
    (MTO) 12, 96-155
    campaigns **12**
    US Army strength **96**, 123
mess kits 49
Midway, naval battle 38, 57
Mindanao 41
Missoula, USS 86
Missouri, USS 41
mobilization training 10
Mobilization Training Program tests
    219-220
Monte Cassino, bombing of 39
Monticello, USS 155
morphine 81

Mountbatten, Lord 170
Mussolini, Benito 39, 41

Nagasaki 41
National Guard (NG) **6**, 10, 16, 43
    federalization 10, 37, 45, 98
    see also infantry
National Service Life Insurance 115
Netherlands 37, 41
New Guinea 38, 40
Nimitz, Chester, Admiral 38, 42
96th Division 216, 228, **247**
    382d Regiment 216-217
        3d Battalion 232
        728th Amphibious Tractor
        Battalion 232
        Hawaii 230-231
        Leyte 231-242, **240**
        Okinawa 242-246
    route, Southwest Pacific Area (SWPA)
    of Operations **218**
97th Division 225
9th Armored Division 225
Nonaggression Pact (Soviet–German) 37
Normandy 40, 184-190
North Africa 117-123, **120**, **121**, **122**, **123**
Norway 37

Oahu 60, 216
Oath of Enlistment 101, 162
oath of allegiance, officers' 228
O'Brien, Michael (165th Regiment, 27th
    Infantry Division) 44-45, 47-56, **51**,
    80-86, 92-93, **95**
    Hawaii 56-61, 71-72
    Makin 61-71
    Okinawa 86-92
    Saipan 72-80
officers 11, 12-13, 16-19, 20-21, 50, 94,
    105, 115

oath of allegiance 228
specialties **232**
training 227-228, **229**
see also Cockrell, Gordon
Officers' Candidate Schools (OCS) 17-18,
219, 221, 227-228
Okinawa 41, 42, 46, 86-92, **86**, **87**, **89**,
242-246
Kakazu Ridge 243-246, **245**
operations, military
Battleace 38
Cartwheel (Rabaul) 39
Cobra 40
Forager 73-80
Goodwood 40
Nordwind 40
Overlord 40
Torch 39
Oran, Algeria 123, **123**
Organized Reserve (OR) 11-13
Organized Reserve Corps (ORC) 16, 17
"overs" 63, 70
see also "friendly" fire

Pacific Ocean Area (POA) of Operations
42-95
campaigns **47**
US Army strength 42-44, **43**
Pacific Theater of Operations (PTO) 12,
42, **47**
US Army strength **43**, **44**
see also Pacific Ocean Area (POA) of
Operations; Southwest Pacific Area
(SWPA) of Operations
"Pact of Steel" (Germany/Italy) 37
"Palace Guard" 118, 135
Papua 39
Paris 40
Patton, General 208

pay
officers' 228
soldiers' **53**, 113, 115, 167, 191
Pearl Harbor 15, 16, 38, 54, 55, 168, 217
Peleliu 40, 42
Philippine Sea (Great Marianas Turkey
Shoot), naval battle 40
Philippines 38, 41
see also Leyte
pillboxes 180-181
Platoon Combat Firing Proficiency
Tests 222
platoon formations **251**
Poland 37, 41
President Grant, USAT 46, 56
Prince of Wales, HMS 38
prisoners of war 41, **55**, 89, 134, **151**,
181, 199
promotion 49, 57, 167, 195
Prüm, Germany 206-207
psychoneurotic/neuropsychiatric
casualties 83, 144, 201-202
Pyle, Ernie
Brave Men 128

quarantine 102
Quebec Conference (Allies)
first 39
second 40

racial segregation 167, 173
Rapido River 131
rationing 173, 223
rations 71, 125, 128, 137, 150, 173,
175-176, 177, 233
Red Beach, Makin 62-63, **63**, **64**
Red Cross 56
symbols 81, **81**, **144**
Regular Army (RA) 9-10, 16, 43, **159**

religious services 45, 50, **53**, 72, 176, 182, **184**, **246**

Replacement Training Centers (RTCs) 9, 102-114

replacements

European Theater of Operations (ETO) 158, 171, 172, **198**, **199**, 199-200, 250

Mediterranean Theater of Operations (MTO) 97, 115, 116, **116**, 118, 123, 135, 136, **137**, 140, 249-250

Pacific Ocean Area (POA) of Operations 84, **84**

Pacific Theater of Operations (PTO) 84, **84**, 242-243, 249-250

Southwest Pacific Area (SWPA) of Operations 242-243

Repulse, HMS 38

Reserve Officers' Training Corps (ROTC) 11, 16, 50

Reuben James, US Destroyer 38

Rhine River 207, 208

rifle company weapons positions **255**

Robin Doncaster, USAT 80, 83

Rommel, Erwin, Field Marshal 38, 39, 40, 96

Roosevelt, Franklin D., President 13, 14, 15, 37, 38, 40, 49, 55, 167

Ruiz, Alejandro, Private First Class 90-91

Saipan 40, 42, 46, 72-80

Santa Cruz Islands, naval battle 39

Savo Island, naval battle 38

Sea Sturgeon, USAT 230

Second Army maneuvers 52, 54-55

Seine River 40

Selective Service Act 13, 14, 37

serial numbers 49, 100-101, 161, 195

service (bugle) calls 49, **52**

Servicemen's Readjustment Act

(GI Bill) 247

Seventh Army 98

71st Light (Pack) Division 224

76th Division 12-13, 114-115

Sicily 39, 123

Siegfried Line **190-191**, 192-195

69th Regiment 45

Slapton Sands, Devon, England 174, **175**

Smith, John (133d Regiment, 34th Infantry Division) 99, **103**, **127**

enlistment 99-102

Italy 123-151

North Africa 117-123

training 102-114

snipers 65, 124

sniperscopes 86-87

The Soldier's Handbook 14, 110, 114, 163

Southwest Pacific Area (SWPA) of Operations 42, 43, 214-247, **218**

campaigns **47**, **215**, 216

US Army strength **43**, **214**

Soviet Union 37, 38, 41

Spanish Civil War 37

squad defensive positions **254**

Stalingrad 39

status reports 149

Stein, Joseph (22d Regiment, 4th Infantry Division) 159, **183**, **203**

England 172-178

France 178-190

Germany 190-212

induction 160-163

training 163-172

Die Suedfront 129

supplies 22, 52, 56, 72, 88, 128, 129-130, 176, 187, 199, 233, 238

Tabontabon, Leyte 234-237, **235**, **241**

tanks 70, 90, **90**, 119, 131, 132, 133, **134**, **135**, 184-185, 187, **188**, **189**, **242**, 245-246

Tassafaronga, naval battle 39
10th Light (Mountain) Division 224
tests
    Army General Classification Test
       (AGCT) 18, 227
    Basic Education Test 227
    classification 18, 100, 101-102, 161,
       219-220
    Mobilization Training Program tests
       219-220
    Officers' Candidate Schools (OCS)
       227-228
    Platoon Combat Firing Proficiency
Tests 222
    proficiency 168-170, 220, 222, 223
34th Division (Iowa Army National
    Guard) 98-99, 123, **124**
    133d Regiment 98, 99
       2d Battalion 118, 136
       100th (Nisei) Battalion
         (attached) 123
       Italy 123-151, **130, 131, 132, 133,**
         134, 135, 137, 140, 141, 142,
         143, 144, 145, 146, 147,
         148, 149
       North Africa 117-123, **117, 118,**
         120, 121, 122, 123
       regimental badges **103**
    135th Regiment 121
Tinian 40
Tobruk 39
    siege of 38
training 10, 11-12, 13, **13**, 14, 15, 52-53,
    136, 172, 174, 220, 221, 222, 223
    amphibious 60, 72, 159, 171, **233**
    Camp Carson 217-220
    Camp Gordon 168-171
    Camp Gordon Johnston 171
    Camp Smith 48, 49
    Camp Wheeler 102-114, **106-107**

    close-combat 221
    combined 222-226
    England 173-174
    Espiritu Santo 84-85
    Fifth Army Battle School 123
    Fort Benning 159, 162-167
    Fort Dix 171
    Fort McClellan 49-50, 53
    Hawaii 43, 46, 56-61, **58, 59, 61**, 71-72,
       230-231
    jungle warfare 60, 72, 85, 216, 231
    live-fire 60, 123
    maneuvers 52, 54-55, 159, 166, 170,
       173-174
    manuals 14
    motorized forces 166
    Oahu 216-217
    officers 11, 12-13, 16-19, 227-228, **229**
    Oran, Algeria 123, **123**
    Ranger 171
    tactical 168
    unit 220-222
transportation 22, **56**, 73, 116, **167**, 172,
    224, 230
    handcarts 224, 225, **225**
Trident Conference (Anglo-American) 39
Tripartite Pact 38
Truman, Harry S. 41, 93, 152
Tunisia 39
    Fondouk 39, 98, 118-121, **120**
    Hill 609 98, 121, 122, **122**
27th Division (New York National Guard)
    45, 46, 52, 53
    cemetery **93**
    165th Regiment, New York National
       Guard 44-46, **45, 51, 53**
       campaigns, Pacific Ocean Area
         (POA) **47**, 47-95
       Hawaii 56-61, **56, 58, 59**, 71-72
       Makin 61-71, **62, 63, 64, 65**

Okinawa 86-92, **86**, **87**, **89**, **90**, **91**, **92**
route, Pacific Ocean Area (POA)
of Operations 46, **46**
Saipan 72-80, **73**, **74**, **75**, **76**, **77**,
79, 83

uniforms 47-48, **53**, **59**, **95**, **103**, **117**, 129,
150, **161**, **188**, **196**, 197-198, **207**
camouflage **60**, **146**
footwear 102, **127**, 136, **140**, 151,
197-198, 204
helmets **57**, 57-60, **103**, 115, 116, **146**
herringbone twill (HBT) **61**, **116**, 150,
164, **183**
issue of **101**, 102, 162
"kitchen police" **163**
leggings 71
lieutenant **203**
private **51**
sergeant **183**
shortages 52
staff sergeant **127**
see also equipment
United Nations 38, 41
United States Military Academy
(USMA) 16
Utah Beach 40, 159, **178**

V-E (Victory in Europe) Day 41
vehicles 70, **167**
Vella Gulf, battle of 39
Vella Lavella, battle of 39
veterans 247
Vienna 41
VJ Day 41
Volturno River 39, 99, 124
Von Arnim, Jürgen 39

Warhawk, USS 231
Warsaw 41

weapons **6**, 57, 60, **60**, 65, **86**, **103**,
105-108, **127**, 136-137, 175, 180
antitank 25, 36, 131
antitank companies 25
bayonets **59**, **61**, **66-67**, 70, **188**
bazookas 24, 185, 186, **188**, 244-245
canon companies 23, 234
flamethrowers 71, 74, **95**, 180-181,
241-242, 244, 245
German 179
grenades **6**, 60, 70-71, 90, 108, **183**,
244-245
heavy weapons companies 20, 25,
32-33, **34**, 34-35, **35**
heavy weapons positions **253**
howitzers 23, 36, 131, 234
Japanese 64, 65, 70, 241
machine gun training **111**, 111-113
machine guns 10, 48, 85, 88, **95**, 115,
143, **253**, **255**
maintenance 50, 71, 85
mines 124-125, 126-128, **129**
mortars 10, 48, **131**, **138-139**, 149-150,
244, **253**, **255**
pineapple grenades **6**, 60, 90
pistols 10, 48, 108
positions **253**, **254**
rifle companies 20, **29**, 30-32, **31**,
33-34, **35**
rifle training 56, 110-111, 118,
163-165, **165**, 219
rifles 10, 48, 50, **51**, **57**, **59**, **103**, 115,
118, **124**, **141**, **142**, **159**, **183**,
185, 218
shortages 52, 166
sniperscopes 86-87
West Wall, Germany **193**
Winter Line Campaign 39

Yamato, Japanese battleship 41
Yap Island 231